SMOKE & PICKLES

SMOKE & PICKLES

EDWARD LEE

RECIPES AND STORIES FROM A NEW SOUTHERN KITCHEN

Artisan

Published by Artisan
A division of Workman Publishing Company, Inc.
225 Varick Street
New York, NY 10014-4381
artisanbooks.com

Published simultaneously in Canada by Thomas Allen & Son, Limited

Library of Congress Cataloging-in-Publication Data
Lee, Edward
  Smoke and pickles : recipes and stories from a new Southern kitchen / Edward Lee.
     pages cm
  Includes index.
  ISBN 978-1-57965-492-4
  1. Cooking, American—Southern style. I. Title.
  TX715.2.S68L4446   2013
  641.5975—dc23
2012039653

Design by Michelle Ishay-Cohen and Kara Strubel

Food styling by Dimity Jones
Handlettering by Jacob Covey

Printed in China
First printing, March 2013

10 9 8 7 6 5 4 3 2 1

CONTENTS

PREFACE

"WHAT DO YOU COOK?"

It's a question I get all the time. There's the short answer and there's the long answer. The short one's easy: I reach for labels like Farm to Table, Field to Fork, Soil to Mouth, Local-Global, New Asian, New Southern, New Anything. . . . I might show photos of my garden in full bloom, woven baskets of fruits and vegetables with a smattering of soil still clinging to the edges, or a handful of the heirloom seeds I've collected over the years. I offer a belabored speech about local farms and

ingredients at the peak of freshness. It's not insincere, but it sure is rehearsed. The simplest questions are the most difficult to answer, because lurking just behind those innocent words is a more complex response. This book is the long answer.

WHAT I COOK IS WHO I AM

My grandmother cooked every day. Her entire life. In our tiny windowless Brooklyn kitchen with just a few pots, mismatching lids, a plastic colander or two, and a fake Ginsu knife, she re-created all the Korean dishes she had learned before she immigrated to America. My grandmother never questioned her identity, culinary or otherwise. She was a Korean widow yearning for a homeland that had been destroyed before her eyes. Her daily rituals of cooking and Bible reading were her last links to an agrarian Korea that no longer existed,

a place that had risen from its ashes into a megametropolis, a place that did not need her. Her food was indelibly linked to that identity. But this is true for most of us, isn't it? Can you separate a Bolognese sauce from the Italian arm that stirs the simmering pot?

Funny thing about my grandmother, though—she refused to make "American food." We always had peanut butter and jelly in the cupboard, but if I wanted a PB&J sandwich, I had to make it myself. I'm not sure whether she was offended by it or if she was quietly, in her own grandmotherly way, guiding me to forge a culinary identity of my own, reflective of the life I would lead as a Korean-American kid. Or I could be reading way too much into it. But it's true that my identity (crisis) would soon enough manifest itself in my language (foulmouthed), my clothes (ripped jeans), my hair (long and messy), and, of course, my food, which started with the PB&J but then wove itself all the way to Kentucky.

The great thing about Americans is not the identity we're born with but our reinvention of it. We start with one family and then, magically, we are allowed to reinvent ourselves into whoever we want to be. As a kid, I'd go to my friend Marcus's house for a meal of Puerto Rican plantains over rice with ketchup and honey. The apartment was loud, the radio always on (we didn't even own one), with people talking over each other. And for that night, I was a Puerto Rican son of a festive family where every meal was a party. Our downstairs neighbors were Jewish, and sometimes they'd watch me when my parents were both working nights. Their food smelled like a hospital, and so did their furniture and their antiseptic gray tabby. But they conveyed love through everything they did. They sat with me and warned me about life, talking to me about being honest and keeping out of trouble. They insisted I read books and learn to play the piano. They were parental and stern and warm all at the same time. It isn't their overcooked string beans I remember most, but their words of nourishment. I felt as though if anything ever happened to my parents, they would have taken me in without a second thought. And, in an odd way, they kind of did.

GRAFFITI WAS MY FIRST CUISINE

All the truants in my junior high were into graffiti, but most of us just scribbled in notebooks. None of us had dared to tag a wall yet. But there was this one mysterious kid, forever in the eighth grade, who was rumored to be a wall artist. He had a shadowy past and facial hair like someone ten years older than us. He smoked, he cursed, he cut school, and it was rumored that he lived alone. Eric (let's call him that) was the coolest kid in a school full of derelicts. We became friends.

There are a million reasons kids deface public property: rebellion, for notoriety, as a cry for attention, boredom. I wanted/needed an identity to call my own, and what was cooler at the time than dark hoodies, backpacks full of Krylons, late-night bombs of hopping fences and scaling exteriors? Mostly I was Eric's lookout, his apprentice. He taught me technique—to use skinny caps for the outline and fat caps to fill in, and to spray without dripping—and he taught me to find my own style, and to write without getting caught. I became someone else overnight, with every stroke of the cold nozzle tracking the city walls. I was a lawbreaker; I was a legend in my own mind. I was anything but that bored Korean kid, good at math, terrible at basketball.

My Korean forefathers' love of pickling is rivaled only by Southerners' love of pickling.

The irony of graffiti is that the permanence of spray paint and china markers lasts only until the next guy decides to write over you. Your tag may survive for a week or a night, or sometimes just a few hours, but inevitably, it is reduced to a memory under the fresh layer of someone else's paint. And most street artists would agree that's the way it should be. Graffiti's never supposed to last. How many remember the art on the L train or a mural on 145th Street? The hardest things to hold on to in life are the ones that want to disappear.

So here I am, twenty years later, far from my Brooklyn childhood, at John Shields's restaurant in Chilhowie, Virginia, with my sous-chef, silent and ruminative, having the meal of a lifetime and wanting it to last more than the few paltry hours I have. Pictures and tweets don't do it justice. This night, too, will become a memory, soon to be painted over by another meal.

I SEEK IMPERMANENCE

I moved to Louisville in 2003. I had to reinvent my identity, both culinary and personal, through the lens of tobacco and bourbon and sorghum and horse racing and country ham. The first time I tried buttermilk, I threw it out because I thought it was sour. It was a revelation to learn that you use it because *it is* sour. And that it tastes nothing like butter. Over time, Louisville, and, by extension, the American South, embraced me as an adopted son. I was not surprised by that. It was effortless. What I didn't expect was how I would come full circle and rediscover myself as a child of Korean immigrants. That all the lovely and resourceful traditions of the Southern landscape would propel me back to the kitchen of my grandmother's spicy, garlicky foods: Soft grits remind me of congee; jerky of cuttlefish; chowchow of kimchi. My Korean forefathers' love of pickling is rivaled only by Southerners' love of pickling. BBQ, with its intricate techniques of marinades and rubs, is the backbone of both cuisines. Buttermilk has become my miso, ubiquitous and endearing. It shows up in everything from dressings to marinades to desserts, but never in the foreground, always as a platform to let other ingredients shine. I found my culinary voice here in Louisville. I found a culture so different and yet not very different at all from the one in which I was raised. I learned to be comfortable in my own skin and to cook the food that flows naturally from my fingers. At the same time, I continue to be astonished by the flavors that surround me. There's an endless history to uncover, and with each lesson I learn, I find myself becoming not only the chef I want to be but also the person I've always wanted to grow into.

One day I was given a curious recipe by a guy here in Louisville who makes jerky for a living. It's really less a recipe than a proclamation:

Take stale cornbread, a shot of sorghum, and a glass of buttermilk, puree it in a blender, and drink it out of a mug. He called it, simply, breakfast. This is the kind of shit that reminds me of my grandmother's attitude and her pride in a tradition that lived in her bones. She never had to explain herself. She was comfortable in her ways. Just like I found comfort in graffiti.

What attracted me to graffiti way back then is the same thing that draws me to the unapologetic land of Kentucky. It's the act of distilling beauty from the imperfections that exist around us. Since we don't have an ocean nearby, we make do with catfish. Since our summers are muggy and hot, we use the climate to age our barrels of bourbon. When our gardens are overrun with wild mint, we happily sit down for an afternoon julep. This is what I mean when I say graffiti was my first lesson in how to approach cuisine as an art. The graffiti movement happened because many small factors (subways, spray cans, hip-hop, etc.) all converged in a city that combusted, to create a subculture that mesmerized a generation.

Most art movements are a product of chance. Graffiti just happened to be everywhere I went as a kid. When I think about food now, I can't help but approach it in the same way those great underground artists did to leave their marks. Instead of succumbing to the causality of time and place, they wrestled an improbable elegance out of all that twisted steel and concrete. I look around now and I see brash mixologists celebrating bourbon; I see country ham producers who are historians; I see chefs and farmers and glassblowers and carpenters and artists all converging to create something both distinct and memorable and, like graffiti, fleeting.

That a Brooklyn kid of Korean lineage can find his place in Louisville is a testament to the city, the time we live in, and cultural forces that are beyond our breadth of knowledge as we live

I continue to be astonished by the flavors that surround me.

through this moment. Something is happening in Louisville right now. Something is simmering wildly throughout the American South. Every time I look around, I see bold new expressions of Southern cuisine waving a proud flag. And this expression of food has captured people's attention, because it is the story not only of Southern cuisine, but also of America's identity. In my short time as a professional chef, I have seen the spotlight pass over every cuisine, from French to Italian to Japanese to Spanish, from nouvelle to comfort to molecular. However, what is happening now in the American South is not part of a trend: It is a culinary movement that is looking inward, not outward, for its inspiration. Every innovation that moves it forward also pulls along with it a memory of something in the past. As Faulkner famously said: "The past is never dead. It's not even past."

What's happening in Southern cuisine is less about technique than about attitude. Take my friend's breakfast, for example. It is tasty but ugly, gluttonous yet frugal, overindulgent but simple. Most of all, though, it is linear. It is history and narrative, full of all the irony and contradictions that make up any good yarn. Some call it tradition—but that's too benign a word.

I ADD A HANDFUL OF SMOKE AND PICKLES

Everyone has a story and a recipe. We cherish them because they are our reinventions. Our recipes convey who we were, are, and want to be. And this is reflected in the food of the best cooks across America, in homes, restaurants, and backyards and at county fairs and tailgates. We are redefining the landscape of how we grow, harvest, name, and eat our very own sustenance. There is a rich diversity in our cuisine—this thing that, for lack of a better term, we call American Cuisine—that is defined by our never-ending search for reinvention.

My story is one of smoke and pickles. Some say umami is the fifth flavor, in addition to salty, sweet, sour, and bitter. I say smoke is the sixth. From the sizzling Korean grills of my childhood to the barbeque culture that permeates the South, I have always lived in an environment where food was wrapped in a comforting blanket of smokiness. My friends found it odd at first that I, a die-hard New Yorker, would move to the South. But for me, it was instinctual. Smoke is the intersection that connects my two worlds. It is

Something is simmering wildly throughout the American South.

found in many incarnations other than the obvious outdoor grill full of charcoal or hardwood. I can add smokiness to any dish by adding bourbon—which picks up toasted notes from the inside of charred oak barrels—or bacon and smoked country hams, or molasses and sorghum, smoked spices, dark beers, tobacco, or meats blackened in a cast-iron skillet. And where there is smoke, there is always a pickle nearby. It's a miraculous thing, the pickle. It's nothing more than a ratio of salt, sugar, sometimes vinegar, and time. But with those few ingredients, you can create an endless array of preserved vegetables and fruits that are the backbone of so many cuisines. In the South, pickles and barbeque go hand in hand because nothing cuts the intensity of smokiness like a sharp pickle. Together they are harmonious, the perfect yin and yang. If I had my way, every dish would start with smoke and pickles—everything else is just a garnish.

Like the Korean-Brooklyn kid in me tugging on a Southern apron, I find connections where others might see contradictions. So these are my stories. Full of holes and inaccuracies, but connected through the recipes. Not like the ones you'll find in the lace-and-antebellum traditional Southern cookbooks. My recipes are filled with smoky flavors and pickles, but they also reflect the people who raise my animals, shoot wild game with me, boil sorghum, pray and sing, and make moonshine. These folks eat and drink like there's no tomorrow. And my recipes grow out of this fecundity. They belong here, in this unique place and time, nowhere else but now.

WHAT I COOK

IS WHO I AM.

Never stick your chopsticks straight up into a bowl of rice; it signifies death.
—KOREAN SUPERSTITION

INTRODUCTION:
RICE & RÉMOULADE

LET'S START WITH THE FOUNDATION,

the fundamental Zen of the Asian table—the bowl of rice that accompanied every meal of my childhood: steamy, chewy, sweet, and comforting. I know memories are supposed to start at age four or five, but I swear I can close my eyes and relive the comfort of those warm bundles of starchy goodness being coaxed into my toothless mouth. Never mind that every baby guide warns that feeding rice to an infant can choke him. Generations of my sinewy, scrappy family were

raised on kilos of sticky rice, and so it was with me. It was rice that would make me strong and smart and allow me to excel in math, science, and history. Rice would make my eyesight sharp, my teeth straight, my fingernails shiny. If I was good, I'd get spicy pork steaming over a bowl of fresh rice. If I was naughty, I'd be threatened with a dinner of cat food—oh, yes, that urban myth of how Asian immigrants, in their quest for thrifty nutrition, ate cat food over steamed rice with soy sauce!

It was drilled into my head that rice was nothing short of a miracle. Every day, our Zojirushi rice cooker steamed away in quiet obedience. During the holidays, my grandmother would throw red beans and chestnuts into the cooker, but other than that, it was always the same. Occasionally, when our trusted rice cooker was on the blink, my grandmother would make rice the traditional way, in a heavy pot, but she didn't like this, because you had to stand over the stove and watch it. And the rice on the bottom would stick to the pot and go from crispy to burnt in the distracted blink of an eye. It was fallible. The rice cooker gave her exactly the same results every time: just follow the preset measurements, push the button, and come back 20 minutes later. The result was always perfect, always consistent. Rice cooked on the stovetop had layers: You'd get light, fluffy rice with a paper-thin skin on top and a crunchy layer on the bottom. (It was customary to eat the fluffy rice for dinner, then add hot barley tea to the pot and scrape up the crunchy bits for an after-dinner treat.) It was fickle, and the rice was different every time. It annoyed my grandmother, this process.

It was as if it reminded her of a lifetime of poverty and chaos and war. She liked the modern convenience of the rice cooker. The consistency calmed her.

But she must have known the rice wasn't as good. Those few times she was forced to make rice in a pot, I'd catch her picking away at the leftover browned bits. The crunch was irresistible. It's the joy of imperfection. This stovetop rice of my childhood is the best recipe to introduce my cuisine. Two ingredients, half an hour, and attention to detail.

Despite my childhood immersion in all things rice, I knew there was more out there. I was twelve. I craved the things you could find in that faraway paradise called Manhattan. At newsstands, I'd peek into issues of *Gourmet* like they were *Playboy,* lusting after lamb roasts and tartes Tatin the same way I lusted after nude women in all their airbrushed glory. I'd whisper the recipes aloud. My head swam with thoughts of exotic ingredients like dried apricots and fresh fennel while I suffered through yet another bowl of rice and cabbage at home. It would take me

RECIPE FOR AN IMPERFECT BOWL OF RICE

The goal when cooking rice this way is to achieve a thin layer of toasted crust in the bottom of the pot. The crispy layer in contrast with the fluffy layer of rice on top is a sumptuous combination. I use a 10-inch cast-iron skillet. You could seek out a stone rice crock like the ones they use in Korean restaurants, but the cast-iron pan works just fine. Make your favorite toppings while the rice is cooking. When the toppings are ready, divide the warm rice, crunchy bits and all, among rice bowls and serve. / **MAKES ENOUGH FOR 4 LARGE RICE BOWLS OR 6 APPETIZER-SIZED ONES**

2 cups Asian long-grain rice
1 teaspoon salt

1 Place the rice in a large bowl and fill the bowl with 4 cups cold water. Using your hands, stir the rice in circles until the water turns cloudy. Drain the rice in a strainer, then return to the bowl and add another 4 cups cold water. Allow the rice to soak for 30 minutes.

2 Drain the rice in the strainer again and shake to release the excess water. Transfer the rice to a 10-inch cast-iron skillet. Add 3 cups cold water and the salt and give it a nice stir. Bring the water to a simmer over medium-high heat. Turn the heat as low as you can, cover the skillet with a tight-fitting lid, and cook for 18 minutes. Turn off the heat and allow the rice to rest for 10 minutes, with the lid still on.

3 Take the lid off the skillet, turn the heat on to medium, and cook the rice, without stirring, for 3 to 5 minutes, until the rice on the bottom of the pan turns amber and crisp. You can keep the rice warm in the skillet until you are ready to serve.

the better part of twenty years and a move to the South to fully appreciate the complexity of all those humble rice bowls, but hey, I was twelve. I was raging hormones, angry and rebellious. I wanted to sink my teeth into venison and gulp cappuccino. I'd been hammering my parents with guilt about how my Jewish friends were getting these super-cool thirteenth-birthday parties called bar mitzvahs and all I had to look forward to was an afternoon of arcade games and a Carvel ice cream cake in the shape of a whale. Where was my Korean bar mitzvah? How would I become a respected physician if I didn't know

how to dine properly? No one would ever take me seriously. Not here in America, where dining out is not a chore but a sport. For my birthday present, my parents were sending me to baseball camp. I hated baseball. I wanted to be on the varsity squad of fine dining! I wanted to go to Sign of the Dove, the pantheon of fine dining back then. Begging would get me nowhere, but money was a more persuasive argument. A dinner at Sign of the Dove would be cheaper than baseball camp. With no risk of expensive injuries. That was that. I made the reservation and we took the L train to my first fancy-pants dinner.

MASTER RECIPE FOR PERFECT RÉMOULADE

Don't be dismayed by the long list of ingredients. All you have to do is throw them all into a bowl and mix them together. This is a master recipe, which means that once this base is done, you can flavor it any way you want. Have fun with it. Use it on everything from burgers to raw vegetables. If you can, make it a day in advance; the flavors will harmonize overnight. / **MAKES ABOUT 3 CUPS**

2 large eggs

1¼ cups mayonnaise, preferably
   Duke's or homemade

⅓ cup finely chopped shallots

½ cup chopped pickled okra
   (substitute chopped cornichons if
   you don't have pickled okra)

2 garlic cloves, grated (use a
   Microplane) or finely minced

1 tablespoon prepared horseradish

2 teaspoons fresh lemon juice

2 teaspoons chopped fresh tarragon

1 teaspoon chopped fresh flat-leaf
   parsley

1½ teaspoons grainy mustard

1 teaspoon ketchup

¾ teaspoon Worcestershire sauce

¾ teaspoon sweet paprika

¼ teaspoon cayenne pepper

¾ teaspoon kosher salt

½ teaspoon sugar

½ teaspoon freshly ground black pepper

Grated zest of 1 orange

Grated zest of 1 lemon

3 dashes Tabasco sauce

1 Put the eggs into a small pot of water and bring to a boil over medium heat. Boil for 4 minutes, then drain and immediately transfer to an ice bath to chill. Drain.

2 Peel the soft-boiled eggs and add to a large bowl. Beat with a whisk; the yolks will still be runny. Don't worry if it's lumpy. Add all the remaining ingredients and mix well with a wooden spoon until the mixture is thick enough to coat the spoon but runny enough to pour out of the bowl. Transfer to a jar and chill in the refrigerator for at least 1 hour before serving. The rémoulade will keep in the refrigerator for up to 5 days.

There are three things I remember about that dinner. The first one was my father drinking scotch and complaining about why it was taking so long. I explained that they did it on purpose so we could have intellectual conversations in between courses. I said it kind of angrily. He didn't speak for the rest of the meal. The second thing was the matching place settings. I was enthralled. Every bread plate had the same pattern on it; the cutlery not only matched, but it was polished, heavy, and neatly aligned. It was, in my innocent estimation, perfection. I touched my cheek to the tablecloth. You see, in our house, every plate, glass, and fork was from a sale rack in some Brooklyn flea market. If a plate broke, you didn't throw out the whole set, you just replaced it with something else about the same size and color. But the imperfection wasn't merely out of necessity or frugality, it was a statement. Our furniture didn't match; our clothes were always either too big or too small; and if the television was out of focus, we

didn't fix it—it was our duty to conform our eyes to the blurry images. I could make some sweeping generalization about Asian culture and the communal versus the individual, but then I'd probably just sound like an ass. Suffice it to say, I longed for something different.

That evening, it came to me in the form of rémoulade. I don't even remember what it was for, just that I'd never had anything like it before: creamy, crunchy, sweet, and sour. I lapped it up, thinking, "What in Buddha's name is this tongue-coating goodness?" It reinforced that nagging suspicion I had that things were indeed better on the other side. We ate mayonnaise; white people ate rémoulade. What other luxuries was I missing? Things I didn't even know existed that other people were taking for granted. I slept restlessly that night and almost every night thereafter for a long time. Somewhere in the folds of that little brain of mine, something clicked, and I knew I would spend the rest of my life chasing the seduction of food. I'd never seen a restaurant kitchen or handled a chef's knife, but I knew I wanted to. I also knew that it would upset the universe my parents had laid out for me. It would make me different, and friends would be hard to come by. Life would become a struggle to find that magical intersection between rice and rémoulade, between the two disparate cultures that overlapped inside me, somewhere neither here nor there, at once flawed and yet desirable. A place like a kitchen.

The recipes in this book are as much about stories as they are about flavors. As I grew up and learned the history of cooking in America, I realized that I was not unique in my discovery of cuisine through the lens of another culture. Evan Jones, author of *American Food: The Gastronomic Story,* described this as "the pattern of bringing from abroad new ways of cooking to be incorporated into an American style that has been evolving since the arrival of the first settlers." So it is as natural for me to baste with fish sauce as it is to cook with Coca-Cola. Both worlds stand at arm's reach.

Everyone has a story and a recipe.

Most of the chapters in this book start with a recipe (or two) that I call, simply, a rice bowl. There are infinite variations. Rice for me is a blank canvas; how you decide on the toppings says a lot about who you are. For me, a rice bowl is both literal and metaphorical, a natural way to express my cuisine. It represents a humble, everyday sort of meal, but I enliven it with modern techniques, global flavors, unusual pairings—basically the sum of everything I've learned and continue to learn. And it is not complete without some sort of a rémoulade on top. After you try a few of my creations, I know you'll get inspired to come up with your own variations defined by your own journey. The chapters are organized so the lighter recipes appear first, followed by those with more complex, bigger flavors. Some of the dishes go best with wine, some with beer, and I give you suggestions where appropriate for both what to drink with the dish and what to serve it with. But feel free to do your own thing. I trust you.

I can't stand the word "fusion," not only because it is dated, but also because it implies a kind of culinary racism, suggesting that foods from Eastern cultures are so radically different that they need to be artificially introduced or "fused" with Western cuisines to give them legitimacy. For as long as I have been cooking in restaurants, it has been common practice for the cooks and waiters to sit down at staff meal and flavor our suppers with curry, salsa verde, soy sauce, Tabasco, mayo, teriyaki, melted butter, and that dreaded plastic bottle of "rooster sauce" (i.e., Sriracha) that exists in every restaurant kitchen. I've always found it funny that we prefer to eat this way, but once the restaurant doors open, we revert to serving a cuisine hampered by traditions and limitations that never acknowledged the modern flavors being embraced by young chefs.

If it is part of our vernacular, then it is part of our pantry. That's a simple mantra that I've tried to follow in my cooking, both at home and at the restaurant. Why exclude anything? If I like pork rinds and I like raw tuna, well, I'll be damned if they don't find a way into a dish together. It isn't forced. My culinary vernacular is broad, and it grows all the time. For now, I surround myself with the bounties of the South and reach back to my roots and to my experiences as a young chef in NYC. That is my story and these are my recipes. I hope you enjoy them.

LAMB & WHISTLES

If you whistle at night,
snakes will come inside
your house and take over
your body.
—KOREAN SUPERSTITION

MY RELATIONSHIP WITH FOOD

developed in three stages: (1) as a memory, (2) as a history, and (3) as an ingredient. Take lamb, for instance. The first memory I have of it is eating it with my sister. Growing up, we never ate lamb. It is not a staple in Korean cuisine, which is odd to me, because lamb goes so well with Korean condiments. It would never have occurred to me to try lamb if not for my sister. She was the adventurous one.

On weekends, she and I would take the subway from Rockaway Parkway to Penn Station and walk eight blocks to the Twenty-sixth Street garment factory our parents managed. You'd call it a sweatshop today, and it sounds horrible to say I spent my childhood weekends in a sweatshop, but it wasn't so bad. I played on the garment racks and spools of plastic dress covers; I ran up and down the fire escapes; and for lunch, Mom would give us each $10 to buy our own meal. For a kid who'd subsisted on rice and cabbage all week, this was a serious treat. We'd come back with burgers or hot dogs, sometimes Chinese food, and Mom would steal a few bites when no one was looking.

My sister was a troublemaker. Every lunch, we'd inch closer to Penn Station, even though (or because?) we'd been told to stay away. This was the 1980s, when Penn Station was rife with drug addicts, swindlers, and criminals of all shades. Every other shop sold porn, and the drunks were already well on their way. It was the weekend, after all. One Saturday, to my mom's horror, we came back with two lamb gyros from the Greek diner. That was bad because (1) Mom knew we'd gone to Penn Station, and (2) she hated lamb. She scolded us and made us promise we'd never go back. She told us lamb was dangerous. She told us it was dirty. But it was too late: I was already hooked. Every weekend became a mission dedicated to finding how to sneak a gyro for lunch without Mom knowing. It's touching now to think back on the way my sister would pull me through a crowd of con artists, drunks, and hookers for our gyro fix. Taped to the greasy tile wall of the diner was a frayed poster of a pretty blond girl eating a Kronos gyro. It was the first thing we'd see as we stepped into the vestibule. My sister would fight her way to a seat at the counter and order us one gyro, extra meat, extra yogurt sauce, extra hot sauce. We'd split it in half and eat it while looking out over a sea of yellow cabs. Then we'd come back to the sweat-shop with slices of pizza we had no appetite for. That was her idea. My sister was the brilliant one.

That is, until she got greedy. Of all the scoundrels populating Penn Station, the dirtiest of all was the three-card monte dealer. Three cards: two black suits and one red suit; a cardboard box for a table; a couple of shills—and you're in business. "Follow the red, not the black." It was wrong, but if we won, we would double our money, not have to split the gyro, and still have leftover cash for a rainy day. "Follow the red, not the black." My sister stood there clenching both bills, watching the dealer's hands as the shills were winning $40, $60 hands. "Follow the red, not the black." How could anyone lose? All one had to do was point to the red card, wait for the dealer to turn it over, and get paid. He wasn't even shuffling very fast. It was easy, too easy. The red card was in the center. It had to be—I'd just followed it with my own eyes. I turned to my sister and pointed. And I saw my lunch money go down on the box, and the ten of spades looking up at the sun. We heard a loud, piercing whistle and, just like that, we were alone on the street corner, stunned, broke, and hungry. From where we stood, we could see the Greek diner. And all the tears in the world wouldn't buy us lunch. We made up a story about dropping our lunch because a car almost hit us. My sister's idea again. Then we sat on a box of cheap dresses and quietly ate bowls of rice and cabbage.

I didn't eat lamb for a long time after that. The next time was in France. I was a cook by then, spending a summer in France traveling through the countryside on my way to Annecy so I could dine at Marc Veyrat's three-star Michelin restaurant. I got a gig at Tante Alice, a quaint little bistro in Lyon where Pierre Gagnaire had gotten his start as a very young chef. There was a picture of him on the wall behind the bar; I can't say if it

was really him or not, but I liked the story. The food was fine but uninspired. The chef was more interested in practicing his English with me than in cooking. After two weeks, sensing my boredom, he sent me to a large brasserie where they rolled out hundreds of covers at both lunch and dinner. At a place like that, you learned to get a quenelle right the first time, every time. The cooks there weren't too fond of me. They said I was just there to learn a few tricks and go back to the States to whore out their recipes for money. They used prostitution as a metaphor for everything. I wasn't getting paid for my work, but every few days, the chef there would give me a little scratch money for beers. I'd save the cash and steal a few swigs of warm pastis from the pantry instead.

The Sunday after I started there was my first day to explore the city of Lyon. It was the gastronomic heart of France, the home of Bocuse, with the best farmers' markets in the country. I'd made a list of everywhere I wanted to visit. It was my only chance to see the city, because in a few days I had to move on to Marseilles, to a seafood restaurant. I was to work in Marseilles for a week before heading to Provence and then to my final destination of Annecy. I showed the cooks my itinerary for Sunday and they cheered me on—better than spending money on a whore, they said. Saturday night, I went to bed like it was Christmas fucking Eve.

If you know anything about Lyon, then you know that everything shuts down on Sunday: all the markets, bakeries, wine shops, and any restaurant worth eating at. I walked for hours with my itinerary slowly turning into a crinkled ball in my clenched fist. This was the cooks' idea of a good joke. Finally I wandered into a busy-looking neighborhood of North African immigrants. I waited in line for thirty minutes at the *tabac* just to smoke some cigarettes—I was that pissed. By the time I found a place to eat, I didn't care that it was a Moroccan joint run by Algerians. I just sat and ate. I ate *braewats* and *bisteeya* and a lamb broth that was so good I nearly fell out of my chair. I smoked and drank tea and listened to cryptic arguments in a language so foreign it sounded like dust. I went home briefly and came back in a few hours for dinner. I ate a lamb tagine and more *braewats* and something that resembled baklava but was much sweeter. It was one of the best meals I had in France. Maybe 'cause I was so hungry. Maybe 'cause it just was. It was lamb in the context of North African history; it was lamb the way they must have eaten it for generations. It was their story; I just got to eavesdrop.

It was their story; I just got to eavesdrop.

The next day, the cooks at the brasserie asked me jokingly how my day off was. I told them to fuck off, and I left a day early for Marseilles so I wouldn't have to say good-bye. I made it to Provence and all the way to Annecy and cooked at Le Belvédère for a week before going to Veyrat's L'Auberge. I treated myself to a long dinner and enjoyed it, but in the way you enjoy something because you know it is costing you so much money. There was lamb on the menu, but I didn't order it. I got the squab instead.

After that, I cooked a lot of lamb, but most of it was mimicry, be it a tagine or a navarin. It only became an ingredient for me after I spent a day with Craig Rogers on his farm in Patrick Springs, Virginia. The flavor of Craig's lamb is unlike anything I'd ever thought of as gamey. Even my mom likes it. It does not need to be boiled for days in perfumed spices. It is a pristine ingredient, and by that I mean a gift. When I first tasted Craig's lamb, it was so mild and creamy and herbaceous that I started to imagine all the different flavors it could play with. It became so much more than ground meat mixed with dried spices and cooked on a rotisserie. It compelled me. And that is how I learned to cook lamb, the long way. It makes me a late bloomer, I know, but sometimes that's just how we have to learn.

Craig doesn't rush himself either. He talks too much and that slows him down, but I like that about him. He gave me a demonstration of how to make sharp whistle calls and I watched his border collies react with military precision. It's their primal instinct to control the flock, and the sheep are happy to oblige. How old is this relationship between dogs and sheep? Almost as old as domestication itself, as old as the first time man settled on a grassy knoll, as old as the first whistle call, as the first swindle. It's funny to think this whole agriculture thing may have started with nothing more than an accidental whistle. Whistles, dogs, sheep, farms, food. Most likely that's not exactly how it went, but it's still nice to think about.

I made all the recipes in this chapter with Craig's lamb. That's important, because unlike some of those earlier lamb preparations that were masked in heavy doses of spices, these are unadorned and simple. We're lucky to have a lot of great lamb producers in the United States now. Try to buy lamb at a farmers' market near you; you want lamb that has grazed on grass, that is hormone free, and that has been raised humanely, not penned. The meat will be slightly paler than commercial lamb, and it should be lean and smell clean.

Good cooking is always simple—not always convenient, but always simple. That's a mantra I've followed over the years. Oh, and the other one is this: Never trade your lunch money for a sleight of hand.

RICE BOWL WITH LAMB

AND AROMATIC TOMATO-YOGURT GRAVY

There is no limit to what a good rice bowl can be. I think this recipe proves that. The meatloaf closely resembles the meat in an NYC-style Greek gyro, the kind that I loved so much as a kid. However, this is a more elegant version, infused with lots of fresh herbs. Don't even bother with dried herbs. I make the lamb in a loaf pan just like you would a traditional meatloaf but then go the extra step of slicing and panfrying it to give it a crispy texture. / **FEEDS 4 AS A MAIN COURSE OR 6 AS AN APPETIZER**

1 pound ground lamb
(85% lean)
1 teaspoon chopped
fresh oregano
1 teaspoon chopped
fresh marjoram
1 teaspoon chopped
fresh rosemary
1½ teaspoons salt
½ teaspoon freshly ground
black pepper
½ teaspoon pimentón
½ cup chopped onion
1 garlic clove, chopped

1 In a medium bowl, combine the lamb, herbs, salt, pepper, and pimentón.

2 Puree the onion and garlic in a food processor. Pour this mixture into a strainer and press out as much of the excess liquid as possible. Knead the onion and garlic mixture into the ground lamb. Chill in the refrigerator for 40 minutes.

3 Preheat the oven to 300°F.

4 Transfer the lamb mixture to a food processor and pulse for 1 minute, or until the mixture is smooth and dense. If you need to pulse for longer than 1 minute, add an ice cube to the food processor so the mixture stays cold. Transfer the mixture to an 8-by-4-inch loaf pan and shape into a loaf with a slightly domed top.

5 Bake the meatloaf for 35 minutes, then turn up the oven to 325°F. Bake for another 10 minutes. Check the internal temperature of the loaf by inserting an instant-read thermometer into the center: It should read between 150 and 160°F. If it doesn't, return the loaf to the oven and check the temperature every 5 minutes.

6 Invert the meatloaf onto a plate, turn right side up, and let cool to room temperature.

7 To make the tomato-yogurt gravy: Heat the olive oil in a medium skillet over medium heat. Add the onions and cumin seeds and sauté for 4 to 5 minutes, until the onions are soft. Add the tomatoes, white wine, tomato paste, ginger, garlic, and bay leaves, bring to a simmer, and cook for 20 minutes. Turn off the heat and let the sauce cool for 5 minutes.

8 Add the yogurt, butter, salt, and pepper to the gravy and whisk thoroughly. Remove the bay leaves and keep the gravy warm until ready to serve.

9 Cut the meatloaf into thin slices. Heat a large skillet over high heat and add ¼ inch of corn oil. Working in batches, add the meatloaf slices and panfry until crispy on the first side, about 4 minutes. Flip and cook for 1 minute longer on the other side. Transfer to paper towels to drain.

10 To serve, scoop the rice into your rice bowls. Place slices of fried meatloaf over the rice. Spoon the gravy over the meat and top with scallion greens. Serve immediately, with spoons—it is best to mix everything together before enjoying.

If you want a classic NYC-style gyro, after frying the meatloaf slices, pile them onto warm pita bread with a bit of cucumber-yogurt sauce, chopped fresh tomatoes, sliced onions, and a liberal sprinkle of hot sauce, and roll it tightly in aluminum foil to catch all the juices.

TOMATO-YOGURT GRAVY
1 teaspoon olive oil
1 onion, finely chopped
½ teaspoon cumin seeds
4 plum tomatoes, chopped
½ cup dry white wine
1 tablespoon tomato paste
½ teaspoon grated fresh ginger (use a Microplane)
1 garlic clove, minced
2 bay leaves
2 tablespoons plain yogurt
1 tablespoon unsalted butter, softened
½ teaspoon sea salt
¼ teaspoon freshly ground black pepper

Corn oil for panfrying

4 cups cooked rice (see page 4)

Greens from 1 bunch scallions, finely chopped

ORANGE LAMB-LIVER PÂTÉ

WITH BRAISED MUSTARD SEEDS

It's a shame we think of pâté as being made only with chicken or duck livers. Lamb's livers are packed with flavor and nutrients. The orange zest in this recipe gives the pâté a delicate perfume. Don't overcook the livers, and always take the extra step of pushing the pâté mixture through a tamis or a fine sieve. The added effort makes the difference between a pâté that's gritty and one with a creamy, velvety texture. / **FEEDS 6 AS AN APPETIZER**

1 To make the braised mustard seeds: Combine all the ingredients in a small saucepan and bring to a boil over medium heat. Lower the heat and simmer for 18 minutes. Transfer to a glass jar, let cool, and refrigerate overnight.

2 The next day, make the pâté: Soak the lamb's liver in a bowl of ice water for at least 1 hour and up to 2 hours.

3 Drain the liver, rinse, and pat dry on paper towels. Cut the liver into 1-inch cubes.

4 Heat a 12-inch skillet over high heat. Add the 2 tablespoons unsalted butter and heat until foamy. Add the onions and garlic and sauté for 2 minutes. Add the lamb's liver and cook for 2 minutes, until lightly browned. Turn the heat to low and add the bourbon and sherry vinegar. Cook until most of the liquid has cooked off, 2 to 3 minutes.

5 Transfer the lamb mixture to a blender. Add the softened butter, grated orange zest, heavy cream, Dijon mustard, salt, and pepper and blend on high for 2 minutes, or until smooth. It should look like a thick milkshake.

6 Gradually pour the contents of the blender through a fine-mesh sieve set over a bowl, pushing on the solids with the back of a spoon; discard the solids.

7 Pour the pâté mixture into six 3-ounce ramekins or small coffee cups. Refrigerate for at least 3 hours before serving. (The pâté can be made up to a day ahead.)

8 To serve, top the pâtés with the braised mustard seeds. Serve with warm toasted bread and the pickled grapes.

BRAISED MUSTARD SEEDS
⅓ cup yellow mustard seeds
⅓ cup brown mustard seeds
½ cup water
½ cup dry white wine
2 tablespoons apple cider vinegar
2 tablespoons sugar
2 tablespoons honey
2 teaspoons Dijon mustard
1 teaspoon sea salt

PÂTÉ
12 ounces lamb's liver
2 tablespoons unsalted butter, plus 2 tablespoons softened unsalted butter
1 cup chopped onions
1 garlic clove, minced
1 tablespoon bourbon
1 teaspoon sherry vinegar
2 teaspoons grated orange zest
½ cup heavy cream
2 teaspoons Dijon mustard
2 teaspoons kosher salt
¼ teaspoon freshly ground black pepper

Warm toasted bread for serving
Pickled Chai Grapes (page 178)

DARKLY BRAISED LAMB SHOULDER

Braising lamb coaxes out deep, hidden notes that yearn for dark flavors like chocolate and sorghum. Using a Dutch oven makes all the difference in a recipe like this, but you can use any heavy pot with a tight-fitting lid. Your lamb shoulder may still have the first three ribs attached to it. The extra bones will add flavor to your broth; you can pull them out before you serve the lamb. Serve this with Soft Grits (page 213) and Red Cabbage–Bacon Kimchi (page 166). / **FEEDS 6 AS A MAIN COURSE**

¼ cup kosher salt

2 tablespoons freshly ground black pepper

1 lamb shoulder roast (3 pounds; see note)

2 tablespoons canola oil

1 cup chopped onions

1 cup chopped carrots

1 cup chopped celery

3 garlic cloves, minced

1 cup chopped button mushrooms

1 jalapeño pepper, chopped (seeds and all)

½ cup bourbon

¼ cup ketchup

1 tablespoon soy sauce

1 tablespoon balsamic vinegar

3 tablespoons sorghum

¼ cup black bean paste (see note)

1½ ounces bittersweet chocolate, chopped

6 cups chicken stock, or as needed

Cooked grits or rice for serving

1 Make a rub by mixing the salt and pepper together in a small bowl. Rub this all over the lamb shoulder and let sit at room temperature for about 30 minutes.

2 Heat the canola oil in a large Dutch oven over medium-high heat. Once the oil is hot, add the lamb shoulder and brown on all sides, about 3 minutes on each side.

3 Add all the vegetables to the pot, tucking them around the meat so they will brown a little. After about 3 minutes, add the bourbon, ketchup, soy sauce, balsamic vinegar, sorghum, black bean paste, chocolate, and stock. The liquid should completely cover the lamb; if it doesn't, add more stock or water to the pot. Bring this to a simmer over medium-high heat. Skim any foam that rises to the top. Lower the heat, put the lid on the pot, and simmer gently for 2½ hours.

4 Take the lid off the pot and cook for an additional 30 minutes. Check for doneness: Does the lamb feel as if it will easily pull off the bone but is not so tender that it will turn to shreds when you try to lift it out of the pan? Good, it is done. Turn off the heat and let the lamb rest for about 15 minutes. (If you want, at this point you can cool and refrigerate this to reheat and serve at a later time; it will actually be better the next day.)

5 Transfer the lamb to a cutting board. Slice the meat against the grain or pull it off the bone in large chunks. Serve it over grits or rice in warm bowls. Ladle the braising liquid with the vegetables over the meat and serve immediately.

If you can't find lamb shoulder, a 3-pound boneless leg of lamb roast will work fine too. You can also use a boneless roast cut into chunks.

Black bean paste is a Chinese condiment made from fermented black or, sometimes, mung beans. It has a salty, tangy, slightly sweet taste. It is too strong to eat right out of the jar, but it does wonders to soups and stews when you want to add a deep umami flavor. You can find black bean paste in the Asian aisle of most grocery stores.

SIMMERED LAMB SHANKS

WITH CASHEW GRAVY

I first started making this dish with lamb necks back when they were easy to come by—farmers were practically giving them away. But chefs caught on to how good the necks taste, and now I almost have to beg Craig to sell me his necks. You might not be able to get necks, so I substituted shanks here; they are just as luscious and easier to find. Of course, if you do find lamb neck at your farmers' market, I encourage you to try it. The cashew gravy is very versatile. I use it on everything from meatballs to chicken wings; it's also great served over roasted cauliflower.

I garnish this dish with fresh cilantro leaves in summer and pomegranate seeds in winter. Try it with a Dogfish Head Imperial IPA for an intense pairing. / **FEEDS 4 AS A MAIN COURSE**

CASHEW GRAVY

3 tablespoons unsalted butter

1½ cups raw cashews

1 cup chopped onions

2 garlic cloves, minced

2 teaspoons grated fresh ginger (use a Microplane)

1 tablespoon garam masala

1½ teaspoons smoked paprika

1 teaspoon cumin seeds

¼ teaspoon turmeric

¼ teaspoon freshly ground black pepper

2 cups chicken stock

One 12-ounce bottle lager beer

1 To make the gravy: Heat the butter in a large skillet over medium heat until it foams. Add the cashews, onions, garlic, and ginger, stir with a wooden spoon, and sauté for 4 minutes, or until the cashews are lightly toasted. Add the spices and continue cooking for another 2 minutes, or until a thick paste forms. Add the chicken stock, beer, coconut milk, and lime juice and bring to a simmer, then turn the heat to medium-low and simmer for 12 to 15 minutes, until the cashews are very soft. Turn off the heat and let the gravy cool for about 5 minutes.

2 Transfer the gravy to a blender. Blend on high for 2 minutes, until a smooth, thick gravy forms. If it is too thick, add water to thin it out: Does it look like peanut butter? It shouldn't. Add water until the gravy will pour out of the blender in a steady stream. Season with salt and pepper.

3 Now brown the shanks: Start by seasoning them with the salt and pepper. Heat the olive oil in a Dutch oven over medium heat. Add the shanks and brown on all sides, about 6 minutes.

4 Turn the heat down to low and pour the cashew gravy to cover the shanks. Cover with a tight-fitting lid and simmer for 2 hours, stirring every 15 minutes so the gravy doesn't burn. (If your lid isn't tight-fitting, you may have to add a little water to the pan to keep the gravy from getting too thick.) After two hours, the meat should be falling off the bone; simmer a little longer if necessary.

5 Serve the shanks over plain or basmati rice with a good helping of the gravy.

1 cup unsweetened
   coconut milk
Juice of 1 lime

4 lamb shanks
   (about 1 pound each)
1 tablespoon kosher salt
1½ teaspoons freshly
   ground black pepper
2 tablespoons olive oil

Cooked plain or basmati
   rice for serving

PULLED LAMB BBQ

The flavor of this lamb BBQ is simple, smoky, and earthy. Lamb is less fatty than pork, so it doesn't beg for a sweet element, which makes it a great vehicle for what I love most about BBQ—the smokiness. You can eat the pulled lamb by itself with just the warm jus on the side for dipping. Or serve it on slider buns topped with caraway pickles and Duke's mayonnaise. You can also serve pulled lamb on plates with Lardo Cornbread (page 208) and Fried Pickles (page 246) for a picnic-style lunch. / **FEEDS 6 TO 8**

SPICE RUB

2 tablespoons kosher salt

1 tablespoon freshly ground black pepper

1 tablespoon dry mustard

1 tablespoon smoked paprika

1 tablespoon ground cumin

1 tablespoon garlic powder

1 tablespoon brown sugar

1 teaspoon cayenne pepper

1 boneless lamb shoulder roast (roughly 3 pounds)

5 cups beef stock

¼ cup apple cider vinegar

1 tablespoon soy sauce

1 teaspoon Tabasco sauce

If you don't have an outdoor grill, you can bypass the grilling step and put the lamb in the roasting pan and then straight into the oven. Increase the cooking time to 5 hours.

1 To make the rub: Combine all the ingredients in a small bowl and mix well. Pat the shoulder all over with the spice rub, applying as thick a layer as you can. Let the meat rest for about an hour. (Any extra rub can be stored in an airtight plastic container in the refrigerator for a month or two.)

2 Heat an outdoor grill until hot. Add some hickory wood chips in the smoker chamber. When the chips start to smoke, place the lamb shoulder on the coolest part of the grill, close the lid, and smoke for 1½ hours. Check the heat occasionally: The grill temperature should not get above 250°F, but it should still be hot enough for the chips to keep smoking. I usually add a handful of chips every time I check the temperature. The rub should now look like a nice dark crust.

3 Meanwhile, preheat the oven to 300°F.

4 Transfer the lamb to a roasting pan. Add the beef stock, cider vinegar, soy sauce, and Tabasco sauce. Cover loosely with aluminum foil. Place in the oven and slow-roast the lamb for 3 hours. It should become very tender and fall easily off the bone.

5 Remove the lamb from the roasting pan (set the pan aside) and shred the meat while it is still hot: Use two forks to pull the meat apart, or put on some disposable gloves and use your hands.

6 Strain the braising liquid, which will have absorbed a lot of the smoky flavor, and use it as a dipping jus.

MAKE A SMOKER ON THE CHEAP

For the best pulled lamb BBQ, use an outdoor grill with an indirect smoker. It requires patience and a little practice, but the key is simply keeping a low constant temperature as the lamb picks up the smoke flavor. If you don't own a proper smoker, there are a number of ways to jerry-rig one on your stovetop.

To make a stovetop smoker, find a large stockpot with a tight-fitting lid. Line the bottom with a double layer of aluminum foil. Add a handful of wood chips and cover with another layer of foil. Find a wire deep-fry basket that has straight sides and set it upside down in your pot. (Sometimes these baskets have handles that would prevent them from fitting inside the pot; just snip them off with wire cutters.) Put your meat on top of the wire basket and cover the pot with the lid. Place the pot over a front burner and turn the heat to high. After 5 minutes, gently lift the lid about half an inch: You should see some wisps of smoke, signaling that the chips are starting to burn. If you don't see any smoke, re-cover the pot, wait another minute, and check again. Once the chips start to smoke, turn the heat to low and seal the lid by wrapping a sheet of aluminum foil around the edges where the lid meets the top of the pot. An improvised smoker like this will get very hot, much hotter than an outdoor grill, so reduce the smoking time by at least half. Once the meat is smoked and lightly crusted, proceed with the recipe, slow-roasting the lamb in the oven.

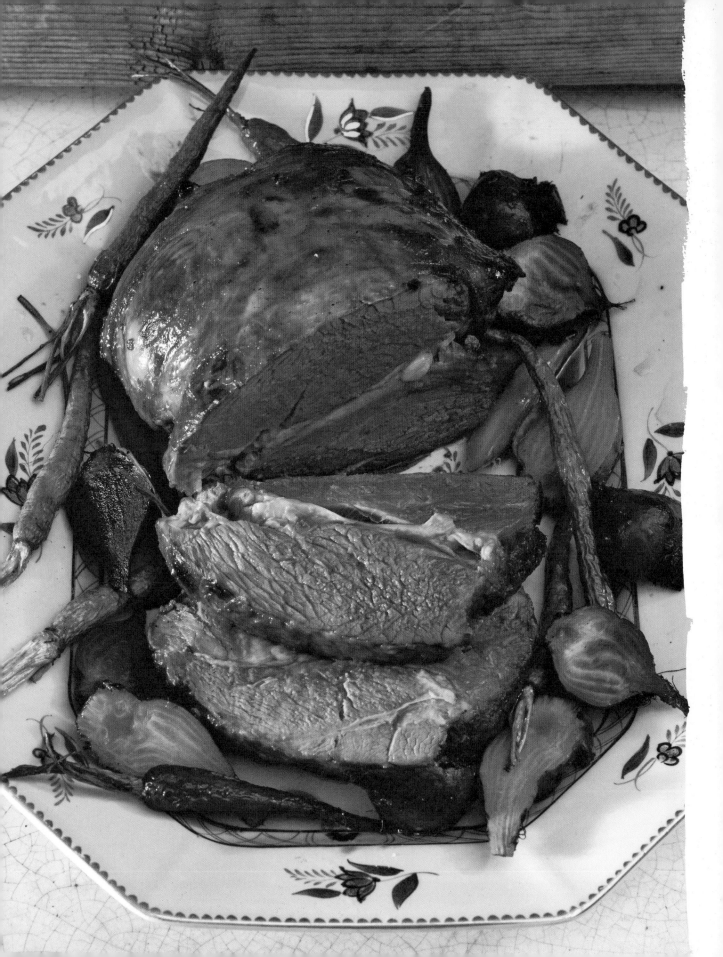

CINNAMON-HONEY ROAST LEG OF LAMB

Many Indian recipes call for yogurt as a marinade to help tenderize meat. Buttermilk has the same effect and also carries the aroma of spices nicely. Everyone has heard of buttermilk-fried chicken, but buttermilk does wonders in tenderizing all kinds of meat, including lamb and pork. This roast doesn't need much else; the cinnamon and honey round it out for balance. It's a subtle, elegant dish that demands you pull out your nice china. Serve the lamb family-style with roasted vegetables and Curried Corn Griddle Cakes (page 209). / **FEEDS 6 TO 8 (OR 4, WITH LEFTOVERS FOR SANDWICHES THE NEXT DAY)**

MARINADE

3 cups buttermilk
1½ cups chopped onions
A small knob of ginger, peeled
2 garlic cloves
Juice of 2 lemons
2 teaspoons cumin seeds
2 teaspoons caraway seeds
2 teaspoons fennel seeds
2 teaspoons sea salt
½ teaspoon freshly ground black pepper

1 boneless lamb leg roast (5 to 6 pounds), rolled and tied up in butcher's twine
2 tablespoons olive oil
2 teaspoons sea salt

HONEY GLAZE

¾ cup honey
2 tablespoons fresh orange juice
½ teaspoon ground cinnamon
¼ teaspoon sea salt

1 Start a day early to marinate the meat: Combine all the marinade ingredients in a blender and blend on medium speed until well combined. Place the lamb leg in a gallon-size resealable plastic bag, pour the marinade into the bag, and seal. (I usually put this into a second bag in case the first one leaks.) Marinate in the refrigerator overnight.

2 The next day, preheat the oven to 325°F.

3 Remove the lamb leg from the bag and rinse thoroughly under cold running water; discard the marinade. Pat the lamb dry. Brush all over with the olive oil and sprinkle with the sea salt. Place in a roasting pan and roast for 1 hour.

4 Meanwhile, make the glaze: Combine the honey, orange juice, cinnamon, and salt in a bowl and whisk to blend. Reserve.

5 After the lamb has spent an hour in the oven, turn the heat up to 450°F and start glazing the roast: Open the oven door and, without removing the lamb from the oven, brush a thick layer of the honey glaze over the top of the roast. Roast for another 15 to 20 minutes, brushing a layer of glaze over it every 5 minutes. Check for doneness: An instant-read thermometer inserted into the middle of the roast should read 135°F for rare, or 140°F for medium-rare. Remove the butcher's twine from the meat and let the meat rest on a cutting board for 10 minutes before slicing and serving.

ROTI WITH SLICED LAMB LEG

(OR, A RECIPE FOR USING LEFTOVER LAMB LEG ROAST)

There are infinite versions of roti; this one, a simplified version that is fast and yummy, was inspired by the street carts of Malaysia. Practice the technique of rolling rotis out very thin. The thinner they are, the flakier and more delicate they will be. Try this roti in place of your favorite sandwich bread, or as an accompaniment for the lamb shanks with cashew gravy (page 20). Wash this down with a bottle of Jockamo IPA from Abita. / **MAKES 5 PIECES OF BREAD**

ROTI
2 cups all-purpose flour
1½ teaspoons salt
½ teaspoon sugar
½ teaspoon ground cumin
¼ teaspoon baking powder
1 cup plain yogurt (see note)

5 teaspoons clarified butter or ghee (see opposite)

FOR EACH SANDWICH
1 large thin slice leftover Cinnamon-Honey Roast Leg of Lamb (page 25)
Sliced cucumbers, sliced roasted red peppers, sliced cooked asparagus, and sliced avocado
A dollop of plain yogurt
A few dashes of hot sauce (Texas Pete is my favorite)

1 To make the roti: Combine all the dry ingredients in a medium bowl and whisk together to combine. Add the yogurt and mix with your hands until the dough comes together. Transfer to a lightly floured work surface and knead for 2 minutes. Divide the dough into 5 pieces and roll out to about ⅛ inch thick.

2 Heat 1 teaspoon of clarified butter per roti in a frying pan over medium-high heat and add the roti dough. Fry until crispy on one side, about 2 minutes. Flip and crisp up the next side, about 2 minutes. Take out of the pan, drain on paper towels, and serve immediately or hold on a plate in a warm oven until ready to eat.

3 To make the sandwiches: Warm the lamb in a 300°F oven for 5 minutes. Place the slices of lamb on top of the fresh roti. Add some sliced cucumbers, sliced roasted red peppers, and sliced avocado to each one, top with yogurt and a few dashes of hot sauce, and roll into a tight cylinder. If you want to get fancy about it, wrap some butcher paper around each sandwich and fold the end over to keep the juices from spilling onto your arms.

Make the roti with plain unstrained yogurt. It will not work with thick Greek yogurt (there's not enough liquid in it).

CLARIFIED BUTTER/
GHEE/DRAWN BUTTER

Clarified butter is butter that has been separated or "clarified" from the milk solids, leaving only the translucent butterfat. In Indian cuisine, it is called ghee. In seafood restaurants, they call it drawn butter. It's all the same. You can find clarified butter in most gourmet shops, and you can find jars of ghee at any Indian market. You can also make it yourself by ever so slowly melting a few sticks of butter in a small pot. The butter will separate into three layers. The top is the whey proteins, which will look frothy—this can easily be spooned off. The milk solids will sink to the bottom. And the golden liquid in the middle is the clarified butter. Gently pour this through cheesecloth into a Mason jar or other container. Stop pouring just before the milk solids leave the pot. There are many advantages to using clarified butter—it can be heated to a higher temperature without smoking, it has a slightly nutty flavor that permeates anything you cook in it, and it keeps for weeks in the refrigerator.

VIETNAMESE LAMB CHOPS

I learned how to make this lamb dish while hanging out with a Vietnamese cook when I was in France. I love the irony of it: I spend four months in France, and one of the favorite recipes I come away with is from a Vietnamese line cook who made an incredibly simple dish from the scraps of lamb that went into the family meal bin. Sometimes he'd collect the scraps for days until he had enough to make a large portion. I think the marinade was supposed to kill off any bacterial growth—I've adapted the recipe a bit so you don't have to use deteriorating meat. / **FEEDS 4**

**8 lamb loin chops,
about 1 inch thick**

MARINADE
½ cup honey
½ cup fish sauce
¼ cup grapeseed oil
¼ cup bourbon
3 tablespoons soy sauce
**2 tablespoons minced
garlic (6 cloves)**
**1 tablespoon ground
coriander**
**1 tablespoon freshly
ground white pepper**
**2 teaspoons fresh lime
juice**

GARNISH
Chopped fresh cilantro
Lime wedges
**Fried Shallots
(opposite)**

**Edamame Hummus
(page 199)**

1 Place the lamb chops in a glass baking dish.

2 To make the marinade: Put all the ingredients into a medium bowl and whisk together until thoroughly combined. Pour the mixture over the lamb chops and gently massage it into the meat. Cover and refrigerate for at least 4 hours, or as long as overnight.

3 Take the lamb out of the refrigerator and let it come up to room temperature. Preheat the oven to 425°F.

4 Transfer the lamb, with the marinade, to a roasting pan. Roast the chops, uncovered, for 15 minutes, or until the glaze is shiny and slightly caramelized. Flip and roast for another 5 minutes.

5 Garnish the chops with cilantro, lime wedges, and the fried shallots and serve with the hummus.

FRIED SHALLOTS

MAKES ABOUT 3 CUPS

5 shallots
1½ teaspoons salt
2 cups corn or peanut oil

1 Slice the shallots as thin as possible (use a mandoline, if you have one, or a sharp chef's knife). Put the sliced shallots into a colander and rinse under cold running water for 1 minute to rinse off any bitter juice that may have collected when slicing. Shake dry, transfer to paper towels, and sprinkle with the salt. Let sit for 10 minutes.

2 Using fresh paper towels, press the shallots to squeeze out as much excess water as possible. Transfer to a plate and separate the strands with your fingers.

3 Heat the oil to 350°F in a large skillet or wok. Fry the shallots in the oil for about 5 minutes, stirring occasionally, until they turn golden brown and crispy. With a spider or skimmer, transfer the shallots to a large plate lined with several layers of paper towels; they will continue to darken and crisp slightly as they cool.

4 The fried shallots are best used right away, but they can be stored at room temperature in an airtight container lined with paper towels.

GRILLED LAMB HEART KALBI

IN LETTUCE WRAPS

I get a lot of goodies from Craig Rogers: lamb entrails, kidneys, prairie oysters . . . but my favorite organ meat by far is the heart. When cooked right, lamb hearts are sweet, juicy, and supple—just the way a good heart should taste. They are high in calories, though, so I like to serve them in these little lettuce wraps, nestled in just the right combination of sweet and spicy. The trick is to cook them rare, or they get tough and chewy.

Don't tell your guests just what they're eating until they ask you what these bits of deliciousness are. To really impress, serve these with a glass of sparkling rosé Prosecco. / FEEDS 6 AS AN APPETIZER

MARINADE

¾ cup chopped onion

¾ cup soy sauce

¼ cup Asian sesame oil

2 tablespoons granulated sugar

2 tablespoons brown sugar

2 tablespoons mirin (sweet rice wine)

3 garlic cloves

A small knob of ginger, peeled and sliced

1 tablespoon toasted sesame seeds

1½ teaspoons red pepper flakes

6 lamb hearts

1 To make the marinade: Combine all the ingredients except the sesame seeds and red pepper flakes in a blender and blend on high for 1 minute. Transfer to a medium glass bowl and stir in the sesame seeds and red pepper flakes.

2 To clean the lamb hearts: Trim off some but not all of the fat from the surface of the hearts. Cut the hearts in half and lay cut side up on a cutting board. Trim some of the veins and arteries from the inside of the hearts. Rinse the hearts under cold running water, add to the marinade, and marinate in the refrigerator for 30 minutes.

3 Meanwhile, make the kimchi puree: Combine the kimchi, chipotle peppers, sesame oil, and lemon juice in a blender and blend on high for 2 minutes, or until a thick puree forms. Transfer to a bowl, cover, and refrigerate until ready to use.

4 Remove the hearts from the marinade and pat dry on paper towels. Heat a large cast-iron skillet over high heat until hot. Add 1 tablespoon of the corn oil and carefully add half the lamb hearts to the pan. Sear very quickly, about 1 minute on each side, until the outside is blackened and caramelized but the inside is still rare. Remove from the heat, then heat the remaining tablespoon of oil and sear the remaining lamb hearts.

5 To make the lettuce wraps: Place a piece of lamb heart on each romaine lettuce spear, top with a spoonful of the kimchi puree, and garnish with a slice of jalapeño and chopped cilantro. Serve immediately.

If you're not quite ready to try lamb hearts, don't despair. This recipe works equally well with thinly sliced lamb loin or, more traditionally, with thinly sliced beef short ribs. Just substitute for the hearts the same amount of lamb loin or beef (about 12 ounces).

KIMCHI PUREE

2 cups Red Cabbage–Bacon Kimchi (page 166)

One 4-ounce can chipotle peppers in adobo sauce

¼ cup Asian sesame oil

1 teaspoon fresh lemon juice

2 tablespoons corn oil

12 romaine lettuce spears, taken from the inside of the head

12 slices jalapeño peppers for garnish

Chopped fresh cilantro for garnish

LAMB BACON

One of the advantages of working with lamb is that it's a manageably sized animal for anyone who wants to get on the nose-to-tail bandwagon. Butchering a 300-pound pig in your kitchen is probably not going to happen. But a whole lamb might be possible—it will weigh 50 to 60 pounds. Lamb bacon is a great beginner's curing recipe, and the results are sublime. / **MAKES ENOUGH FOR 6 PEOPLE**

1 cup kosher salt

½ cup sugar

2 pounds lamb bellies
  (roughly 2 pieces)

A handful of fresh
  rosemary sprigs

Hickory wood chips,
  soaked in warm water

Make large batches of this bacon and keep the extra in your freezer. It will stay good for up to a month.

1 Combine the salt and sugar in a bowl. Trim the bellies of any loose pieces of fat or sinew and rub the salt-sugar cure all over them. Layer the bellies in a shallow dish with the skin side down, adding some rosemary sprigs between each layer. Sprinkle the extra cure and the last of the rosemary over the top and put in the back of the refrigerator. Leave uncovered for 2 days; the bellies will absorb the salt and leach out liquid.

2 After the 2 days, remove the bellies from the cure and discard the rosemary. Rinse the bellies under cold water and transfer to a large tub. Cover with cold water and soak for 2 hours.

3 Light your charcoal grill. Remove the bellies from the water and pat dry on paper towels.

4 Place some soaked wood chips right on top of the hot coals; 2 handfuls of chips should be enough. Once the wood begins to smoke, fit the grill rack over the chips. Scatter another handful of soaked wood chips over the grill rack and place the lamb bellies skin side down over the wood chips. This prevents the bellies from cooking directly on the hot metal grill rack. Cover the grill and smoke the lamb bellies for 2 to 3 hours. Monitor the temperature—it should stay between 160 and 200°F—and add more wood chips to the hot coals if necessary. The bellies are done when they are slightly blackened; the flavor will be smoky but mild, and the meat will have a little resistance but ultimately give way in your mouth as you bite into it.

5 Chill the bacon in your refrigerator before slicing it and using it in any dish where you would use pork bacon. To store it, wrap each belly individually in plastic wrap and store in the refrigerator for up to a week or in the freezer for up to a month.

Rub the cure over the entire surface of the lamb.

Store the lamb in a shallow dish.

Rinse the lamb under cold water.

Cook the lamb belly skin side down.

SPINACH SALAD

WITH SPICED PECANS, LAMB BACON, CLEMSON BLUE CHEESE, AND BOURBON VINAIGRETTE

Lamb bacon is an elegant variation on pork bacon. The subtlety of the bacon pairs nicely with salads that want a more delicate flavor, like this one. If you're not in the mood to put lamb bacon in a salad, I wouldn't necessarily pair it with plain-old breakfast eggs, unless the eggs were shirred, with a little Roncal and chervil. Oh, that might be nice. But try this salad first. / FEEDS 4

BOURBON VINAIGRETTE

¼ cup bourbon

¾ cup olive oil

2 tablespoons apple cider vinegar

1 tablespoon maple syrup

¼ teaspoon sea salt

½ teaspoon freshly ground black pepper

SALAD

8 ounces Lamb Bacon (see page 32), cut into small cubes

8 ounces spinach

½ cup pecans

1 green apple, cored and cut into matchsticks

1 breakfast radish, sliced into thin rounds

4 ounces Clemson blue cheese or other mild artisan blue cheese, crumbled

1 To make the vinaigrette: Start by pouring the bourbon into a small saucepan and bringing it to a boil over medium heat. Be careful, because the alcohol in the bourbon could ignite. If that happens, to tamp out the flame, simply put a tight-fitting lid over the pot—the lack of oxygen will suffocate the flame; remove the lid after a few seconds. Boil to reduce the liquid to about 2 tablespoons. Transfer the bourbon to a ramekin and refrigerate until well chilled.

2 Combine the olive oil, vinegar, maple syrup, salt, and pepper in a small bowl. Whisk in the reduced bourbon. Keep refrigerated; bring to room temperature when ready to use.

3 To make the salad: Put the lamb bacon in a small skillet and cook, stirring, over medium-low heat just until it becomes crispy on the outside, 5 to 6 minutes. Transfer to a paper towel to drain what little fat will render from the bacon.

4 Combine the remaining salad ingredients in a large bowl and add the lamb bacon. Toss gently with the bourbon vinaigrette and serve immediately.

In winter, I make this salad using kale instead of spinach and warm the vinaigrette just slightly.

CURRIED LAMB PROSCIUTTO

This recipe is ambitious. It requires an extra refrigerator (see Curing, page 40). Take out all but the top rack, which is what you will use for hanging the leg of lamb. Turn the temperature up as high as it will go, usually around 38° to 40°F, and you have a safe environment that will hold a few lamb legs.

I like curing lamb because it takes a lot less time than pork. A pork leg prosciutto will require you to wait 18 months—talk about delayed gratification. But a lamb leg will be ready in a mere 66 days. And you'll look like a charcuterie god when you serve this lamb sliced tableside to your guests. You can make it without the curry paste, but the curry adds a seductive aromatic. You'll be amazed at how soft the curry notes become. This is great on its own or in the following salad recipe. It lasts for about a month in my house, but depending on how often you serve it, it could be gone in a couple of weeks. / **MAKES 1 LAMB PROSCIUTTO**

1 bone-in leg of lamb,
    about 6 pounds

FIRST CURE
1 cup kosher salt
½ cup sugar
½ cup freshly ground black
    pepper

SECOND CURE
1 cup kosher salt
½ cup sugar
Curry Paste (recipe
    follows)

1 Trim off any excess fat and sinew from the surface of the lamb leg. Make the first cure by combining the salt, sugar, and black pepper in a small bowl. Put the leg in a large tub that holds it comfortably and rub the cure generously over the entire surface of the leg; it is best to wear disposable gloves when doing this. Scoop up the excess cure that falls to the bottom of the tub and keep rubbing the lamb leg with it. Cover the tub with plastic wrap and put it in the back of your regular refrigerator for 18 days; turn the leg every 2 days or so.

2 After 18 days, remove the lamb leg from the tub and rinse it under cold running water for 10 minutes. Make the second cure by mixing the salt and sugar together in a small bowl. Rub this cure over the lamb leg (wearing disposable gloves) just like you did the first time. Then smear the curry paste over the entire surface of the leg. Cover the tub with plastic wrap and put it in the back of your regular refrigerator for another 8 days.

3 After 8 days, remove the lamb from the tub and rinse it under cold running water for 10 minutes. Transfer the lamb leg to a clean large tub and fill it with cold water. Soak the lamb leg for 1 hour.

4 Take the leg out of the water and pat it dry with paper towels. At this point, the lamb leg is cured, but it needs to hang in a cool, dry environment with good air circulation to dry out. Tie it up with twine, then suspend it, fatter end down, from the rack in your curing refrigerator for at least 40 days.

5 After 40 days, the lamb prosciutto is ready to slice and serve. You can continue aging it for up to another 30 days if you want, or cut it into chunks and freeze it. Store leftovers in the refrigerator for up to 2 weeks.

Slicing cured meats is an art unto itself, but suffice it to say, slice it as thin as you can.

CURRY PASTE

MAKES ABOUT 1 CUP

4 garlic cloves
A knob of ginger, peeled and sliced
¼ cup canola oil or other neutral oil
3 tablespoons unsweetened coconut milk
2 tablespoons tomato puree
2 tablespoons soy sauce
1 teaspoon sea salt
1 teaspoon sugar
1 teaspoon cayenne pepper
1 teaspoon garam masala
1 teaspoon ground cumin
1 teaspoon ground coriander
½ teaspoon turmeric
½ teaspoon freshly ground black pepper

Combine all the ingredients in a blender or a food processor and blend until a thick paste forms. The paste can be made ahead and stored in an airtight container in your refrigerator for up to a month.

SALAD OF CURRIED LAMB PROSCIUTTO

WITH DRIED APRICOTS, PINE NUTS, FENNEL, AND TARRAGON VINAIGRETTE

Fennel is a nice foil for salty curried lamb. Here the fennel adds brightness to the salad, while the apricots lend a layer of sweetness. But you can be creative with the mix: Try it with fresh figs, washed-rind cheeses from Alsace, or pickled watermelon rind. And enjoy the salad with a crisp Pinot Blanc. / FEEDS 4

VINAIGRETTE

3 tablespoons fresh tarragon leaves, finely minced

1 teaspoon minced garlic

1 tablespoon Dijon mustard

½ teaspoon kosher salt

¼ teaspoon freshly ground black pepper

3 tablespoons rice vinegar

6 tablespoons extra virgin olive oil

1 large fennel bulb, stalks removed

½ teaspoon kosher salt

8 to 10 slices Curried Lamb Prosciutto (page 36)

4 dried apricots, sliced very thin

¼ cup toasted pine nuts

1   To make the vinaigrette: Combine all the ingredients in a small bowl and whisk together until emulsified. (The vinaigrette can be made ahead and stored in a glass jar in the refrigerator for up to 1 week.)

2   To make the salad: Using a mandoline, shred the fennel as fine as possible. Transfer to a large bowl, add the salt, and toss gently. Allow to wilt at room temperature for 15 minutes.

3   Toss the wilted fennel with enough of the vinaigrette to just moisten.

4   Arrange the lamb slices on a plate. Layer the fennel on top and scatter the apricots and pine nuts over it. Drizzle with the remaining vinaigrette.

CURING

I never know how to explain why I love the process of curing so much. We make a lot of cured meats at my restaurant, from country hams to duck breasts—we even cure sea urchin roe. It's the most gratifying form of cooking I know, because it takes the most time to complete. I'm always trying to teach our guests how to do it. I'll start by saying, "It's easy. If a caveman could do it, so can you. It's nothing but salt and sugar." Then I go on about salt solutions and fermentation and the philosophy of preservation, and next thing I know, I've lost them. Yet to me, the greatest gift of a chef is the ability to distill a complex process into a few simple steps that anyone can wrap their brain around. Yes, the sublime art of charcuterie and salumi, with its infinite permutations and flavor combinations, requires a lifelong dedication to a craft that most chefs, including me, will never completely master. *But* (and here is where you come in), just because you may never make the perfect culatello, that shouldn't prevent you from participating in the great pleasure of curing. So let's take all the smoke and mirrors away and bring it down to brass tacks.

Curing is a process that results in an absence of moisture, which is what bacteria need to multiply. Salt is your tool to draw moisture out of a piece of meat. The bigger your piece of meat, the more salt and time you need to cure it. The most important ingredient when curing meats is patience. When you eat a slice of properly aged ham, you are tasting the culmination of time passing. You are eating a slice of the past, of history. Damn it, I'm getting all dreamy about curing again.

There are three important things to remember about curing.

1 Nitrates are helpful but not necessary for the curing process. They're a chemical agent used mostly to preserve the appealing color of the meat. I do not use nitrates for any of my cured meats.

2 Most meat from commercial sources has been properly air-chilled to kill harmful bacteria, but some organically grown meats slaughtered at small family-run abattoirs will not have been. So, just to be safe, before curing any cut of meat, freeze it until the meat gets down to 42°F; putting the meat in your freezer overnight will usually do the trick. Thaw the meat completely before curing it.

3 Traditional curing requires a vermin-free environment in which to store the meat at a constant temperature of between 50 and 60°F, with humidity at around 75 percent and constant air circulation. If you have an environment like this to hang your meats, that's great. A wine refrigerator is perfect. Most of us don't have a wine fridge, though. If you really want to get into curing, you could buy an extra no-frills refrigerator for it. The lower temperature of the refrigerator, around 30 to 34°F, means it'll require more time for the curing process to happen, but it will ensure that you won't have a bacterial outbreak. Remove all but the top rack from the refrigerator. Set the temperature to its highest setting, usually about 38°F. Hang your meats by tying them to the top rack with butcher's twine. Be sure to leave plenty of space between the meats for air circulation. If there's anyone in your house you think might interfere with your curing process, put a padlock on the refrigerator door.

THE CHEESEMAKER

I first met Pat Elliot at an American Cheese Society Conference in Louisville. For most of us, one profession is enough to keep us busy. Pat has three—physician, farmer, and cheesemaker—and she is brilliant at all of them. She raises her own sheep, and as a physician, she looks at animals with an added perspective that the average farmer does not have. I love that about her. Conversation topics with her can skip rapidly from animal feed to medicine to the density of cheese rinds. I have used her cheeses from the day we opened 610 Magnolia. If Pat is in a good mood, she'll send me some samples of unpasteurized sheep's-milk yogurt with the cheese delivery. That doesn't stay at the restaurant, though—it comes straight home with me.

"Sheep are not dumb. They are not weak. They are stoic animals. They have an incredible ability to withstand pain without showing it. This is because they are flock animals, and the wolves always go after the weak ones. Over time, sheep evolved to show no pain, even when they were sick, so they wouldn't be singled out by predators. Farmers who raise sheep sometimes complain that their sheep will drop dead out of the blue without showing any symptoms. That is not true. You just have to observe them more closely, because they hide their pain when they get sick. They are extraordinary animals."

—PAT ELLIOT, CHEESEMAKER
(AND PHYSICIAN),
EVERONA DAIRY, RAPIDAN, VIRGINIA

COWS & CLOVER

If you eat lying down,
or fall asleep right after
a meal, you will be
reincarnated as a cow.
—KOREAN SUPERSTITION

★ ★ ★

BEEF HAS BEEN BOTH MY FAVORITE

meat and my biggest disappointment. Korean barbeque—the holy trinity of salt, sweet, and smoke—still acts as a sensory trigger for me that starts with that first bite of tangy, charred meat and ends in a cradle of childhood euphoria, when I could eat beef to my heart's delight without the worry of indigestion or lipids. Kalbi, with its charcoal-fired sweet-soy-and-pungent-garlic aftertaste, was the reason my family would venture out to Koreatown. Those trips provide some

of my fondest memories of being a kid. So naturally, when I opened a restaurant, I tried my hand at a Korean BBQ joint, in a location on Mott Street that no one else wanted.

What started as a tiny place to sell hot plates of kalbi soon became a full-blown hipster restaurant. We added salads and desserts, then we added wines and cocktails to supplement our original offering of OB beer and Heineken. I was twenty-five and still very green. My original plan was to sell Korean BBQ to white people and make a little money so I could enroll in cooking school. But within a few months, I was entertaining celebrities and fashionistas and selling lychee martinis by the dozens. I was making too much money to close, and I was having too much fun to stop. Every night, we started out as a marginally respectable restaurant, but by midnight someone was dancing on the bar or making out in the kitchen, and suspiciously long lines would develop for the bathroom.

I hung out with artists and designers, I dated a Japanese actress, I watched the sun rise with random people who became my friends, and I got to spend one idiotically epic night with Joe Strummer and Bob Gruen. My culinary aspirations were on hold—actually they were marinating in a tequila bottle.

On one particularly chaotic night, in walked Jeremiah Tower. For those of you too young to remember him, Tower was the other half of Chez Panisse. He and Alice Waters propelled Chez Panisse from a neighborhood Berkeley restaurant to one of the most important institutions in the history of American cuisine. Their eventual split was very public and very acerbic. Like Kobe and Shaq, they both moved on to great careers, but never as blindingly bright as during their heyday at Chez Panisse. If I'm sounding like a sycophant, it's because I am. For a young chef like me, they represented the pinnacle of what could be accomplished when a restaurant and a committed philosophy of agriculture come together. They were revolutionary, and they inspired a generation of chefs to follow their lead.

I was born the year Jeremiah Tower started at Chez Panisse, and here he was sitting in my tiny hipster restaurant. I wanted to impress him. But with what? Some watercress and a dying Asian pear? There was a girl passed out on the bar; she happened to be my waitress. I had some frozen skate in the cooler and a badly butchered duck in the back of the reach-in. I decided to stick with my ace in the hole: grilled kalbi short ribs. We sold bus tubs worth of them every night. I had a packed restaurant devouring them. I sent out a heaping sizzle plate of short ribs, along with our tray of condiments. I drank a beer and waited for the accolades. But they never came. What did come back was a plate of cold, congealed, barely touched short ribs. All he'd eaten was the rice and condiments. Orders were flying in on my board, but I didn't care. I sat on a milk crate and died. All that revelry and cash started to feel like failure.

I took a bite of my own kalbi; the sweet-and-salty marinade was pretty good, but the meat underneath was remarkably bland. God, I'd just wrecked everything Tower ever stood for. I went to his table expecting the worst. But he was polite, gentle even. He had nothing negative to say, but nothing glowing either (which, of course, said it all). He asked me a few harmless questions about the restaurant, looked around at the drunken hipsters spilling out of their chairs, and smiled indifferently before skipping out into the evening.

It was one night, one customer. Best to shrug it off and keep going. But it bugged me, and the feeling festered; it was taking the fun out of all the fun I was having. I called my purveyor and ordered the best beef he could find. I asked him where the meat came from. He said Iowa. I asked where in Iowa. He said he didn't know. I hung up the phone and called another purveyor. I asked more questions; I asked what the cows were fed. I got silence. I hung up and called another purveyor. That guy lied to me. I called farm after farm, and after two hours on the phone, I found a guy in upstate New York who could sell me Hereford beef—but I'd have to take a quarter of the whole animal and he could only deliver on Tuesdays. And it was double the price of what I was paying. I looked around my tiny kitchen and saw my chickens and eggs and pork ribs and squid and celery and mangoes and carrots and spices and beans and rice and . . . and I thought, "Oh, this is gonna suck."

I didn't transform my kitchen overnight. It's been a long road, and any chef out there who starts down that path knows that the rabbit hole is very, very deep. But once you start, it's almost impossible to turn back. The hardest part is the first step, and the best part is turning a disappointment into an inspiration.

I was a literature major, so I like to see things as metaphors. The beef was only the surface of this hulking mass of a disappointment I'd built. I'd thought things were all going my way, and they kinda were. But I knew inside that there was more to life than grilled meat and tequila shots. Three years of the restaurant had gone by in a blink.

All that revelry and cash started to feel like failure.

My girlfriend had moved to Italy; my new friends were creepy. And then two planes reduced the Twin Towers to ashes. I lost a dear friend. I lost all the money I'd saved. I needed a break.

I don't remember exactly why I decided to go to the Kentucky Derby. For a city kid from Brooklyn, that seersucker-and-bourbon spectacle somehow seemed like the panacea to my urban hell. A friend of a friend knew of a restaurant in Louisville that would hire me for the weekend of the Derby, so I could make a little cash and see a bit of the bluegrass. I wanted to take my shoes off and walk barefoot through fields of clover. I wanted to walk alongside the cows that grazed on the same grass that was below my feet. I packed my bag for a week. And it was a week that would change my life forever.

RICE BOWL WITH BEEF,

ONIONS, COLLARDS, FRIED EGG, AND CORN CHILI RÉMOULADE

Whenever I can succesfully marry my love for Asian BBQ with my favorite Southern ingredients, I know I've made something special. The marinade for this beef was inspired by the popular Korean bulgogi sauce, and the collards are a true Southern icon. The history of collard greens begins with the African roots of the slaves in the colonial South, and the need to feed families with a hearty and nutritious green that was easy to farm, but it has grown into a tradition of abundance, celebration, and comfort. And here the collards seem right at home in a simple but satisfying rice bowl. / **FEEDS 4 AS A MAIN COURSE OR 6 AS AN APPETIZER**

CORN CHILI RÉMOULADE

1 teaspoon unsalted butter

2 ears corn, shucked and
    kernels removed

¼ cup Perfect Rémoulade
    (page 6)

1 teaspoon chili powder

MARINADE

1 garlic clove, grated
    (use a Microplane)

1 teaspoon grated fresh
    ginger (use a Microplane)

3 tablespoons soy sauce

1 tablespoon Asian
    sesame oil

2 teaspoons fresh lemon juice

2 teaspoons sugar

½ teaspoon salt

½ teaspoon freshly
    ground black pepper

One 1-pound flat-iron steak,
    thinly sliced

COLLARDS

1 tablespoon olive oil

1 tablespoon unsalted butter

1 cup diced onions

1 To make the rémoulade: Melt the butter in a small sauté pan over medium heat. Add the corn and sauté for 3 to 4 minutes, until tender. Remove from the heat, stir in the rémoulade and chili powder, and set aside.

2 To marinate the beef: Combine all the marinade ingredients in a bowl. Add the steak slices, turning to coat. Allow to marinate for 20 minutes at room temperature.

3 While the steak is marinating, cook the collards: In a large skillet, heat the olive oil and butter over medium heat until the butter melts. Add the onions and cook for 8 to 10 minutes, until caramelized and nicely browned. Add the collard greens, salt, and vinegar, and sauté for 5 minutes, or until the collard greens are wilted. These aren't braised collards, so don't cook all the color out of them—they should be wilted but still with enough crunch to keep your mouth happy. Transfer the collards to a warm plate and cover to keep warm.

4 Cook the steak: Heat the sesame oil in a large skillet over medium heat. Add the steak slices, with the marinade, and cook, stirring constantly, for 3 to 5 minutes, until the beef is browned and cooked all the way through. Transfer the beef to a bowl and keep warm until ready to serve.

5 To cook the eggs: In the same skillet, melt the butter. Fry the eggs sunny-side up one at a time. Keep warm until ready to serve.

6 To serve, scoop the rice into your rice bowls. Spoon the collard greens over the rice and place the beef over the greens. Place a fried egg over the beef in each bowl and spoon about a tablespoon of the rémoulade over the egg. Serve immediately, with spoons—it is best to mix everything together before enjoying.

If you can't find flat-iron steak, sirloin or boneless short ribs work just as well. But stay away from tougher cuts like flank, because they'll seize up and become very chewy, which isn't the texture you want alongside soft, fluffy rice.

1 bunch collards
   (12 ounces), ribs
   removed, roughly
   chopped
1 teaspoon salt
1 teaspoon apple cider
   vinegar

1 tablespoon Asian
   sesame oil

EGGS
1½ tablespoons
   unsalted butter
4 large eggs,
   preferably organic

4 cups cooked rice
   (see page 4)

STEAK TARTARE

WITH A SIX-MINUTE EGG AND STRAWBERRY KETCHUP

This is one of the few "restaurant-style" dishes in the book, but most of the prep can be done ahead of time, so when it comes to serving, it's really about timing the egg just right. When the runny egg yolk breaks, it's super sexy, and it brings all the other ingredients together. The Strawberry Ketchup adds an unexpected twist. The typical tomato ketchup relies on the concentrated sweetness of the tomato, a fruit. This version replaces the tomatoes with strawberries, which have an umami-rich sweetness of their own when cooked. Think of it as ketchup for grown-ups. I like to drink an earthy Oregon Pinot Noir with this dish. / **FEEDS 4 AS AN APPETIZER**

TARTARE

8 ounces boneless beef
    eye-of-round, tri-tip,
    or rib-eye
¼ cup minced shallots
¼ cup chopped fresh
    flat-leaf parsley
1 tablespoon Asian
    sesame oil
1 teaspoon Dijon mustard
¾ teaspoon kosher salt
½ teaspoon freshly ground
    black pepper

4 large eggs,
    preferably organic
¼ cup Strawberry Ketchup
    (opposite)
4 slices brioche,
    toasted and cut into
    4 triangles each
Juice of 1 lime
A handful of arugula
    for garnish
Coarse sea salt

1 To make the tartare: Mince the beef as fine as you can with a sharp chef's knife. Put the meat in a chilled bowl, add the shallots, parsley, sesame oil, mustard, salt, and pepper, and gently toss with a rubber spatula. Cover and refrigerate until chilled.

2 While the tartare is chilling, gently place the eggs in a small pot and cover with cold water. Bring to a simmer over medium-high heat and set your timer for 6 minutes. When the eggs are cooked, carefully remove them from the water and let cool in an ice bath. Then carefully peel the shells off under cold running water.

3 To serve, spoon a tablespoon of the strawberry ketchup to one side of each plate. Place a piece of toast in the center of the plate. Spoon the beef tartare over the toast, and squeeze lime juice over the tartare. Carefully place 1 egg over the tartare on each plate. Garnish with the arugula, sprinkle some sea salt over the eggs, and serve immediately.

Strawberry ketchup is a great way to use slightly older, slightly bruised strawberries. Sometimes I can get them at the farmers' market for a nice price toward the end of the season, when they aren't as pretty but are still delicious. No one else wants them, but I buy as many as I can. Try strawberry ketchup with cured hams, corn dogs, and fried okra.

STRAWBERRY KETCHUP

MAKES 2 CUPS

1 pound fresh strawberries, washed
　　and hulled, sliced or halved

½ cup chopped onion

½ cup apple cider vinegar

½ cup packed brown sugar

2 teaspoons soy sauce

1 tablespoon distilled white vinegar

1 teaspoon ground ginger

1 teaspoon kosher salt

½ teaspoon freshly ground white
　　pepper

½ teaspoon smoked paprika

½ teaspoon ground cumin

¼ teaspoon ground cloves

1 Combine the strawberries, onion, cider vinegar, brown sugar, and soy sauce in a small pot, bring to a simmer over medium heat, and cook for 14 minutes, until the strawberries are soft and broken down.

2 Transfer the berry mixture to a blender and puree on high. Strain through a fine-mesh sieve into a bowl. Discard the solids.

3 Add the white vinegar, ginger, salt, white pepper, paprika, cumin, and cloves. Whisk well. Transfer to two small jars, cover, and refrigerate. The ketchup will keep for up to a month in the refrigerator.

LIME BEEF SALAD

Beef doesn't always have to be a caveman dish. It can be delicate and accompanied by crunchy, colorful, healthful produce. Serving meat with a salad satisfies the carnivore in you but it doesn't make the meat the star of the show: the veggies are. Use good-quality fish sauce—and don't be afraid of this ingredient: It's the secret element that adds depth to the salad. This refreshing but earthy salad is perfect with an Austrian Grüner Veltliner. / **FEEDS 4**

VINAIGRETTE

5 tablespoons fresh lime juice (from about 3 limes)

1½ tablespoons brown sugar

2 teaspoons fish sauce

2 teaspoons Asian sesame oil

2 teaspoons grated fresh ginger (use a Microplane)

½ teaspoon soy sauce

¼ teaspoon freshly ground black pepper

SALAD

8 ounces green cabbage, shredded as thin as possible

1 plum tomato, halved lengthwise and sliced into thin half-moons

1 mango (find one that is slightly underripe and still firm), peeled, pitted, and cut into thin matchsticks

1 tablespoon chopped fresh mint

1 teaspoon black sesame seeds

1 red Fresno chile or jalapeño pepper, finely chopped

1 To make the vinaigrette: Combine all the ingredients in a bowl and whisk together. Cover and chill.

2 To make the salad: Combine all the ingredients in a bowl and toss well. Cover and chill.

3 To make the beef: Put the water, ginger, garlic, and salt in a small pot and bring to a boil over high heat, then turn the heat to low and simmer for about 15 minutes while you pound the beef.

4 Cut the beef into thin slices: you should get about 8. One at a time, place each slice between two sheets of plastic wrap and pound with the bottom of a small saucepan or a rolling pin until paper-thin. Transfer to a plate.

5 Remove the chilled vinaigrette from the refrigerator. Using chopsticks or tongs, gently drop a few slices of beef into the simmering water and cook for just 10 seconds, or even less if you like your beef a little on the rare side. Remove the beef slices and immediately drop into the chilled vinaigrette. Repeat with the remaining beef slices.

6 Add the beef and vinaigrette to the salad. Toss gently and arrange on small salad plates. Top with the cilantro and peanuts and serve immediately.

BEEF

8 cups water

A small knob of ginger

1 garlic clove

1 teaspoon salt

5 ounces boneless beef,
   sirloin or eye-of-round

1 small bunch cilantro,
   coarse stems removed,
   leaves and tender stems
   finely chopped

1 tablespoon chopped
   peanuts

Cilantro stems are
edible! I go crazy when
I see cooks pick just
the leaves and throw
away the stems. Cilantro
stems are delicate and
crunchy, and they taste
even better than the
leaves. If you don't want
long cilantro stems in
your dish, pull off the
leaves and finely snip
the stems like you would
with chives.

BEEF BONE SOUP

WITH KABOCHA DUMPLINGS

Korea is famous for its soups and stews, especially during the fall and winter, when we all crave steaming-hot comfort food. So much of Western cooking is about clarity in broths. This is the exact opposite: the bones are simmered hard so that the fat—the meat and marrow—emulsifies into the broth, and what you get is a broth that has a satisfying mouthfeel. The brightness of the pumpkin is a great way to balance the rich broth. I don't generally like wine with hot soups; instead, reach for a flavorful beer like Spring Street Saison from Avondale Brewing. / FEEDS 4

4 pounds beef bones, with a little meat still on them

8 ounces daikon radish, peeled and sliced into ¼-inch-thick rounds

½ white onion, sliced about ¼ inch thick

Kosher salt and freshly ground black pepper

12 Kabocha Dumplings (recipe follows)

1 cup watercress sprigs

1 Place the bones in a pot and add enough cold water to cover. Let sit at room temperature until all the blood has seeped out of the bones and meat, about 1 hour.

2 Drain the bones, then fill the pot with enough cold water to cover the bones by 1 inch. Bring to a boil over high heat, lower the heat to a simmer, skim off any foam that rises to the surface, and keep at a rolling simmer for about 3 hours, until the broth is reduced to 8 cups; continue skimming off foam diligently. The broth should be cloudy and milky white.

3 Transfer the bones to a large bowl. Strain the broth through a fine-mesh sieve, then return it to the pot. Pull off any meat from the bones, chop it into small pieces, and add it to the soup. Discard the bones.

4 Bring the soup to a simmer, add the daikon and onion slices, and simmer until the daikon is tender but still holds its shape, about 15 minutes. Season to taste with salt and pepper.

5 Add the dumplings to the soup and simmer until cooked through, about 3 minutes. Divide the soup among four bowls (3 dumplings for each bowl). Garnish with the sprigs of watercress and serve immediately.

→ CONTINUED

KABOCHA DUMPLINGS

MAKES 12 DUMPLINGS

2 cups ½-inch pieces peeled
    kabocha squash
2 tablespoons unsalted butter,
    softened
1 teaspoon Asian sesame oil
Sea salt
1 teaspoon black sesame seeds
12 round wonton wrappers

If you can't find kabocha, use pumpkin or butternut or acorn squash. I'd stay away from spaghetti squash or any of the lighter gourds, as they don't have as much flavor. Frozen squash will work well in a pinch, but do not use squash that comes out of a can, please.

1 Preheat the oven to 450°F.

2 Spread the squash on a baking pan and roast for 35 minutes, or until lightly golden and tender. Let cool.

3 Transfer the squash to a blender, add the butter and sesame oil, and puree until thick and smooth, adding water by the tablespoonful if necessary. It should be the consistency of mashed potatoes that can hold a shape on a plate. Season to taste with salt. Transfer to a bowl and stir in the sesame seeds. Chill until cool.

4 Lay the wonton wrappers on a work surface. Place 2 teaspoons of the kabocha filling in the center of each wrapper. Moisten the edges of each wrapper with water, then fold in half and press to seal the edges. Cook the dumplings right away, or transfer to a lightly floured baking sheet and keep covered with plastic wrap or a damp kitchen towel until ready to use; use them within a few hours, or they will start to dry out. (You can freeze the dumplings on a tray with ample room until hard, then transfer to a freezer container or bag.) Note: Extra puree can be frozen and used for soups, fillings, or to make more dumplings.

GRILLED KALBI

It took me forever to get this recipe from my mom. She doesn't write down measurements, so whenever I asked for a recipe, she'd say something like, "Add a little bit of this and just enough of that." But even without a recipe, her kalbi always tastes the same, and it's always a treat to have her make it, versus eating it at a restaurant. I guess that's just a mother's touch. Finally, to get her recipe, I had to sit and watch her make it, taking notes as she mixed her ingredients together. Nowadays I make this when my friends want traditional-style kalbi. And I've stopped using measuring cups too. The marinade keeps well, so you can make it in advance to save some time. / **FEEDS 6 TO 8 AS A MAIN COURSE**

1 To make the marinade: Combine all the ingredients in a blender and pulse to a chunky puree; you want a little texture. (The marinade can be covered and refrigerated for up to 2 days.)

2 Layer the short ribs in a casserole, pouring some of the marinade over each layer and making sure every rib is nicely covered. Cover and let marinate in the refrigerator for at least 4 hours, or as long as overnight.

3 Remove the ribs from the refrigerator and let come to room temperature.

4 Prepare a very hot fire in a charcoal or gas grill; a quick char is what you want here.

5 Grill the ribs for about 2 minutes on each side, until charred on the outside but still a touch rare in the middle. Serve with the rice and kimchi.

The grilling part of this recipe is key. You really have to watch the ribs because, depending on the thickness of the meat, it can overcook in seconds. You can broil these if you do not have a grill, but be mindful because the broiler can also quickly overcook them.

MARINADE
1½ cups soy sauce
¼ cup granulated sugar
¼ cup packed brown sugar
¼ cup mirin (sweet rice wine)
⅓ cup Asian sesame oil
1 small onion, chopped
6 garlic cloves, chopped
A small knob of ginger, grated (use a Microplane)
3 scallions, finely chopped
2 tablespoons toasted sesame seeds
1 teaspoon red pepper flakes

5 pounds bone-in English-cut short ribs, cut about ⅓ inch thick (you can have your butcher do this)
Cooked white or brown rice (see page 4)
Spicy Napa Kimchi (page 169)

BRAISED BEEF KALBI

WITH EDAMAME HUMMUS

Kalbi can be made a number of ways, not just marinated and cooked on the grill. One popular method is to use beef short ribs that are cut thick and braise them slowly for a long time. It's a winter dish in Korea and one that is normally served for special occasions or celebrations. The fat from the short ribs gives this a melt-in-your-mouth texture. Traditionally you might serve it with brown or white rice, but I like to pair it with Edamame Hummus (page 199). / **FEEDS 6 TO 8**

4 pounds English-cut bone-in
   short ribs
4 cups water
2 tablespoons corn oil
1 tablespoon Asian
   sesame oil
1 large onion, chopped
5 garlic cloves, chopped
A small knob of ginger, peeled
   and minced (about
   1 tablespoon)
¾ cup soy sauce
¾ cup chicken stock
½ cup mirin (sweet rice wine)
2 tablespoons sugar
2 teaspoons honey
2 teaspoons freshly ground
   black pepper
4 carrots, peeled and coarsely
   chopped
3 parsnips, peeled and
   coarsely chopped
⅓ cup pine nuts
2 tablespoons golden raisins

2 cups Edamame Hummus
   (page 199)

1 Place the short ribs in a large pot and add the water. Bring to a boil, then reduce the heat and simmer for 8 minutes. Remove the ribs from the water, pat dry, and set aside. Strain the liquid and reserve 2 cups of it.

2 Rinse and dry the pot and return it to the stove. Add the corn oil and sesame oil and heat over medium-high heat. Working in 2 batches, add the short ribs and brown on all sides, about 5 minutes per batch. Return all the short ribs to the pot, then add the onions, garlic, and ginger and cook for 3 minutes.

3 Add the soy sauce, chicken stock, mirin, and the 2 cups reserved cooking liquid and bring to a slow simmer. Stir in the sugar, honey, and pepper and simmer, partially covered, turning the ribs occasionally, for 1 hour.

4 Add the carrots, parsnips, pine nuts, and raisins and continue to simmer, partially covered, until the ribs are tender and the braising liquid is thickened and flavorful, about 1 hour longer.

5 Serve with a dollop of edamame hummus.

Like many slow-braised meat dishes, this one will taste better the next day, so try to make it a day in advance.

OXTAIL STEW

WITH LIMA BEANS

When I was a kid, my grandmother would boil oxtail to within an inch of its life and serve it in a casserole with rice and kimchi. I would sit at the table for as long as it took to clean off the bones, gnawing and sucking on them. Oxtail was dirt cheap back then. It was a meat that mostly immigrants bought, because all that cartilage made for a hearty dish that would fill the tummies of a large family for little money. But oxtail has grown quite trendy these days, and it's on the menus of some of the best restaurants across the country. My grandmother would have a fit if she saw the price of oxtail today.

This dish is both complex and peasant-like. You can use a fork for the beans, but I'd recommend eating the oxtail with your hands. Serve with Red Cabbage–Bacon Kimchi (page 166). / FEEDS 4 OR 5

3 pounds oxtails, cut into
    2-inch segments
1½ tablespoons all-
    purpose flour
2 tablespoons corn oil
2 tablespoons unsalted
    butter
1 large onion, coarsely
    chopped
10 ounces carrots
    (about 2 large carrots),
    peeled and coarsely
    chopped
2 green bell peppers,
    cored, seeded, and
    coarsely chopped
3 garlic cloves, chopped
3 tablespoons minced
    fresh ginger
1 habanero pepper,
    finely chopped

1 Trim most but not all of the fat from the outer layers of the oxtail pieces. Soak in cold water in a large bowl for 30 minutes at room temperature.

2 Drain the oxtail pieces, rinse, and pat dry with paper towels. Place them in a large bowl, sprinkle the flour over them, and toss gently to coat. Heat the corn oil in a large heavy pot over high heat. Working in 2 or 3 batches, add the oxtail pieces and brown on all sides, about 5 minutes. Transfer to a large plate.

3 Pour out the fat and wipe the pot clean. Melt the butter over medium heat. Add the onion, carrots, green peppers, garlic, ginger, and habanero pepper. Sauté for 4 minutes, or until the vegetables soften up just a bit.

4 Add the browned oxtail pieces to the pot, along with the tomatoes, black bean paste, sherry, star anise, sugar, and pepper. Add the stock and allspice. Bring to a simmer and skim off any foam that rises to the top. Simmer, uncovered, for 3 hours. If the liquid reduces too much, add a little water to keep the oxtail pieces submerged. The meat should be falling off the bone and the liquid should be starting to thicken up a little. Carefully remove the oxtail pieces, transfer to a deep platter, and keep warm.

5 Add the lima beans to the pot and simmer the braising liquid for 20 minutes, or until it thickens to the consistency of a light gravy.

6 Pour the black bean gravy over the oxtail pieces and serve warm with lots of paper towels; these are meant to be eaten with your hands.

3 plum tomatoes, coarsely chopped

8 ounces (¾ cup) black bean paste (see note, page 19)

1 cup dry sherry

2 whole star anise

1 tablespoon sugar

1 teaspoon freshly ground black pepper

4 cups chicken stock

1 teaspoon ground allspice

1 cup fresh or frozen lima beans

BRAISED BRISKET
WITH BOURBON-PEACH GLAZE

I made this recipe with my dear friend Ashley Christensen, of Poole's Diner in Raleigh, for a fund-raiser dinner for the Southern Foodways Alliance. We served it with sorghum-glazed carrots, Sea Island peas, butter beans, and a mess of bourbon. Afterward, we sang karaoke at her house, and I lost my shirt, literally, and the cops came and shut down the party. I hope your night is just as epic when you make this at your home. Serve the brisket with Quick Caraway Pickles (page 173) and Braised Bacon Rice (page 193). / FEEDS 12 TO 15

RUB
3 tablespoons kosher salt
2 teaspoons freshly
　　ground black pepper
½ teaspoon smoked
　　paprika
¼ teaspoon ground
　　cinnamon

BRISKET
1 flat brisket (7 to
　　8 pounds; see note)
3 tablespoons grapeseed
　　oil
1 large onion, coarsely
　　chopped
6 garlic cloves, smashed
2 large carrots, coarsely
　　chopped
3 celery stalks, coarsely
　　chopped
3 plum tomatoes, coarsely
　　chopped
Two 12-ounce bottles stout

1　To make the rub: Mix all the ingredients together in a small bowl.

2　Cut the brisket in half, against the grain. Put it on a baking sheet and rub the brisket all over with the spice rub. Don't be gentle with it—use all the rub in the bowl. Let stand in the refrigerator for 2 hours to give the brisket a quick cure.

3　Position a rack in the upper third of the oven and preheat the oven to 350°F.

4　In a rondeau or a large shallow pot big enough to hold both brisket pieces in one layer, heat 2 tablespoons of the oil over high heat. Add the onions and garlic and sauté for 5 minutes, or until the onions pick up a little color. Transfer the onions and garlic to a plate.

5　Add the remaining tablespoon of oil to the pot and heat until it's nearly smoking. Add the brisket, fat side down, and allow it to brown, untouched, for 5 to 6 minutes. Lift one corner of the brisket and check it; it should be nicely browned. Using tongs, flip both brisket pieces.

6　Add the onions and garlic to the pot, along with the carrots, celery, tomatoes, stout, bourbon, soy sauce, balsamic vinegar, brown sugar, beef stock, and thyme leaves and bring to a simmer over high heat.

→ CONTINUED

1½ cups bourbon

½ cup soy sauce

2 tablespoons balsamic
vinegar

½ cup packed light brown
sugar

8 cups beef stock

A handful of fresh thyme
leaves with small stems

GLAZE

One 10-ounce jar peach
jam or preserves

1 tablespoon bourbon

½ cup reserved braising
liquid

Pinch each salt and freshly
ground black pepper

A whole flat brisket will
come cleaned, so there's
no trimming needed.

7 Cover the rondeau with a double layer of aluminum foil and transfer to the oven. Cook for 4½ hours. Resist the temptation to peek under the foil. Remove the pot from the oven and slowly pull back the foil. The brisket should be very tender to the touch but still hold its shape. Transfer the brisket to a platter and tent it with foil to keep it moist.

8 Strain the braising liquid. Reserve some of the cooked vegetables and ½ cup of the braising liquid for the glaze and return the rest to the rondeau. Turn the heat up to high and reduce the braising liquid for about 15 minutes.

9 Meanwhile, to make the glaze: Combine the peach jam, the bourbon, and the strained braising liquid in a blender and blend until a smooth puree forms. Season with the salt and pepper.

10 When the brisket has cooled a bit, using a sharp paring knife, score the fat side of the brisket by making slits about ¼ inch deep in a crosshatch pattern.

11 Preheat the broiler. When the braising liquid has reduced, return the brisket to the rondeau, fat side up. The liquid should only come about three-quarters of the way up the brisket, so that the meat is submerged but the fat is exposed; this is very important, so if it is not the case, take the brisket out and reduce the liquid as necessary. Glaze the top of the brisket with the peach glaze, using 3 to 4 tablespoons. Transfer the rondeau to the broiler and check frequently: You want to brown the glaze without burning it; it should take only about 4 to 5 minutes.

12 Transfer the brisket to a cutting board. Slice against the grain into thick slices and place on a large platter. Ladle some of the braising liquid around the brisket. Drizzle a little bit more of the peach glaze over the brisket and serve with the reserved cooked vegetables.

WHAT IS FISH SAUCE?

You probably have seen fish sauce: It's that bottle of reddish-brownish funk with a label you can't read, and it's always there in the Asian food section of the grocery store with all the other unfamiliar stuff you have no idea what to do with. If you actually dare to open a bottle and take a whiff, you smell what can only be described as funkiness. The remarkable thing about it, though, is that fish sauce makes everything taste better, and I mean everything—but it only takes a few drops for its concentrated funk to permeate a dish and miraculously transform it into umami flavor. Umami is that mysterious fifth taste that is indescribable by itself, but in the context of a whole dish, it is the depth, roundness, and savory element. Sometimes I simply call fish sauce liquid flavor. And, contrary to what you might think, fish sauce is best used in meat, not fish, dishes. Italians use fermented anchovies to add flavor in the same way, and so do the Scandinavians. Fish sauce is the Southeast Asian equivalent, simply fermented fish; it's usually anchovies, but it comes in other versions too, based on squid or shrimp. Some of the cheaper brands use collected fish guts, not my favorite.

Cuong Pham makes the best fish sauce I've had this side of the Pacific. His company is called Red Boat (see Resources, page 279), and he makes what he calls a first-press fish sauce on an island in Vietnam where the temperature stays at a constant 80 to 90°F, with strong headwinds. Cuong's fish sauce has only two ingredients: anchovies and salt. Salt is added to the anchovies, and the salt pulls the liquid from the anchovies as they sit in wooden vats for a year to ferment. It takes five pounds of anchovies to yield enough fish sauce to fill one 500-ml bottle. The process requires true patience, so maybe fish sauce really has three ingredients.

Fish sauce is as essential to Southeast Asian cuisine as good olive oil is to Italian cuisine. I use it to finish soups, sauces, stews, and dressings. A couple of dashes will bring to life an otherwise dull sauce. If only the rest of life were that easy.

BOURBON-AND-COKE MEATLOAF SANDWICH

WITH FRIED EGG AND BLACK PEPPER GRAVY

Southern Living asked me to share a meatloaf recipe with their readers a while back. I didn't want to admit it at the time, but I'd never made meatloaf in my life. I went home and made six different versions, none of which I liked. I took a break, poured myself a bourbon and Coke, and had a eureka moment. This bourbon-fueled meatloaf was the result, and it's my favorite by far. It's also the starting point for an intense, manly sandwich that you won't soon forget. This sandwich goes great with a badass wheat ale like Gumballhead from Three Floyds Brewing Co. / FEEDS 8

MEATLOAF

1 tablespoon unsalted butter

1 cup finely chopped onions

¼ cup finely chopped celery

1 garlic clove, minced

3 ounces bacon, diced

1 cup chopped button mushrooms

1 pound ground beef chuck (80% lean)

½ cup fresh bread crumbs

1 large egg

1 large egg yolk

¼ cup ketchup

2 tablespoons Coca-Cola

1 tablespoon bourbon

1 teaspoon Worcestershire sauce

¾ teaspoon kosher salt

¼ teaspoon pepper

GLAZE

¼ cup ketchup

½ tablespoon soy sauce

1 tablespoon brown sugar

1 Preheat the oven to 350°F.

2 To make the meatloaf: Melt the butter in a large skillet over medium-high heat. Add the onions, celery, and garlic and sauté for 3 minutes, until softened. Add the bacon and mushrooms and sauté for another 4 minutes, until soft. Transfer the mixture to a large bowl. Let cool to room temperature.

3 Add the ground beef, bread crumbs, egg, yolk, ketchup, cola, bourbon, Worcestershire sauce, salt, and pepper to the bacon mixture. Mix with your hands until evenly blended. Form into a loaf and transfer to a 9-by-5-inch loaf pan.

4 To prepare the glaze: Mix the ketchup, soy sauce, and brown sugar together. Brush it over the top of the meatloaf. Bake for about 1 hour and 10 minutes, or until an instant-read thermometer inserted in the center reads 145°F. Remove the meatloaf from the oven and carefully pour the drippings into a small bowl by holding the meatloaf in the pan and tipping it slightly. You should get about a cup of drippings; save this for your gravy. Let the meatloaf cool for about 20 minutes. Leave the oven on.

5 While the meatloaf is cooling, make the gravy: Melt the butter in a small saucepan over medium heat. Whisk in the flour until smooth, then whisk in the drippings and chicken stock. Bring to a simmer, whisking, and simmer for 2 minutes. Add salt to taste, the black pepper, and a few drops of lemon juice to brighten the gravy. Turn off the heat and keep the gravy warm until ready to use. (The gravy keeps very well in the refrigerator for up to a day. Rewarm it in a small saucepan and add a few drops of water to help smooth it out.)

6   To make the sandwiches: Arrange the bread slices on a baking pan and toast in the oven until nicely browned, about 6 minutes. Let cool.

7   Unmold the meatloaf and cut eight ¾-inch-thick slices from it.

8   Smear a tablespoon of mayo on each toast, then top with a slice of meatloaf and a slice of tomato.

9   In a large skillet, melt a little butter over medium heat. Fry the eggs sunny-side up, 2 eggs at a time, about 3 minutes. Using a spatula, lay a fried egg over each slice of meatloaf.

10 Drizzle the gravy over the eggs and top with some chopped parsley. Eat right away.

Texas toast is double-thick white bread. You can use normal white bread if you can't find Texas toast.

BLACK PEPPER GRAVY
1½ tablespoons unsalted butter
1 tablespoon all-purpose flour
1 cup reserved meatloaf drippings
½ cup chicken stock
Kosher salt
1 teaspoon freshly ground black pepper
A few drops of fresh lemon juice

SANDWICHES
8 slices Texas toast (see note)
½ cup mayonnaise, preferably Duke's
8 thick slices tomato
3 tablespoons unsalted butter
8 large eggs, preferably organic

Chopped fresh flat-leaf parsley

T-BONE STEAK
WITH LEMONGRASS-HABANERO MARINADE

Every once in a while, I like to dig into a big, fat, bloody steak. I might feel terrible the next day, but it's so tasty when I'm eating it. One problem I find with a big steak is that after a few bites, it starts to taste dull. So I like to add a bright acidic marinade for a contrast with all that meatiness. The acid actually accentuates the umami element in the steak and gives it a punch that is quite addictive. Serve with Collards and Kimchi (page 200) and a glass of Circus Boy from Magic Hat Brewing. / **FEEDS 4 NORMAL PEOPLE OR 2 VERY HUNGRY ONES**

1 To make the marinade: Combine all the ingredients in a blender and blitz on high until well blended.

2 Generously salt and pepper the steaks. Place in a glass baking dish and pour half of the marinade over the steaks. Marinate at room temperature for 20 minutes.

3 In a large cast-iron skillet, heat the butter and peanut oil over high heat until just barely smoking. Add the steaks, cover the pan with a lid, and cook for 3 minutes. Uncover, flip the steaks, and reduce the heat to medium. Cook the steaks, uncovered, for another 2 minutes or so. Do the steaks look caramelized and moist and shiny from the marinade? Good, they are ready to eat. Remove the steaks from the pan and let rest on a cutting board for 2 minutes.

4 Spoon the pan juices over the steaks; serve immediately.

A T-bone steak is a decadent cut. You can easily substitute 8-ounce rib-eye or tenderloin steaks. Or, try this with sirloin cut into thin strips and stir-fried, using the remaining marinade to deglaze the pan.

MARINADE
6 garlic cloves
3 lemongrass stalks, trimmed to within 2 inches of the root end and finely minced
2 habanero peppers, halved and seeds removed
Juice of 1 lemon
Juice of 1 orange
2 tablespoons Asian sesame oil
1 teaspoon soy sauce
½ teaspoon salt

Salt and freshly ground black pepper
Two 10-ounce T-bone steaks, ¾ inch thick (see note)
1 tablespoon unsalted butter
1 teaspoon peanut oil

ROPA VIEJA

IN CAROLINA RED RICE

When I was in New York City, Miguel was a line cook I worked with in various restaurants. He taught me about Latin cooking. Because of Miguel, I've grown to love chicharrones and salsa verde. This recipe is my version of a classic Cuban dish; Miguel would be proud. / **FEEDS 4 TO 6 AS A MAIN COURSE**

ROPA VIEJA

2 pounds flank steak, cut into 4-inch-wide sections against the grain

4 cups beef or chicken stock (use beef for a heartier stew, chicken for a lighter version)

¼ cup sherry vinegar

¼ cup soy sauce

1 large onion, thinly sliced

3 stalks celery, thinly sliced

4 garlic cloves, chopped

1 jalapeño, chopped (with the seeds)

1 tablespoon ground cumin

1½ teaspoons ground coriander

1 teaspoon smoked paprika

1 teaspoon kosher salt

½ teaspoon freshly ground black pepper

2 tablespoons unsalted butter

2 cups Carolina rice (see note)

2 cups water

1 cup canned crushed tomatoes

1 red bell pepper, cored, seeded, and sliced into ribbons

¼ cup grated Parmesan (1 ounce)

2 tablespoons chopped fresh flat-leaf parsley

Kosher salt and freshly ground black pepper

1. To make the ropa vieja: In a large pot, combine the flank steak, stock, vinegar, soy sauce, onion, celery, garlic, jalapeño, cumin, coriander, paprika, salt, and pepper. Cover, bring to a simmer, and simmer over low heat for 2 hours.

2. Remove the lid and cook for another 40 minutes. Remove from the heat.

3. Transfer the meat to a large bowl or other container. Let cool for about 20 minutes.

4. Using a fork, pull the flank steak apart into bite-sized pieces, without completely shredding it, and return to the bowl. Pour the warm cooking liquid and vegetables over the meat.

5. Rinse and dry the pot the ropa vieja cooked in. Melt the butter in the pot over medium heat. Add the rice and toast, stirring, for 2 minutes. Add the water, crushed tomatoes, and red pepper, then pour in the cooking liquid from the ropa vieja—don't worry if some of the meat goes into the rice, it's all going to get mixed in at the end. Cook for about 12 minutes, until the rice absorbs the liquid and is cooked through.

6. Add the meat and vegetables to the rice. Stir in the grated Parmesan and parsley. Cook for a few more minutes, until you get the thickness you want; it should be loose and a bit runny, but not soupy at all. Season with salt and pepper and serve immediately.

You can buy authentic Carolina rice online (see Resources, page 279), but any long-grain rice will work fine here, though you may need to adjust the cooking time. I wouldn't recommend Arborio rice for this dish.

THE EDUCATOR

Fred Provenza of Utah State University is one of the leading proponents of managing an herbivore ecosystem. I've followed his lectures for years. He explains how the special taste of a cow's meat or milk is inseparable from its diet, which is the grass it eats and the soil it grows in. Clover is like candy to cows. One of the indicators of a good cattle farm is seeing robust clover in a field where the cows graze—as well as alfalfa, trefoil, timothy, fescue, and more. Most cattlemen will tell you that grain and corn in a cow's diet is not a bad thing so long as they can graze on healthy grass as well. And healthy grass needs good soil. We tend to think of the importance of soil only when it comes to growing produce, but actually it is an essential nutrient for all herbivorous animals: cows, sheep, deer, rabbits, goats, birds. Even pigs, though actually omnivores, are kept on a herbivore diet on farms.

There is a circular Zen-like philosophy in starting with a patch of grass on a field and linking it all the way through cows and milk and human sustenance and back to grass. Getting into the chemical composition of soil is probably not what you're reading this for, so suffice it to say, if you were potting an herb that you wanted to eventually use in your food, you wouldn't dump a bunch of pesticides in it, would you? Think about that the next time you dump weed killer on your lawn. Clover, after all, is a weed.

"The vitality of land influences the species and behaviors of organisms that live in soil. Soil health affects the varieties, chemical characteristics, and behaviors of plants. That in turn affects the nutrition and health of herbivores. Ultimately, the health and well-being of people is intertwined with the health of soil through plants and herbivores."

—FRED PROVENZA,
DEPARTMENT OF WILDLAND RESOURCES,
UTAH STATE UNIVERSITY

If anyone but the shooter carries out the dead bird, no one will shoot a bird for the rest of the day.
—COMMON HUNTING SUPERSTITION

★ ★ ★

BIRDS & BLUEGRASS

TAKE A CITY KID OUT OF HIS

hood and drop him in the middle of the Bible Belt without a lick of knowledge about his environs, and you've got me when I moved to Kentucky. I was in the land of fried chicken, bourbon, and country ham; college hoops; bluegrass music; horse racing; mint juleps; and deep religion. The first thing I did when I got there was to sign up for horseback-riding lessons. I figured that's what everyone did on the weekends. I nearly broke my groin the first day. I suffered three more weeks

of soreness and steady humiliation in the hopes of impressing some old-time Kentuckians with my equine abilities. When I finally got a chance to meet a true blue-blooded, white-haired, bourbon-sipping gentleman of unquestionable lineage, I hardly waited for an introduction before I made my announcement. I told him I'd be happy to accompany him on a sunny afternoon of riding. His wife gave me that "Oh, bless his heart" kind of look. He laughed through his mustache and replied, "Son, we don't riiide haw-ses, we buy 'em." I canceled my lessons.

Eddie and Sharon were the original proprietors of 610 Magnolia, the storied restaurant that I would inherit. It was their idea that I leave New York City to start anew in Louisville. During my visit in 2002, they had seen in me something that I could not see myself: the will to succeed. I was eager but broken, curious but jaded. They

offered me an opportunity to reboot. They offered me 610 Magnolia: their baby, which they'd spent the last twenty-seven gutsy years nurturing with an elegance and sass only they could get away with. How could you say no to that? Well, I did. I stayed in New York and festered away in a restaurant I didn't want anymore. Every few weeks I'd get a call from Eddie checking in on me. They were polite but aimless conversations, I thought, yet all the while he was gauging my level of misery. One weekend, he casually mentioned that a man by the name of Brook happened to be passing through New York City and that it would behoove me to have lunch with him. I knew enough not to decline.

When Brook called, I was butchering chickens. He was cautious and courteous, but you can tell a person's standing by how they invite you to lunch. There's never any indecision about it. It's not, "Well, I was thinking of trying . . ." It's more like, "I got us a table at Balthazar at noon." I washed my face and did my best imitation of "I'm too cool to dress up for this lunch but I'm respectful enough to wear a clean shirt, which if you knew me, you'd know is huge, because I don't put on a clean white shirt for just anyone." We sat down and got into some oysters. Brook was slow to start and let me do the talking at first. Then we got into some Châteauneuf-du-Pape and steak frites. I was ready for a pitch, for talking numbers, percentages, all that. Instead, he talked about trains and how they leave the station, and when they leave the station, you are either on the train or left behind on the platform. He talked about horses and jockeys and betting on winners and how you have to start from the rear sometimes to see the field before you can begin your sprint. We got into a second bottle of wine. He talked about music and contemporary art and California wine. Everything was a Kentucky allegory, and I was getting hazy and thinking, "What does any of this have to do with me?" Brook talked about my success as a foregone conclusion, like I was already in Kentucky, like I'd already made up my mind. He talked and talked, and one sentence found its way into ten more without any break. By the time I finally lifted my face out of my wineglass, I was shaking his hand, like a pilgrim to the pope. "Welcome to Louisville," he said, and grinned.

And that's how I got here.

After I quit riding horses, I was itching to do something else. Hunting was next on my list. People warned me that I'd lose my appetite for birds by being so close to the kill—that the violence would be too much to stomach. I worried too. Guns, where I came from, were used on people, not animals. Rifles and camouflage were for zealots. Why go out and kill a beast in the wild when everything we need is neatly wrapped up for us in supermarkets? Hunting seemed at best inhumane, at worst a window into the depravity of the human soul.

"Welcome to Louisville," he said, and grinned.

I arrive before dawn for my first duck hunt, wearing jeans and a hoodie and carrying a flask of bourbon, which I've been sipping on since 4 a.m. Liquid courage is better than no courage at all. Mike is the one guy I know. He introduces me to the rest of the crew and we shake hands, illuminated only by the headlights of their Jeep Cherokees. We drive to Simpsonville with bags of beef jerky and Skoal Bandits littered across the dashboard.

There's a lot to do before a duck hunt besides finding the nearest pond. You have to map out the ducks' flight patterns, set out the decoys, find cover to hide the blinds, test the calls, and load the 12-gauge. Most of this is done in darkness. We share a quick slug of bourbon before sliding into our blinds just in time to see the first pulse of dawn lifting out through the maples. I shove a pinch of chaw into my cheek and wait for the waterfowl. I'm alone in my blind. The shotgun is resting on my right shoulder, safety off. I hear the guys bantering back and forth, but they're talking to the sky and sounding distant. The only thing close is my breathing. I'm worried I won't be able to bounce up out of the blind and pull the trigger. There's no time to aim. It's five shotguns screaming at a formation of ducks. What if I miss? What if I spook them before they get close enough? I nod off to sleep. Then I hear a voice checking on me. I answer that I'm A-okay. They heard me snoring. I have to pee, but I don't dare suggest getting out of my blind. The sky is the perfect color for an alfresco brunch. I'm thinking how much I love ricotta pancakes and cantaloupe when it is just freshly sliced, before it turns opaque and tastes like the inside of a refrigerator.

Out of nowhere, Mike starts his duck call. Chris is waving flags. The rest of the crew is sounding their calls. I wrap my finger around the trigger. From the north comes a small formation so far away the ducks may as well be clouds. They pass us by in slow motion and disappear behind the trees. "They'll be back," Mike says, and he keeps blowing into the blank sky. Sure enough, they come back, much closer now. They are circling in wide arcs, pitching, then retracing the pattern. They disappear behind me for so long it seems they've forsaken us, but they come back again, even closer now. I lose them in the sun, but I can hear them. The duck calls are hitting a crescendo. I'm ready to jump out of my skin. They're about thirty yards out and they set their wings, their legs extended like landing gear. The blinds split open and I hear shots explode in unison. Mine goes off a half second behind. I see feathers and carcasses. I have one more shot. I lean in too close, and this time the gun kicks back and punches my right cheek. I'm blinded for a second as I shake the pain out of my head. When I clear the smoke out of my eyes, I see that I've shot a decoy. Shot the bejeezus out of him.

The guys had a good laugh over the decoy. They actually gave it to me as my first kill. We dressed the three real ducks and put them on ice in a cooler, then sat down to breakfast. The conversation turned to cooking different fowl, from ducks to wild turkeys to chukars and doves. Each hunt has its own vocabulary, its own dogma. Each one is a different set of thrills. It hit me that far from being zealots, these guys were gourmands. They were lawyers and real estate agents and traders. But beyond that, they were a tribe of men sharing in the process of a feast. It felt good to laugh, to be included. They sent me home with bags of frozen game from past hunts, and later that week I made them pheasant and dumplings, fried quail, venison sliders, and roast duck. We ate huge that night. No spouses, no outsiders. Just us and some wine and whiskey and lots of stories, some so unbelievable the person telling them couldn't even keep a straight face.

There are certain salutations in Louisville that feel like hugs. From the very beginning, every time I would go out of town and return, Eddie and Sharon would say to me, "Welcome home." It was a nice thing to hear, even when I didn't believe it myself. But little by little, it started to ring true. I learned to ask people how they were doing and really mean it. I waved at strangers. They waved back. Amazing. The more I felt at home in Louisville, the more I became curious about its history and what its environs had to offer. I was eager to explore this new world outside the four walls of my kitchen. And soon I would get to explore the rabbit hole as deep as it would take me.

RICE BOWL WITH CHICKEN,

ORANGE, PEANUTS, AND MISO RÉMOULADE

The chicken patties in this recipe are mixed with grated daikon radish, which lightens the texture and adds a vegetal note to it. The patties are not limited to this dish alone. Shape them into meatballs for a great snack, or form them into larger patties and you have the beginnings of a killer chicken burger. Miso and chicken are a natural pairing; the nutty saltiness of the fermented soybeans contrasts with the mild creaminess of the chicken. Use organic chicken, please. With all that we now know about the added hormones and antibiotics in commercially raised poultry, there's no excuse not to use organic. / **FEEDS 4 AS A MAIN COURSE OR 6 AS AN APPETIZER**

MISO RÉMOULADE

2 tablespoons red miso

1 tablespoon Asian
    sesame oil

⅓ cup fresh orange juice

½ teaspoon soy sauce

½ teaspoon sugar

¼ cup Perfect Rémoulade
    (page 6)

CHICKEN SAUSAGE TOPPING

1 pound ground chicken,
    preferably organic chicken
    breasts

½ cup finely grated daikon radish
    (see note), excess water
    squeezed out

1 garlic clove, finely grated (use a
    Microplane)

4 teaspoons Asian
    sesame oil

2 teaspoons soy sauce

2 teaspoons whole milk

1 teaspoon Worcestershire sauce

1 teaspoon maple syrup

½ teaspoon fish sauce

1 To make the rémoulade: Whisk together the miso, sesame oil, orange juice, soy sauce, and sugar in a small bowl, blending well to make a creamy sauce. Mix in the rémoulade and refrigerate.

2 To make the chicken sausage: Put the ground chicken in a large bowl, add all the remaining ingredients and, using your hands, mix well. Form into small quarter-sized patties and place on a baking sheet.

3 Heat a large skillet over medium heat. Add about 1 tablespoon olive oil to the pan. Place only as many patties in the pan as will fit without crowding and fry for 3 minutes on each side, until browned and cooked through. Transfer to a plate lined with paper towels to drain oil. Repeat with the remaining olive oil and patties.

4 To serve, scoop the rice into your rice bowls. Place 2 or 3 chicken patties over the rice in each bowl. Place a few orange segments next to the chicken. Spoon about a tablespoon of the miso rémoulade over the chicken. Scatter a few bean sprouts over the sauce and sprinkle with a small amount of crushed peanuts and a pinch of nori matchsticks. Serve immediately with spoons. It is best to mix everything together before enjoying.

¾ teaspoon salt

½ teaspoon freshly ground
   black pepper

½ teaspoon sugar

3 scallions, finely chopped

About ¼ cup olive oil for
   panfrying

4 cups cooked rice (see
   page 4)

1 orange, cut into segments

2 ounces fresh bean sprouts

1½ ounces crushed peanuts
   (approximately ¼ cup)

1 sheet nori, cut into thin
   matchsticks

If you don't have daikon radish,
use raw turnips instead.

MISO-SMOTHERED CHICKEN

This recipe incorporates miso and chicken again (see page 74) but in a totally different way. The braising technique allows the dark meat of the chicken thighs to absorb the miso, which cooks down to an almost peanut-butter-like flavor. It is meltingly tender, and every time I make it, I always find someone back in the kitchen scraping the last bits from the pot. I suggest making more than you need and storing the extra in an airtight container in your fridge. It will keep for at least 5 days. / **FEEDS 4 AS A MAIN COURSE**

½ cup all-purpose flour

1 teaspoon kosher salt

1 teaspoon cayenne pepper

1 teaspoon garlic powder

4 bone-in chicken thighs

2 tablespoons vegetable oil

2 cups chopped yellow onions

1 tablespoon minced garlic

⅓ cup bourbon

2 cups chicken stock

½ cup fresh orange juice

2 tablespoons soy sauce

1 tablespoon dark miso

8 ounces shiitake mushrooms, stems discarded, thinly sliced

Cooked rice for serving
Pineapple-Pickled Jicama (page 172)

1 In a shallow dish, mix together the flour, salt, cayenne, and garlic powder. Coat the chicken thighs evenly with the mixture.

2 Heat the oil in a medium Dutch oven over medium heat until it shimmers. Add the chicken pieces skin side down and cook, turning once, until golden on both sides, 8 to 10 minutes. Transfer the chicken to a paper-towel-lined plate.

3 Pour off all but 2 tablespoons of oil from the pot. Add the onions and cook over medium-low heat, stirring occasionally, until softened and golden, 12 to 15 minutes. Stir in the garlic and cook for 1 minute. Add the bourbon and cook until all the liquid has evaporated, about 2 minutes.

4 Stir in the chicken stock, orange juice, soy sauce, and miso and bring to a simmer. Return the chicken to the pot, cover, and simmer until the chicken is cooked through and tender, about 30 minutes.

5 Add the mushrooms and simmer, uncovered, until the mushrooms are tender and the sauce is thickened, to the consistency of a gravy, 10 to 15 minutes longer. Serve with rice and the pickled jicama.

MISO

Miso is found everywhere in Asian cookery. In China, it is called *dòujiàng*; Koreans call it *daen-jang.* The basic ingredients of most commercially made misos are soybeans and rice that are mixed with koji (a starter enzyme that breaks down the proteins) and salt and left to ferment for months, but miso can also contain wheat, barley, buckwheat, or millet. My friend Sean Brock, in Charleston, makes miso using fermented pecans and black walnuts!

Like many of the Asian condiments I use on a daily basis, miso adds a haunting umami element to anything it touches. There are many kinds, but the most important distinction is between light or white (*shiro*) miso and dark or red (*aka*) miso. White miso, which is actually a blond color, is very delicate, and I use it for recipes that are made with little or no heat, like vinaigrettes, dressings, and light broths. I use red miso, which is a dark mahogany color, for stews and soups that call for long cooking times or glazes that will be cooked under a hot broiler or over high heat. Don't worry about the brand—or the Japanese writing that you can't understand on the label—just remember this distinction, and you'll be fine when shopping for miso.

POTATO-STUFFED ROAST CHICKEN

The perfect roasted chicken had always eluded me. There's no way to cook the thighs through without drying out the breast. I had gone through all the recipes I could try, but I'd never quite felt satisfied with any of them. Then I started trying out the technique in this recipe (see step-by-step photographs on the following pages) in the privacy of my home kitchen. It makes sense: the potatoes insulate the breasts, the fat from the skin flavors the potatoes, and the breasts stay incredibly moist. And the potatoes become an extra component without any more work. I've made this recipe twenty different ways, and this is my favorite. It's so easy you could do it in your sleep the second time around. My latest adjustment is to skip trussing the legs. The chicken may look a bit obscene when done, but allowing the legs to remain free allows more air to circulate around the thighs so the skin gets crispier and the meat cooks faster, in perfectly paced harmony with the insulated breasts.

For the ultimate comfort food dinner, serve the chicken with Bourbon-Ginger-Glazed Carrots (page 215) and Spoonbread with Kale and Bacon (page 204). / **FEEDS 4 AS A MAIN COURSE**

1 large Yukon Gold potato (about 11 ounces), peeled

1 tablespoon unsalted butter

2½ teaspoons kosher salt

¾ teaspoon freshly ground black pepper

One 3- to 3½-pound roasting chicken

2 teaspoons olive oil

1 Using the large holes of a box grater, grate the potato onto a cutting board. Wrap the grated potato in a square of cheesecloth and wring out as much water as possible.

2 Melt the butter in a large cast-iron skillet over medium heat. Add the grated potatoes, season with ½ teaspoon of the salt and ¼ teaspoon of the pepper, stir gently with a wooden spoon, and cook for exactly 2 minutes, no longer. Quickly transfer the potatoes to a plate and let cool.

3 Position a rack in the upper third of the oven and preheat the oven to 400°F.

→ CONTINUED

4 Place the chicken on your work surface with the legs facing you. Starting at the tail end of each breast, use your fingers to gently loosen the skin from the flesh. Slide one finger in between the breast meat and the skin and move it from side to side to release the skin from the meat. Yes, this will feel funny, but carry on. Be careful not to tear the skin, but if it does rip a little, don't worry; it's not the end of the world. Rotate the bird so the breasts are now facing you and do the same thing starting at the neck end of the breasts, so that all of the breast skin is released from the meat.

5 Gently stuff the cooled potatoes into the space between the skin and breasts (see opposite): Stuff half of them from the top and the remaining potatoes from the bottom. Now even out the potato layer: Place both your hands over the skin of the breasts and massage it to smooth and flatten the potatoes into an even layer. Rub the chicken with the olive oil and season with the remaining 2 teaspoons salt and ½ teaspoon pepper.

6 Wipe out the cast-iron skillet with a paper towel and heat it over medium heat. Place the chicken breast side down in the hot skillet, press it gently against the bottom of the pan, and hold it there for a bit while it browns lightly, about 3 minutes. Gently flip the chicken onto its back; the skin on top should be lightly browned. Slide the skillet into the oven and cook for 50 minutes to 1 hour. To check for doneness, insert an instant-read thermometer into the upper part of a thigh. I like my chicken when the thigh meat is at 155°F, but you may want yours at 160°F if you don't like any pink at all. Allow the chicken to rest in the pan for 10 minutes.

7 Transfer the chicken to a cutting board. Cut each breast away from the bones, being careful not to disturb the potatoes under the crispy skin. Slice each breast into 3 chunks and arrange on a platter. Carve the legs and add them to the platter, along with the wings.

> Once you've tried this recipe, you'll make it again and again. I promise. To vary the recipe, add about a teaspoon of chopped fresh rosemary or thyme to the potatoes while cooking them.

Grate the potatoes on a box cutter.

Squeeze out excess water from the grated potatoes.

Without tearing the skin, stuff the potatoes in the space between the skin and the breast.

Sear the chicken breast side down in a hot cast-iron pan.

ADOBO-FRIED CHICKEN AND WAFFLES

I'm not sure who first thought of serving fried chicken and waffles together, but if adding waffles helps you to feel better about eating fried chicken for breakfast, I'm all for it. This is a Filipino adobo, not the Spanish version. The vinegar brightens the richness of the fried chicken and helps with digestion. Add more or fewer chiles, depending on how much heat you like.

This is my kind of soul food. Serve with Kabocha Squash Mac 'n' Cheese (page 202) and Tank 7 Farmhouse Ale from Boulevard Brewing Company. And invite me over if I happen to be in your town. / FEEDS 6

WAFFLES
1 cup all-purpose flour
1 teaspoon sugar
1 teaspoon baking powder
½ teaspoon kosher salt
¼ teaspoon paprika
¼ teaspoon freshly ground
    black pepper
3 tablespoons unsalted
    butter, melted and
    cooled
2 large eggs
1 cup buttermilk

DIPPING SAUCE
¼ cup water
3 tablespoons fresh lemon
    juice
2 tablespoons maple syrup
2 tablespoons fish sauce
1 tablespoon soy sauce
2 fresh Thai bird or
    habanero peppers,
    thinly sliced

1 To make the waffles: Preheat your waffle maker and lightly oil it. Meanwhile, in a medium bowl, whisk together the flour, sugar, baking powder, salt, paprika, and black pepper. In a small bowl, whisk together the melted butter, eggs, and buttermilk. Pour the wet ingredients into the dry ingredients a little at a time, whisking constantly.

2 Cook the waffles according to your waffle maker's instructions. Cut the waffles into 2-inch-wide wedges and reserve on a plate at room temperature or keep warm in a low oven until ready to serve.

3 To make the dipping sauce: Combine all the ingredients in a small bowl. Cover and refrigerate until ready to use.

4 To make the adobo broth: In a large pot, combine all the ingredients, cover with a tight-fitting lid, and bring to a simmer over medium heat. Simmer for 5 minutes, then turn the heat down as low as it will go.

5 Arrange the chicken pieces on a work surface and season them with salt. Add the chicken pieces to the gently simmering broth, cover, and poach for 15 minutes, turning once halfway through. You want the chicken to poach gently and stay moist while picking up the flavor of the broth, so make sure the liquid does not get hotter than a gentle simmer. Turn off the heat and allow the chicken to cool in the liquid, covered, about 20 minutes.

→CONTINUED

ADOBO BROTH

2½ cups distilled white
  vinegar

1½ cups water

3 garlic cloves, finely
  minced

4 bay leaves

1½ teaspoons black
  peppercorns

1 teaspoon sugar

¼ cup soy sauce

½ teaspoon red pepper
  flakes

1 teaspoon salt

FRIED CHICKEN

2 pounds chicken, thighs
  and/or drumsticks, plus
  wings if desired (do not
  use breasts)

Salt

2 cups buttermilk

1 cup all-purpose flour

1 teaspoon paprika

½ teaspoon freshly ground
  black pepper

About 8 cups peanut oil for
  deep-frying

6 Remove the chicken pieces from the adobo broth (discard the broth) and transfer to a plate lined with paper towels. Pat dry.

7 To fry the chicken: Pour the buttermilk into a large shallow bowl. In another bowl, combine the flour, 1 teaspoon salt, the paprika, and the pepper. Dip each chicken piece in the buttermilk, shake off any excess liquid, dredge in the flour mixture, turning to coat, and transfer to a large plate. Let stand at room temperature for 15 minutes. The flour coating will turn a little soft—that's a good thing.

8 Meanwhile, fill a large, deep cast-iron skillet about half-full with peanut oil. Heat the oil to 365°F. Cook the chicken pieces 2 or 3 at a time for 8 to 10 minutes, turning every minute or so, depending on how thick the pieces of chicken are; wings will cook faster and drumsticks will take the longest. Be sure to keep the oil temperature at around 350 to 365°F. The chicken is cooked when the internal temperature reaches at least 165°F. Using tongs, lift the chicken out of the oil and drain on paper towels. Season again with a little salt, and transfer to a platter.

9 Serve the fried chicken with the waffle pieces and the dipping sauce. Eat it hot!

Fried chicken is good cold too. Eat the
cold leftovers the next day with a dash
of Tabasco and a squeeze of lime juice.

FRYING AT HOME, WITH THE QUARTER RULE

Frying in a pot of hot oil is one of the more frightening undertakings in a home kitchen. We've all heard those stories of people trying to fry a turkey in a vat of oil, only to have the house burn down. There are two rules to remember when frying. The first concerns volume displacement. All that means is that you need to make sure you are using a pot or pan big enough to hold the oil and whatever you are going to fry in it. Rule number two relates to heat transference: simply make sure your oil is hot. Frying only works when the oil is hot enough to create a violent steam around the food being fried. That layer of steam around its surface is what keeps the food being fried from absorbing too much oil.

Restaurants use large deep fryers because they fry vast amounts at a time and in quick succession. At home, a heavy pot or deep skillet filled with about 2 inches of oil will give you a perfectly crisp result. The key is to make sure that the oil never drops far below the appropriate frying temperature, which is usually a minimum of 325°F and a maximum of 400°F. The best way to ensure this is to fry in small batches. I have a rule that'll help you when frying: If the amount of food you are frying at one time would cover more than a quarter of the bottom of the pot or pan, you are probably going to drop the temperature of the oil so much that it will not recover in time to achieve a crispy exterior, no matter how long you leave the food in the oil. So if you are frying more than that, fry in batches—and wait at least 2 minutes between sessions to give the oil enough time to get hot again.

Here are a few other rules to remember when deep-frying:

- Always keep a lid that fits the pot handy. If the oil catches on fire, turn off the heat, immediately cover the pot with the lid, and let it stand for a few minutes to extinguish the flame. Never put water on a grease fire—it will only make it worse.

- Different oils smoke at different temperatures. Use an oil that has a high smoking temperature—peanut oil is best, but corn, canola, safflower, or grapeseed oils will work well too. Frying in animal fats like lard is also highly recommended.

- Watch the oil carefully: If it smokes, it's too hot. If your thermometer says it's not too hot, you're using the wrong oil.

- Salt foods right out of the fryer—they'll absorb the salt better. If you wait too long, the salt will simply bounce off the crispy skin and wind up on your cutting board.

- Always drain fried foods on paper towels or wire racks immediately out of the fryer. Even better, toss them gently a few times to allow cool air to circulate around the fried surfaces.

- When you've finished frying, try to skim off any bits still floating in the oil. It's this stuff that will denature your oil. If you keep the oil clean, you can reuse it a few times. Denatured oil will turn dark and smell rancid; don't ever fry in this oil. Store the cooled oil in the container it came in, in a cool, dark place.

- Fried foods taste better when you eat them with your hands.

KENTUCKY FRIED QUAIL

The technique of double-cooking poultry gives it that extra crispiness. Just as in the Adobo Fried Chicken and Waffles (page 82), here you poach the bird first before frying it. This allows some of the fat to render out, and it also shrinks the skin. Then your frying time will be less, so the meat won't be overcooked. It's a nifty trick—try it. Quail is often treated as a luxury item, adorably trussed and served on pretty porcelain plates. I love taking quail out of that context and serving it on newspaper with a dipping sauce and a mound of seasoned salt, letting people eat with their hands.

The Fragrant Salt used here is popular in Chinese cuisine; it can be used to flavor anything from scallops to popcorn. The quail is extra tasty paired with Pickled Garlic in Molasses Soy Sauce (page 181). / **FEEDS 4 AS AN APPETIZER**

FRAGRANT SALT
¼ cup sea salt
4 teaspoons Szechuan peppercorns
1 tablespoon five-spice powder

DIPPING SAUCE
2 tablespoons soy sauce
1 teaspoon sugar
Juice of 1 lime

4 semi-boneless quail (see note)
2 to 3 cups peanut oil for deep-frying

1 To make the fragrant salt: Combine all the ingredients in a spice grinder or a blender and grind until fine. Transfer to a small bowl.

2 To make the dipping sauce: Combine all the ingredients in a bowl and whisk together. Set aside at room temperature.

3 Bring 4 cups of water to a boil in a wide pot and add 1 tablespoon of the fragrant salt. Add the quail to the water and boil for 2 minutes. Drain on paper towels and pat thoroughly dry; transfer to a plate.

4 In a large, heavy pot, heat the oil (enough to barely cover the quail) to 390°F over medium-high heat. Cook the quail one at a time, and keep a lid handy; if the oil splatters too much, simply cover the pot with the lid. Add 1 quail to the pot and fry for 1 minute, then flip the bird and fry for another 30 seconds. It should crisp up very fast and turn a dark, shiny amber. Drain on paper towels, pat dry with more paper towels, and immediately sprinkle some of the fragrant salt over the quail. Repeat this process with the rest of the quail.

5 Serve the quail with the dipping sauce and the remaining fragrant salt on the side.

Semi-boneless quail have been partially boned, leaving the wing and leg bones intact. If you are using wild-caught quail, simply remove the back bones and leave the breast meat on the breastbone.

PHEASANT AND DUMPLINGS

Birds in the wild will be tougher and leaner than farm-raised varieties. Although it takes longer to cook them, they will always have more flavor. But this recipe was tested with farm-raised pheasant because, in all likelihood, that's what you'll be using. If you can get wild-caught game, increase the cooking time by about 20 minutes.

The dumplings here get a burst of flavor from fresh horseradish. Fresh horseradish can be found at most specialty shops. Prepared horseradish has too much added sugar and vinegar to use in this dish. If you can't find fresh horseradish, just omit it. Sometimes it's better to just leave an ingredient out rather than to substitute an inferior version. This stew is good with mugs of Winter White Ale from Bell's Brewery. / **FEEDS 4 AS A MAIN COURSE**

PHEASANT

2 tablespoons unsalted
    butter
1 cup chopped onions
2 celery stalks, chopped
1 cup small-diced carrots
2 garlic cloves, minced
2 tablespoons all-purpose
    flour
8 cups chicken stock
2 cups dry white wine
1 pheasant (about
    2½ pounds), cut in half
6 ounces oyster
    mushrooms
2 cups diced butternut
    squash
A small handful of fresh
    sage leaves, chopped
A small handful of fresh
    thyme leaves, chopped

1 To make the pheasant: In a large pot, heat the butter over medium heat until frothy. Add the onions, celery, carrots, and garlic and cook until just softened, about 4 minutes.

2 Add the flour to the pot and cook, stirring, for 1 minute to make a roux. Reduce the heat to medium-low, add the chicken stock and white wine, stirring constantly, and bring to a simmer. Add the pheasant halves and cook, uncovered, for 1 hour and 15 minutes, skimming occasionally, until the meat is tender and falling off the bone.

3 Gently remove the pheasant from the pot and let cool for 5 minutes on a cutting board, then pull the meat from the bones and shred it with your hands. Return the shredded meat to the pot, and discard the bones.

4 Add the mushrooms, squash, sage, and thyme to the pot and simmer for another 15 minutes.

5 Meanwhile, make the dumplings: Combine the flour, baking powder, and salt in a bowl. Add the horseradish, milk, and butter and mix with a wooden spoon until just combined. It should only take a few swift, strong strokes. The dough will be a little lumpy—that's okay. Resist the temptation to keep mixing, or you will have flat, rubbery dumplings.

6 Using a teaspoon, scoop up small balls of dough and drop them into the simmering broth. Add the peas and continue to simmer for another 12 minutes, or until the dumplings are cooked all the way through. Season with salt and pepper to taste.

7 Ladle the stew into warm bowls. Garnish with celery leaves, sprinkle with red pepper flakes, and serve with crusty bread.

The last step of any slow-simmered stew like this is to taste and give it a final seasoning of salt and pepper. Slow-cooked dishes, which happen to be my favorite kind, change so dramatically every few minutes that it's important to season the food right before the dish is served. Sometimes the difference between a good dish and a great one is just a pinch of salt.

1 cup frozen peas
Sea salt and freshly ground
    black pepper

DUMPLINGS
1 cup all-purpose flour
1 teaspoon baking powder
1 teaspoon salt
1 tablespoon grated fresh
    horseradish
⅓ cup whole milk
1 tablespoon unsalted
    butter, melted

Small sprigs of celery
    leaves for garnish
Red pepper flakes
Crusty bread for serving

BRAISED TURKEY LEG, HOT BROWN-STYLE

The first thing people ask you when you move to Louisville is, "Have you tried a hot brown yet?" It's as if eating a hot brown is an initiation that solidifies your identity as a true Louisvillian. The story goes that the hot brown was invented in the Brown Hotel in the 1920s, and it's been expanding belt sizes ever since. It truly is a monster of a sandwich: Texas toast, turkey, bacon, cheese, and gravy. Finishing one is a monumental feat, and something you probably only need to do once or twice a year.

This is my take on the hot brown, still rich but a little less daunting, and just as tasty. Because the dish is so devilishly filling, it needs a spicy bourbon with a few cubes of ice in a large rocks glass. / FEEDS 4

4 slices thick-cut bacon, finely diced

2 tablespoons unsalted butter

2 bone-in turkey drumsticks (about 2 pounds)

Sea salt and freshly ground black pepper

2 carrots, finely diced

2 celery stalks, finely diced

2 leeks, white part only, finely chopped

3 tablespoons sorghum

2 cups apple cider

1 cup chicken stock

2 fresh sage sprigs

2 slices Texas toast (regular white bread works fine too), cut into rectangular ½-inch-thick croutons

1 Preheat the oven to 325°F.

2 Warm a Dutch oven or a large cast-iron skillet over medium heat. Add the bacon and cook until it renders its fat and begins to crisp, 4 to 6 minutes. Remove the bacon and drain on a paper towel; leave the bacon fat in the pan.

3 Add the butter to the pan and melt over medium heat. Season the turkey legs generously with salt and pepper. Add to the pan and brown on all sides, 8 to 10 minutes. Transfer the turkey legs to a plate.

4 Pour off all but 2 tablespoons of the fat from the pan. Add the carrots, celery, and leeks and cook, stirring occasionally, until they begin to brown, about 5 minutes.

5 Add the bacon and turkey legs to the pan, then add the sorghum, apple cider, and chicken stock and bring to a simmer. Add the sage, cover with the lid, and transfer to the oven. Bake for 45 minutes.

6 Check the turkey legs. If they're not totally immersed in liquid, flip them over and replace the lid. Cook for an additional 35 minutes, or until the meat is falling off the bone. Transfer the turkey to a plate and let cool slightly. Set the braising liquid aside. (Leave the oven on.)

7 Meanwhile, spread the croutons on a baking sheet and toast in the oven for 8 to 10 minutes, just until slightly browned. Remove from the oven.

8 Pull the skin off the turkey legs and discard. Remove the meat from the bones and shred it with your hands.

9 To serve, divide the braised turkey meat among four bowls. Add the cheese to the braising liquid and whisk until combined, then season with salt and pepper. Ladle about ½ cup of the braising liquid into each bowl. Top each serving with some croutons, a spoonful of the diced tomato, a pinch of the fresh herbs, and some bacon bits. Dust each bowl with paprika and serve immediately.

⅔ cup grated semi-firm cheese, such as Gouda

GARNISH
½ cup diced tomato
Chopped fresh sage and thyme
2 slices bacon, cooked until extra crispy and broken into bits
Smoked paprika

If you are using store-bought low-sodium chicken broth, I recommend concentrating it a bit to intensify the flavor. Pour the broth into a pot and reduce it by one-third over high heat. The reduced broth can be stored in your refrigerator for up to one week.

HONEY-GLAZED ROAST DUCK

Chinese roast duck is one of those dishes that people tend to eat only in restaurants. The perception is that making it involves numerous steps and lots of industrial equipment. I went through many a duck trying to modify the traditionally complex recipe so that it was feasible to make at home. Why bother? Well, I think there's no meal that's more fun than tearing into a roast duck with a table full of friends. I serve the duck with lots of condiments. I like the abundance. I like fighting for it at the table. Try and find a duck with the head still attached. Yes, the neck is delicious. And it makes for a dramatic presentation.

Invite a lot of friends over and open some Tsingtao beer, a few bottles of Mollydooker Shiraz, and a flask of reliable whiskey, and take the time to enjoy life. / FEEDS 6

DUCK
One 5-pound duck
¼ cup kosher salt
15 garlic cloves, peeled
Salt and pepper

GLAZE
½ cup honey
2 tablespoons fresh
    orange juice
2 tablespoons soy sauce

FOR SERVING
(CHOOSE ANY OR ALL)
Hot Sauce (opposite)
Hoisin sauce
Pineapple-Pickled Jicama
    (page 172)
Bourbon-Pickled Jalapeños
    (page 175)
Fresh cilantro sprigs
Fresh basil sprigs
Sliced cucumbers

1 Preheat the oven to 325°F.

2 Remove the gizzards from the duck and save for making a broth another day (see note). Rinse the duck under cold running water and pat dry. Using a very sharp knife, score the skin, making a diagonal crosshatch pattern across the breast. I basically just let the weight of the knife sink into the breast fat as I swipe it; be careful not to cut into the meat. Place the duck in a colander in the sink.

3 Bring 4 cups water and the salt to a rolling boil in a saucepan. Set the pan of boiling water near the sink. Using the largest ladle you have, slowly pour the boiling water over the duck; it will look like you are giving the duck a spa treatment, and the skin will shrink and curl up a bit. This renders fat from the skin without cooking the meat so the skin gets crispier.

4 Scatter the garlic cloves over the bottom of a large cast-iron skillet or a roasting pan. Season with salt and pepper. Set the duck, breast side up, on the garlic. Roast for 45 minutes.

5 Flip the duck over and roast for 15 minutes. Flip the duck back, so the breast is facing up again, and roast for another 15 minutes.

6 Meanwhile, make the glaze: Combine the honey, orange juice, and soy sauce in a small bowl and whisk together.

7. Take the pan of duck out of the oven, carefully tilt it, and pour as much of the rendered duck fat as possible into a bowl. (Store the fat in a lidded jar in the refrigerator, for a worthy friend who will appreciate the privilege of having you cook for him or her potatoes or eggs in duck fat.) Brush the glaze generously over the breast and legs of the duck. Turn the oven up to 450°F and roast the duck for 15 minutes, brushing a little more glaze over it once or twice till you've used all the glaze.

8. Take the duck out of the oven and baste with any glaze remaining on the bottom of the pan. Serve immediately, with all the accoutrements and the roasted garlic.

When you have finished eating the duck, save the carcass to make a rich stock for soups, sauces, and more. The next day, put the carcass and the reserved gizzards into a pot, cover with water, and add aromatics like onions, carrots, bay leaves, and a few pieces of star anise. Bring to a boil, simmer for 2 hours, and strain. The stock keeps in the refrigerator, covered, for 1 week.

HOT SAUCE

MAKES ALMOST 4 CUPS

1 pound mixed red jalapeño peppers, fresh Thai bird peppers, and habanero peppers
6 garlic cloves
2 cups apple cider vinegar
1 Red Bull (an 8.4-ounce can)
1 cup water
¼ cup hoisin sauce
¼ cup sugar
4 teaspoons fish sauce
4 teaspoons Asian sesame oil

1. Trim the stems from the peppers. Combine all the ingredients except for the Asian sesame oil in a medium pot and bring to a boil, cover, then reduce the heat and simmer for 15 minutes.

2. Transfer the contents of the pot to a blender and puree until smooth, adding water as needed to create a smooth sauce. Add the sesame oil and blend well. Transfer to a jar and store in the refrigerator. The sauce will keep for up to a month.

We drink a ton of Red Bull in my kitchen. It keeps us going through the sluggish afternoon hours. Some days, it seems to be the most prevalent ingredient in the kitchen, which always gets me thinking about ways to use it in a recipe. I used to put ginger ale in this hot sauce, but I like it better with the Red Bull. It's sugary, citrusy, and loaded with caffeine. What's not to like? If you are one of those people who are wary of the product, you can substitute ginger ale or Sprite.

CHICKEN AND COUNTRY HAM PHO

Pho is one of those deceptively simple dishes that when done right is astoundingly satisfying. It is basically a clear meat broth that is ubiquitous in Vietnam. But making a good broth is like standing naked before your audience: There's nothing to hide behind, no fancy garnishes, no sauces to mask mistakes. It is all about fresh ingredients, technique, and patience. A good pho should never be insulted by more than a drop or two of hot sauce. / **FEEDS 4 AS A MAIN COURSE**

BROTH

2 onions, halved

A large knob of ginger (about 3 inches by 1 inch), thinly sliced

4 cloves

2 star anise

1 tablespoon coriander seeds

1 tablespoon black peppercorns

One 2- to 3-pound chicken, quartered and skin removed

3 quarts water

2 tablespoons fish sauce

1 tablespoon sugar

6 ounces rice noodles

2 cups fresh bean sprouts

½ cup fresh basil leaves

½ cup fresh cilantro leaves

2 serrano chile peppers, thinly sliced

4 slices country ham or prosciutto

4 lime wedges

Hot sauce for serving

1 Preheat the broiler. Place the onions and ginger on a small aluminum-foil-lined baking sheet. Broil 3 to 4 inches from heat, turning once, until nicely charred, 5 to 7 minutes. Transfer to a large stockpot.

2 Toast the cloves, star anise, coriander seeds, and black peppercorns in a small dry skillet over medium heat until fragrant, about 2 minutes. Add to the stockpot. Add the chicken, water, fish sauce, and sugar and bring to a simmer. Simmer, skimming the foam from the surface frequently, until the chicken is cooked through, about 30 minutes. Remove the chicken from the pot, leaving the broth to simmer, and transfer it to a large plate to cool slightly.

3 When the chicken is cool enough to handle, pull the meat from the breasts and legs. Transfer the meat to a plate, cover with plastic wrap, and refrigerate. Return the bones to the pot.

4 Continue to simmer the broth gently until it is slightly reduced and flavorful, about 1 hour and 15 minutes longer. Strain the broth through a cheesecloth-lined sieve and discard the bones and vegetables.

5 Meanwhile, place the noodles in a heatproof bowl, cover with boiling water, and let stand for 3 minutes; drain.

6 Divide the noodles and broth among four large bowls and garnish with the chicken, bean sprouts, basil, cilantro, chile, and country ham. Or serve the broth and noodles in bowls with the garnishes on a plate. Add a squeeze of lime and a few drops of your favorite hot sauce to each bowl and serve.

THE CRAFTSMAN

Robert Clifft is one of a rare breed of master turkey callers and box call makers. He lives and works in Bolivar, Tennessee. His box calls are a work of art: hand-carved mahogany, cedar, poplar, or butternut. Each one is different and requires a bit of getting used to. His call techniques are so realistic they give me goose bumps. When I have a free afternoon, I call him up and put him on speakerphone. We'll both sit around with our box calls, and he'll train me by making me mimic the sounds he makes. I've had more than a few people ask me if I'm raising turkeys in my office.

"Some folks say the best way to kill an old gobbler is to find one that wants to die. You will hunt a lot of times and not kill a turkey. Patience is something you must have. You are hunting in his living room, and he has all day. It has been said the difference between a deer and a turkey is a deer thinks every man is a stump and the wild turkey thinks every stump is a man."

—ROBERT CLIFFT,
MASTER TURKEY CALLER AND
MAKER OF HANDMADE TURKEY CALLS
APTLY NAMED THE LAST CALL

PIGS & ABATTOIRS

If you dream about a pig, you will soon have good fortune.
—KOREAN SUPERSTITION

IT'S HARD TO IMAGINE A DECENT

restaurant these days that does not engage in building relationships with local farmers. To do so is simply our responsibility. To me, a menu is nothing more than a written promise that, to the best of our abilities, we will cook with seasonal foods, procure our ingredients from farmers we trust, and nurture relationships with purveyors who give back to the land as much as we take from it. Wendell Berry, the writer, political activist, humanist, farmer, and philosopher, has often

been quoted as saying, "Eating is an agricultural act." And no other five words have made more of an impact on my career. With that one sentence, Berry turned a passive daily ritual into an ecological, political, and moral mission. For the average person, this is probably the last thing you want to think about as you bite into your burrito (and I have been guilty of it myself), but because I am a purveyor of gourmet food, part of my job is to deliver food that not only tastes good but also has a link with accountability. I ought to be able to trace our ingredients back to their source and ensure that every stage along the way has been scrutinized to a standard that makes me, the chef, comfortable—not just the FDA. This is the driving message behind the movement called "farm to table."

If there is one thing about this current feel-good movement that makes me uneasy, it is the gaping hole in the middle between the farm and the table that is oftentimes ignored. That missing link is the abattoir, or slaughterhouse. It's not a place

we want to think about as we cut into our pork chops, but how else would that happy, tail-swishing pig turn into porchetta? It had to go through an FDA-certified slaughterhouse, a place so abhorrent that the word itself has become synonymous with torture. It is a place entrenched in secrecy and invisibility, in order to give us the privilege of enjoying our dinner guilt-free. What horrors must lurk inside! Things we are better off not even knowing about. There is a neighborhood in Louisville called Butchertown. I figured the name was some quaint carryover from a time past when men with handlebar mustaches owned butcher shops that supplied the immigrant population. But it is actually where JB Swift operates a large commercial pig processing plant today. There are certain times of the day in Butchertown when the smell from the pigs will sit in the air and permeate every fiber of your clothes. It is the smell of commercial death. This is not a place where they give tours. It is not an agricultural act.

I get my pigs from a couple of farms around Louisville: Red Wattles from Kathy Botroff in Horse Cave and Durocs from Ashbourne Farms in LaGrange. And today I am going to help Jim Fiedler slaughter the black heritage-breed pigs that he brought down from Rome, Indiana. I am driving to Boone's Butcher Shop in Bardstown, Kentucky. Most of the local farmers here process their animals at Boone's. It was surprising to me that when I asked if I could help with the slaughter, all Jim had to do was put a call in to Boone's, and they were open to the idea. Jim is a kind, affable man with a dinner-table's-worth of stories behind him. He raises a breed that is hard to find and even harder to make money from, but they are his: stubborn pigs for a stubborn man. Jim is never on time, because he tends to do the herding, driving, and unloading all by himself. He drives a white pickup truck with a red trailer rigged to the back. Today he's bringing twenty pigs, and the morning chill will slow him down for sure. It's a two-hour drive from his farm. I leave Old Louisville at five a.m. to meet him at Boone's. It's a pretty drive, the road flanked by uneven hills interrupted by evergreens and the Jim Beam distillery pumping steam into the sky. The houses along the freeway are simple and sad. Every time I breathe, I fog up my windshield: it's that cold.

I smell Jim's pigs before he arrives. They live on unique soil: more loam, more grass and clover than most. They get to play around in mud, and it cakes onto their quill-like hairs. Their ears are so large they drape over their eyes, so all you see are their quivering snouts. They smell like shit—a rich, fecund, herbaceous shit. Our first order of business is to move the pigs from their trailer to the holding pens. I'm new at this and am slowing down the process. The workers at Boone's are baffled, if not annoyed, that I'm here slowing down their day. I'm thinking the same. Until today, I've enjoyed the privilege of turning processed pigs into pretty food.

I've never killed a pig. Will doing so make me a better chef? Does a carpenter need to cut down trees? Probably not. But if killing is a ritual, it's one that I need to experience. What I find is that it's less a ritual than a process.

From the pens, we bring in the pigs, one at a time, to the kill floor. There they meet an electric rod that shoots 1.5 amps into their necks. It takes two to three minutes for the legs to stop kicking. Once dead, the pig is hoisted by its rear legs with a chain onto a conveyor belt, where its throat is slit and the blood drains out. The tricky part is making sure the animal is dead. If it is not, it endures the pain of the hoist and the bleed-out. This is where most of the animal rights activists' justified outrage stems from.

And that's what brings me to the kill floor. I need to see firsthand what happens to these animals, to take part in that agricultural act that links the farms to my table. I find the process to be remarkably mundane. The animals are handled one at a time, and death, though never the same, has a disturbing predictability to it. The animals drop, shake, and sputter out in a routine that goes from violent to quiet. After its trip on the conveyor belt, each pig's carcass goes into a four-minute 150°F scalding bath, where rubber paddles remove most of the hairs. The entrails are removed and checked for parasites by a USDA inspector. The last remnants of hairs are burned off with a torch. Then it's back onto the conveyor belt, where the carcass is chainsawed in half, washed, and sprayed with a lactic acid solution, then moved to a cooling room to hang overnight before being butchered. This process takes less than ten minutes and is handled by a crew of three.

When the crew breaks for lunch, I duck out back to the holding pens for a cigarette. The remaining pigs are huddled together, a soft medley of oinks in the air. They are used to humans and hardly pay me any attention. I'm sad for them, not because they are about to die, but because there is no fanfare for them in these last moments of life. These pigs will wind up at the best restaurants in the region, brined, roasted, or cured, and sliced with culinary charm. Their meat will be praised and photographed for magazines and books. But here they are, patiently waiting, quarantined and anonymous. There used to be rituals and prayers and celebrations for pigs about to be turned into feasts. Nowadays we take it for granted that these beautiful breeds are plentiful and ready for delivery at the drop of a phone call.

It's bewildering how much we concentrate on the life of the animal but think so little about its death.

It's bewildering how much we concentrate on the life of the animal but think so little about its death. For all the talk about animal husbandry, the last fifteen minutes of an animal's life will have a profound effect on the meat. Electric prods, canes, and other instruments of force will bruise the meat of the already frightened animals, who then produce greater amounts of blood chemicals like cortisol and epinephrine, which have negative effects on the quality of the meat as well. Temple Grandin has been the most outspoken pioneer of a movement to persuade processing plants to adopt a humane standard of slaughtering. She works tirelessly to convince the slaughterhouse industry that animal welfare is inseparable from meat quality, that humane transport and kills are profitable, and that the only standard is a humane one. Animals, far from being just property, are sentient beings. Temple has a mind-blowing Web site offering free information about everything you will ever want to know about slaughterhouses. I encourage you to visit it at www.grandin.com.

I was listening to Temple give a lecture in northern Virginia last year, and one of the things she said to farmers and abattoir owners was quite revolutionary: She encouraged them to take videos of their animal slaughters and post them on the Web. She asked them to be vigilant and transparent about their responsible actions. She urged them to be proud of their efforts and to share them with the public. She made a case for turning the act of slaughtering into a public ritual: from invisibility to an agricultural act.

We killed more than thirty pigs that day at Boone's. By comparison, a big company like Swift can process more than a thousand pigs an hour. The difference between the two is like that between a small artisan cheese dairy and Kraft. As consumers, it's easy for us to group them all together under the umbrella of animal killers, but there is a difference when it comes to volume that affects how the animals are handled. Killing the first few pigs was a shock to me. It's not easy to watch anything die. The pace was fast, but not so fast that I didn't have time to notice how one pig had ears that were lopsided, how one had a longer tail than the one before it. Maybe it doesn't matter at that point, but it was a small consolation for me to notice these things.

I've been back to Boone's, and to other abattoirs in the region, and when I occasionally tell people about these experiences, I get a range of reactions, some curious, some disgusted. What's a chef doing killing animals? Shouldn't I be in the kitchen? I know I don't belong in the kill room. But where do I belong? On a farm, picking berries? Behind an expo line shouting orders? In front of a camera, talking nonsense? Or maybe in front of my computer writing about it to give some public voice to a process that generally goes unnoticed, to a group of unnamed pigs who became delicious meals. This is my attempt at an agricultural act.

RICE BOWL WITH SPICY PORK,

JICAMA, CILANTRO, AND KIMCHI RÉMOULADE

I started to make pork sausage patties to mimic the red pork you see in Chinese restaurants. That red pork generally gets its color from food coloring. In my recipe, grated beets give it both the tantalizing color and a sweetness. These sausage patties are good for more than the rice bowl. They make great appetizers for a party. And the kimchi rémoulade can be used on anything from tacos to crab cakes. / FEEDS 4 AS A MAIN COURSE OR 6 AS AN APPETIZER

KIMCHI RÉMOULADE

1 teaspoon grated fresh
   ginger (use a Microplane)
½ cup finely chopped Spicy
   Napa Kimchi (page 169)
5 tablespoons Perfect
   Rémoulade (page 6)

PORK SAUSAGE PATTIES

1 pound ground pork
¼ cup red beets, grated
1 garlic clove, grated
   (use a Microplane)
1 tablespoon Asian sesame oil
1 tablespoon soy sauce
1 teaspoon fish sauce
1 teaspoon sorghum
½ teaspoon salt
½ teaspoon sugar
¼ teaspoon freshly ground
   black pepper

About ¼ cup olive oil for
   panfrying
4 cups cooked rice (see
   page 4)

GARNISH

5 ounces jicama, peeled and
   cut into matchsticks (1 cup)
Fresh cilantro sprigs (optional)

1 To make the kimchi rémoulade: Mix the ginger with the chopped kimchi in a small bowl. Stir in the rémoulade. Cover with plastic wrap and refrigerate.

2 To make the sausage: Put the ground pork in a large bowl, add all the remaining ingredients, and, using your hands, mix well. Form into small quarter-size patties and place on a baking sheet.

3 Heat a large skillet over medium heat. Add about 1 tablespoon olive oil to the pan. Place only as many patties in the pan as will fit comfortably and fry for 3 minutes on each side, until browned. Transfer to a paper-towel-lined plate to drain the fat. Repeat with the remaining patties, adding more oil as needed.

4 To serve, scoop the rice into your rice bowls. Place 2 or 3 pork patties over the rice in each bowl and spoon about a tablespoon of the kimchi rémoulade over the pork. Scatter a few pieces of jicama over the sauce and garnish with a few sprigs of cilantro, if using. Serve immediately with spoons. It is best to mix everything together before enjoying.

CURRY PORK PIES

When I was a kid, there was a shop on Bayard Street in Chinatown where they used to sell tiny crescent-shaped pork pies for something like 60 cents. The bakery was in an amazing storefront that had been built in the 1960s and never changed. I would sit there with a 50-cent cup of tea and eat their buns and pies until I was stuffed, and it cost me maybe $3. I missed that place so much I created my own version of their pork pie, except I use a Southern piecrust and bake the pies in muffin tins (see step-by-step photographs on the following pages). I make a dozen at a time, and while that may seem like a lot, believe me, these pies don't last very long. Times change; the place on Bayard Street got a makeover, and I think the pies now sell for a dollar. / **MAKES 12 INDIVIDUAL PIES**

FILLING

½ cup chopped bacon

¾ pound ground pork

¾ cup chopped onions

¼ cup diced green bell pepper

¼ cup diced carrots

1½ tablespoons minced fresh ginger

1 garlic clove, chopped

1 tablespoon all-purpose flour

¾ cup chicken stock

2 teaspoons curry powder

2 teaspoons soy sauce

½ teaspoon salt

¼ teaspoon freshly ground black pepper

1 To make the filling: Heat a large cast-iron skillet over high heat. Add the bacon and cook for 3 minutes, or until the bacon is lightly crisped and some of the fat has rendered out. Add the ground pork, onions, bell pepper, carrots, ginger, and garlic and sauté for 5 minutes, or until the vegetables have started to soften and the pork is cooked through.

2 Sprinkle the flour over the vegetables and pork and cook, stirring, for 1 minute. Add the chicken stock, curry powder, soy sauce, salt, and pepper, stir well, and cook for about 2 minutes. Has the liquid cooked off but the filling still looks moist? Good. Transfer it to a bowl and let cool in the refrigerator while you make the crust.

3 Preheat the oven to 425°F. Grease a 12-cup muffin tin with a little soft butter. Keep chilled in the refrigerator until ready to use.

4 To make the piecrust: Measure the flour and salt into a bowl. Add the shortening and butter and, using a fork or your fingers, work them into the flour until you have a granular texture (like cornmeal). If the butter starts to soften, stop and chill the mixture in the refrigerator. Add the water gradually and work it in just until the mixture clumps together to form a wet dough; don't overwork the dough. Dust with a little extra flour and divide the dough in half. Shape into 2 disks, wrap in plastic wrap, and chill for 30 minutes before rolling out.

→ CONTINUED

PIECRUST

10 tablespoons unsalted butter, cut into cubes and chilled, plus softened butter for the muffin tin

4 cups all-purpose flour

2½ teaspoons kosher salt

⅔ cup cold vegetable shortening

8 to 10 tablespoons ice water

1 large egg

1 tablespoon vegetable oil

2 tablespoons whole milk

5 Remove one disk of dough from the fridge and put it on a floured surface. Using a rolling pin, roll the dough to a 15-by-20-inch rectangle about ⅛ inch thick. Using a biscuit cutter or a glass jar, punch out twelve 5-inch rounds of dough, rerolling scraps if necessary. Line the prepared muffin tin with the dough rounds. Make an egg wash by whisking the egg with the oil and milk in a small bowl. Brush the inside of each crust with some of the egg wash to seal it, reserving the remaining egg wash for the top crusts.

6 Spoon about 2 tablespoons of the chilled filling into each piecrust.

7 Roll out the second disk of dough on the floured surface about ⅛ inch thick. Using a slightly smaller biscuit cutter or a 3-inch ring mold, cut out 12 rounds. Drape a round over each pie and use your fingers to crimp the edges together. Brush the tops with the reserved egg wash. Use a fork to poke holes, or a sharp paring knife to cut an X, in the top of each pie.

8 Bake for 15 minutes, or until the pies are puffed and golden; you should see a little bit of the juices bubbling up through the holes. This will make you hungry, so take them out of the oven and let cool for 10 minutes before removing from the tins to prevent them from crumbling. Serve immediately.

Once they have cooled, you can freeze the pies in an airtight container. To reheat, bake at 400°F for 12 to 15 minutes, or until the center is warm.

Roll out the dough and punch out circles.

Line the muffin tin with the dough rounds.

Add the pork filling to the dough.

Top each pie with a smaller round and hand crimp the edges.

PORK RIBS AND SAUERKRAUT

WITH HORSERADISH

Louisville sits at the intersection of many different cultures. There's Southern soul food rising up from the south, a German influence coming down from the north, and country cooking spreading from Appalachia. This is a dish that embodies all of these cultures. I serve the ribs with roasted potatoes and pair it with the classic German-style Altbier from Bluegrass Brewing Company in Louisville. / **FEEDS 4 OR 5 AS A MAIN COURSE**

One 5-pound rack pork
    spareribs

RUB
4 teaspoons kosher salt
2 teaspoons freshly
    ground black pepper
2 teaspoons five-spice
    powder

One 2-pound bag
    sauerkraut
    (about 4 cups)
One 12-ounce bottle
    pilsner beer
2 cups chicken stock
½ cup water
½ cup apple cider
3 tablespoons Dijon
    mustard

HORSERADISH CREAM
¼ cup prepared
    horseradish
1 cup sour cream
2 tablespoons mayonnaise

1 Position a rack in the middle of the oven and preheat the oven to 335°F.

2 Using a sharp chef's knife, slice the rack of ribs into individual ribs.

3 To make the rub: Mix together the salt, pepper, and five-spice powder in a small bowl. Use your hands to massage the rub all over the ribs. Now is not the time to be coy—be forceful about it.

4 Transfer the ribs to a casserole or a roasting pan. Top with the sauerkraut, juice and all. Add the beer, stock, water, cider, and Dijon mustard. The liquid should just barely cover the ribs: If it doesn't, add water until it does.

5 Cover the roasting pan loosely with aluminum foil and poke holes In the foil with a fork. Transfer to the oven and bake for 1½ hours.

6 Remove and discard the aluminum foil. Turn the oven up to 450°F. Return the roasting pan to the oven, uncovered, and bake for about another 30 minutes: When ready, the ribs should be meltingly tender. The sauerkraut will be lightly browned. The braising liquid should be reduced to a delicious jus. If you want a thicker sauce, simply ladle a few cups into a small saucepan and reduce until thickened.

7 Meanwhile, make the horseradish cream: Combine all the ingredients in a small bowl and whisk together until smooth. Leave out at room temperature until ready to use.

8 Transfer the ribs and sauerkraut to a platter, along with the jus. Serve with the horseradish cream dolloped on top or on the side.

PORK CRACKLIN'

This is not so much a recipe—it's just me telling you how I make my cracklin'. There's nothing difficult about it, but it does require patience. Once done, the cracklin' can sit out at room temperature for days, but I promise it'll never last that long. Technically cracklin' is the skin of the pork belly, but over the years, I've made it with every part of the pig. Basically, whatever scraps are left over from butchering and trimming a hog can become cracklin'. Be very careful doing this in your home kitchen: as with any prolonged deep-frying recipe, you have to watch the oil constantly. / **MAKES 1 QUART**

1 Freeze the pork skin for at least an hour, not so that it is frozen solid but so that it is at least pretty stiff. Slice into slivers about ¾ inch thick and about 1 inch long.

2 Heat the peanut oil and lard in a large cast-iron pot over medium heat to around 340°F. Add the pork a little at a time, making sure not to let the hot oil splash. Monitor and regulate the temperature of the oil so that it doesn't fall below 300°F and doesn't go above 350°F. As the pork cooks, it will render more fat. Cook for 20 to 25 minutes, gently turning the pieces of pork, until the pork is floating in the oil. I use a set of long wooden chopsticks to flip the pork, or a pair of long tongs. The cracklin' should be dark and crispy. Gently scoop the pork out of the oil with a skimmer or slotted spoon and drain on paper towels. Season immediately with salt, nothing else. Let cool to room temperature.

3 Store the cracklin' in jars or resealable plastic bags at room temperature.

2 pounds pork belly skin and other trimmings
1 cup peanut oil, or just enough to cover pork pieces
1 cup lard or bacon fat
Salt

BRINED PORK CHOPS
WITH PEACH-GINGER GLAZE

This is one of those homemade dinners that will make you feel like you're dining out. Since you can make the brine the night before, go ahead and make the glaze and the gremolata then too. The next day, all you'll have to do is cook the pork and pull it all together. (The glaze and the gremolata will both keep for up to a week in the fridge.) Serve with Parsnip and Black Pepper Biscuits (page 206), if you like.

One of my favorite beers in all the land is Lazy Magnolia's Southern Pecan Nut Brown Ale, and it has never tasted better than with this dish. / **FEEDS 4 AS A MAIN COURSE**

BRINE
1 cup gin
2 cups water
¼ cup kosher salt
3 tablespoons sorghum
3 tablespoons brown sugar

Four 1-inch-thick pork loin
  chops (about 11 ounces
  each)

GLAZE
3 peaches
¼ cup dry white wine
2 teaspoons grated
  fresh ginger (use a
  Microplane)
2 teaspoons honey
Pinch each of salt and
  freshly ground black
  pepper

1 To make the brine: Bring the gin to a boil in a small saucepan over medium heat and boil until reduced to about ¼ cup. Add the remaining ingredients and stir over low heat just to dissolve the brown sugar. Take off the heat and allow to cool to room temperature.

2 Place the pork chops in a gallon-size resealable plastic bag and pour the cooled brine into the bag. Close the bag and brine the pork chops in the refrigerator for at least 4 hours, or up to 24 hours.

3 To make the glaze: Peel the peaches, cut each peach in half, and remove the pit. Cube the flesh and transfer to a small saucepan. Add the wine, ginger, honey, and salt and pepper, bring to a simmer, and cook for 10 minutes, or until the peaches are very soft. Let cool for about 15 minutes.

4 Transfer the peaches and liquid to a blender and puree on high until smooth. The smell of the sweet peaches and ginger should fill the room. Transfer to a bowl and refrigerate until ready to use.

5 To make the gremolata: Combine all the ingredients in a food processor and pulse about 10 times to a rough paste; you can also grind them in a mortar with the pestle. Refrigerate until ready to serve.

6 Preheat the oven to 400°F.

7 Remove the pork chops from the brine (discard the brine) and pat dry with paper towels. Heat the olive oil in a large cast-iron skillet over medium heat. Add the pork chops and cook for 3 minutes on each side, until browned and nicely caramelized.

8 Brush a dollop of the peach glaze over each pork chop. Sprinkle a generous even layer of the gremolata over the glaze. Transfer the pan to the oven and bake for 12 to 14 minutes, until the pork is cooked to medium-rare. The juices should run clear when a chop is pierced with a knife close to the bone. The glaze will be set and the gremolata should look just a shade brown and crunchy on top. Let the cooked chops rest in the pan for 5 minutes.

9 Carefully transfer the pork chops to plates and serve immediately.

PISTACHIO GREMOLATA
1 cup pistachios
¼ cup dried bread crumbs
Grated zest of 1 lemon
1½ tablespoons chopped fresh flat-leaf parsley
1 garlic clove, finely chopped
1 teaspoon Dijon mustard
1½ teaspoons olive oil
1 teaspoon salt
¼ teaspoon freshly ground black pepper

2 tablespoons olive oil

CHICKEN-FRIED PORK STEAK

WITH RAMEN CRUST AND BUTTERMILK PEPPER GRAVY

I love anything that is "chicken-fried." It sounds so redneck, but to me it's a Southern version of the famous Japanese dish called *tonkatsu,* which uses panko bread crumbs, a sweeter version of regular bread crumbs. Tonkatsu is Japan's version of the breaded and fried pork cutlet that came there from Europe in the late nineteenth century. It always fascinates me to see how different cultures latch onto a simple concept and interpret it uniquely. The bottom line is we all love meat that is pounded, breaded, and fried. I use dried ramen noodles as the crust; it sounds nuts but it is crazy good.

Pair with a great wine. I love Jim Clendenen's opulent Chardonnays from Au Bon Climat. / **FEEDS 4 AS A MAIN COURSE**

BUTTERMILK PEPPER GRAVY

3 tablespoons unsalted
   butter
3 tablespoons all-purpose
   flour
1¼ cups ham broth
   (see note, page 192)
   or chicken stock
¼ cup whole milk,
   or as needed
1 tablespoon buttermilk
1 teaspoon salt, or to taste
1¼ teaspoons freshly
   ground black pepper,
   or to taste

1 To make the gravy: Melt the butter in a small skillet over low heat. Sprinkle the flour over the melted butter and stir with a wooden spoon until smooth. Cook for 1 to 2 minutes to cook off the raw flour taste, but don't allow the roux to color.

2 Take the skillet off the heat and continue to stir for a minute to cool it down slightly, then add the ham broth, milk, and buttermilk. Return the skillet to medium-low heat and cook, stirring, until the gravy thickens and coats the back of the spoon, 5 to 6 minutes. Season with the salt and pepper. Taste. Gravy preferences are wide-ranging: Add more milk to make a thinner gravy; adjust the salt and pepper to your liking. I like mine really salty.

3 Place one pork chop between two sheets of plastic wrap and pound firmly but not violently with a mallet or the bottom of a skillet until you get an even ¾-inch-thick cutlet. Repeat with the other chops. Season the pork on both sides with the salt and pepper.

4 Set up a breading station: Put the flour in a shallow dish. Next to that, whisk the egg and milk in a medium bowl. Next to that, combine the ramen crumbles with the bread crumbs in a shallow bowl. Dredge one pork cutlet in the flour, turning to coat, then put it into the egg mixture. Lift the cutlet out of the egg wash with a fork, letting the excess drip off, transfer to the ramen crumbles, and press as much of this crust onto the pork as possible. Transfer to a plate. Repeat with the remaining pork cutlets. Let sit at room temperature for 15 minutes before frying.

5 Preheat the oven to 350°F.

6 In the largest cast-iron skillet you have, heat the oil over high heat. Fry the pork cutlets one or two at a time, depending on how large your skillet is, for about 2 minutes on each side. The ramen crust will burn pretty quickly, so watch it carefully. Transfer to a baking sheet and pat dry with paper towels.

7 Transfer the cutlets to the oven and bake for 10 minutes until the pork is cooked all the way through. Meanwhile, reheat the gravy over low heat.

8 Remove the chops from the oven and serve immediately, with the gravy. If you feel any guilt about eating this rich dish, sprinkle a little fresh parsley over the top.

There are infinite varieties of ramen, but try to use one that has thin noodles, as they will crisp up better. If you can't find ramen, substitute 1 cup panko bread crumbs.

4 boneless pork rib chops (cutlets)
2 teaspoons sea salt
1 teaspoon freshly ground black pepper
1 cup all-purpose flour
1 large egg
½ cup whole milk
One 3.5-ounce package dried ramen noodles, pounded until crumbled but not pulverized
¼ cup dried bread crumbs
3 tablespoons peanut or vegetable oil
Chopped fresh flat-leaf parsley (optional)

COLA HAM HOCKS

WITH MISO GLAZE

Ham hocks are hard to find fresh, but not impossible. My butcher can usually get them for me. You may find them more easily in their smoked form, which can be used to flavor all sorts of veggies and soups, but it's worth the effort to find them fresh for this dish. When roasted slowly, the meat becomes impossibly tender and flavorful. And special. It's not every day you see a whole ham hock on a plate.

Serve these with Butter Beans with Garlic-Chile and Celery Leaves (page 212) and Pickled Corn–Bacon Relish (page 182). / **FEEDS 4 AS A MAIN COURSE**

4 ham hocks (about
    1 pound each; see note)
2 tablespoons peanut or
    vegetable oil
1 small onion, chopped
2 garlic cloves, minced
1½ cups dry vermouth
One 12-ounce can cola
¼ cup rice vinegar
2 tablespoons soy sauce
1 star anise
1 teaspoon black
    peppercorns
2 bay leaves

MISO GLAZE
¼ cup red miso
½ cup apple cider
½ cup packed brown sugar
3 tablespoons sorghum
2 tablespoons soy sauce

1 Soak the ham hocks in cold water for 30 minutes; drain and pat dry with paper towels.

2 In a Dutch oven, heat the oil over medium heat. Add the ham hocks and brown on all sides, about 5 minutes. Don't worry if they get a little burned on the outside; you're going to cook the hell out of these hocks.

3 Add the onions and garlic to the pot and sauté for 2 minutes. Add the vermouth, cola, vinegar, soy sauce, star anise, peppercorns, and bay leaves, bring to a boil, and skim off the foam that rises to the top. Cover with a tight-fitting lid and lower the heat to medium-low. Braise for 2 hours while you read some Walt Whitman poems.

4 Just before the hocks are done, prepare the glaze: In a small saucepan, combine all the ingredients, bring to a simmer, and simmer, stirring until thick and syrupy, 5 to 6 minutes. Keep warm.

5 After 2 hours, check the ham hocks: The skin should be soft and amber in color and the meat should be falling off the bone. If not, continue to cook for another 20 minutes or so.

6 Preheat the broiler. Carefully transfer the ham hocks to a baking pan. Brush the glaze onto the hocks and transfer to the hot broiler. Broil until the glaze starts to bubble and caramelize, usually 3 to 5 minutes—but this will really depend on the strength of your broiler, so check frequently. Transfer to large warm bowls and serve with a small ladle of the braising liquid.

A ham hock is usually cut from just above the ankle and just below the part of the bone where a traditional ham starts. They can come from either the back or front legs of the pig. I always try to get the back-leg ham hocks since they are a bit larger, but tastewise they are the same. When ordering, just make sure they don't give you the ham hock with the foot still attached, as I have sometimes seen butchers do. It generally makes people squeamish. If you don't want all the fat, you can take the skin off the hocks before you transfer them to the broiler and just glaze the meat instead of the skin. Give the skin to your pooch; he'll love you forever.

PULLED PORK SHOULDER

IN BLACK BBQ SAUCE

Oven-roasting pork shoulder is a great way to get that soft pulled-pork texture without having to smoke it for hours. The Black BBQ Sauce that flavors the pork is something I came up with a few years ago after a trip to Owensboro, Kentucky, home to some of the best BBQ in the region. I noticed how every BBQ joint had a signature sauce they could call their own. Most BBQ sauces are too sweet for me; I like the saltiness of Asian BBQ marinades. So I started tinkering with conventional notions of BBQ and added some Asian spices to a Southern BBQ sauce recipe. We have had some variation of this sauce on our menu ever since.

Serve the pulled pork with Lardo Cornbread (page 208) and Quick Caraway Pickles (page 173), or stuff it inside hot dog buns and top with Spicy Napa Kimchi (page 169) and Pork Cracklin' (page 109). There are endless ways to enjoy this stuff. / FEEDS 6 TO 8

BLACK BBQ SAUCE

2 tablespoons unsalted butter

1 teaspoon olive oil

1 pound onions, chopped

5 garlic cloves, chopped

2 jalapeño peppers, chopped (seeds and all)

⅓ cup raisins

½ cup bourbon

½ cup dark coffee

½ cup cola

½ cup ketchup

¼ cup soy sauce

¼ cup balsamic vinegar

2 tablespoons molasses

2 tablespoons Worcestershire sauce

1 To make the BBQ sauce: In a Dutch oven, melt the butter with the olive oil over low heat. Add the onions, garlic, jalapeño peppers, and raisins. Cover the pot and cook over medium-low heat, stirring occasionally, until the onions start to brown and caramelize on the bottom of the pot, about 5 minutes. Deglaze the pan by adding the bourbon, coffee, and cola. Scrape up the brown bits from the bottom of the pot with a wooden spoon and simmer until the liquid has reduced by about half.

2 Add the ketchup, soy sauce, balsamic vinegar, molasses, Worcestershire sauce, and black bean paste and simmer over low heat for about 5 minutes. Add the mustard, allspice, black pepper, cayenne pepper, and smoked paprika and simmer for about 10 minutes. Turn off the heat and allow the sauce to cool for about 15 minutes.

3 Transfer the sauce to a blender, add the lime juice and sesame oil, and puree on high until you achieve a smooth, thick sauce. Taste. Is it good? Adjust the seasonings to the way you like it. Transfer to a bowl and refrigerate; bring to room temperature when ready to use. (The sauce will keep in an airtight container in the refrigerator for up to a month.)

4 To make the rub: Combine all the ingredients in a bowl.

5 Put the pork shoulder in a large baking dish or other container and pat a thick layer of the rub over the entire surface. Let stand in the refrigerator for at least 2 hours to give the pork a quick cure.

6 Preheat the oven to 425°F.

7 Wrap the shoulder loosely in aluminum foil and set in a roasting pan. Pour a little water, about ½ cup, into the foil package. Roast for 2½ hours. Check the meat. Does it pull away from the shoulder-blade bone when you poke it with a fork? It is done.

8 Carefully transfer the pork to a cutting board. It is easier to pull the meat while it is still hot. Use two forks: one to hold the shoulder in place and the other to shred the meat, using a downward motion.

9 Moisten the meat with just enough BBQ sauce to flavor it but not so much that it overpowers the pork. Transfer to a platter and serve hot.

2 tablespoons black bean paste
1 tablespoon dry mustard
2 teaspoons ground allspice
2 teaspoons freshly ground black pepper
2 teaspoons cayenne pepper
1 teaspoon smoked paprika
Juice of 1 lime
¼ cup Asian sesame oil

RUB
¼ cup kosher salt
1½ tablespoons ground cumin
1½ tablespoons smoked paprika
1½ tablespoons freshly ground black pepper

One 5-pound pork shoulder roast, skin on

PIGGY BURGERS

WITH SUN-DRIED TOMATO KETCHUP

A few years ago I was in San Sebastián, in northern Spain, home to arguably the best food in Europe and the epicenter of Basque culture. So it was pretty horrifying when I found myself having lunch at the only McDonald's in the city, but I had a good reason. They serve a pork burger there—a fast-food pork burger—and I had to have one. Alas, it wasn't as good as I wanted it to be, so I came up with one myself. These are great with cold root beer. / **MAKES 4 LARGE BURGERS**

BURGERS

1 pound ground pork
   (85% lean)
2 tablespoons hoisin sauce
Greens from 3 scallions, finely
   chopped
1 teaspoon salt
½ teaspoon freshly ground
   black pepper

SUN-DRIED TOMATO KETCHUP

6 ounces sun-dried tomatoes,
   chopped
2 dried pasilla peppers, stems
   and seeds removed
1 garlic clove, chopped
½ cup balsamic vinegar
½ cup dry red wine
¼ cup packed brown sugar
1 tablespoon soy sauce
¼ teaspoon sea salt
¼ teaspoon freshly ground
   black pepper
About ¾ cup water

2 tablespoons peanut oil

FOR SERVING

4 hamburger buns
Spicy Napa Kimchi (page 169)
Fresh bean sprouts
Fresh cilantro leaves
Pork Cracklin' (page 109)

1 To make the burgers: Combine all the ingredients in a large bowl. Form the meat into 8 thin patties (about 2 ounces each); the patties should be thin enough to use 2 per burger. Stack the patties between squares of wax paper and refrigerate for at least 30 minutes before cooking. (The patties can be wrapped, stacked, and stored in the freezer for up to 1 week; pull some out whenever you feel like a burger.)

2 While the patties are chilling, make the ketchup: Combine all the ingredients except the water in a medium saucepan, bring to a simmer, cover, and cook for 15 minutes over low heat.

3 Transfer the tomato mixture to a blender and puree on high, slowly drizzling in enough water to create a smooth puree. Transfer to a bowl and refrigerate until ready to use. (Leftover ketchup will keep in the refrigerator for up to 2 weeks.)

4 Heat a large cast-iron skillet over medium heat and add 1 tablespoon of the peanut oil.

5 Add 4 of the pork patties to the pan, and cook for 2 minutes on the first side, then flip and cook for another minute on the other side, until cooked through. Transfer the cooked burgers to a plate and keep warm in a low oven. Cook the remaining patties in the same way.

6 To assemble the burgers, smear a little of the ketchup on the bottom of each bun and top with a pork patty. Spread some ketchup on each patty and top with the remaining patties. Top each one with some kimchi, a few bean sprouts, a couple of cilantro leaves, and a small fistful of pork cracklin'. Serve immediately.

COUNTRY HAMS

I stopped using prosciutto the day I discovered country ham. There's a bit of confusion about what exactly a country ham is, so let me clarify: A country ham is a dry-cured pig leg, salted and hung to dry for about a year, much like Italian prosciutto. The difference is that prosciutto is only salted, never smoked, while many American country hams are smoked as well as salt-cured, and most also have some form of sugar in the cure. And country hams are packed in salt for almost twice as long as prosciutto is, though usually not aged as long, making them saltier than their Italian counterpart. That is why the producer usually suggests soaking the ham in water or beer before cooking to draw out some of the salt. Cooking the ham might seem odd because you'd never think to cook a prosciutto, and it also leads some people to conclude that country hams are unsafe to eat "raw," but the soaking and cooking is because of the saltiness (the soaking takes out the salt, but then the ham needs to be cooked to intensify the flavor). The hams are, in fact, safe to eat raw, sliced thin and enjoyed with pickles and compotes and mustards. Country ham is very different from a city ham, also sometimes known as a spiral ham, which is a wet-brined, often injected, ham that is not aged long at all, very moist, and fully cooked or smoked (so you don't have to cook them, but you often do anyway).

Country hams have existed in America in some form ever since Hernando de Soto, the famous Spanish explorer, brought pigs to North America from Europe in 1539. They were first made in Virginia, where Smithfield took up residence, but they soon spread to North Carolina, Tennessee, Georgia, Kentucky, and beyond. There are countless farms making country hams today, both small producers and commercial giants. Each region has, over the years, developed its own particular style, and eating through them is a revelation. It's sort of like eating through the colonial history of America.

Pictured opposite are my favorite hams from Kentucky. All of them are aged for at least 10 months, most over a year. Each one is a bit different, which you can see from their shades of smoke. Hams like these are no farther away than our backyard of the American South. See Resources, page 279, for a list of my favorite ham purveyors; Newsom's is also a great source of information on hams.

BACON PÂTÉ BLT

New York City is filled with Greek diners, where you can get anything from a meatball hero to chicken souvlaki to a BLT. The waiters shout orders at the kitchen in a coded language that mesmerizes me—orders like "a Jack Tommy on whiskey all the way" (grilled cheese with tomato on rye with a side of fries). I waited tables in diners all through college, and I'd always sit down after the lunch rush and have a BLT with extra bacon, griddled tomatoes, and a black-and-white milkshake (vanilla ice cream with chocolate syrup). This recipe grew out of my cravings for that rich, unctuous BLT. I cut these into 1-inch squares, and serve them warm as an appetizer with a flute of Schramsberg Blanc de Blanc. / **MAKES 6 SANDWICHES; SERVES 10 TO 15 PEOPLE AS A CANAPÉ**

BACON PÂTÉ

1 pound good-quality bacon, diced

1 medium onion, diced

10 sun-dried tomatoes, chopped

¼ cup dry red wine

¼ cup Dijon mustard

2 tablespoons sherry vinegar

1 teaspoon sorghum

3 scallions, finely chopped

3 ounces foie gras (see note)

1 teaspoon freshly ground black pepper

12 slices rustic whole-grain bread, preferably from a day-old bread loaf

Dijon mustard

¼ cup grated aged Gruyère cheese

¼ cup corn oil for panfrying

1 To make the pâté: Heat a medium skillet over medium heat. Add the bacon and onions and sauté for about 5 minutes, until the onions are soft. Drain off some but not all the fat, leaving about 2 teaspoons. Add the sun-dried tomatoes, red wine, mustard, sherry vinegar, sorghum, and scallions, bring to a simmer, and simmer gently for 6 to 8 minutes.

2 Transfer the bacon mixture to a food processor and puree to a coarse paste. With the processor running, add the foie gras and pepper and process until well combined. Transfer to a bowl or other container and let cool to room temperature before transferring to the refrigerator to fully chill. (The pâté can be refrigerated, tightly covered, for at least 2 weeks.)

3 To make the sandwiches: Lay out the slices of bread on a surface. Spread a little Dijon mustard on each slice and sprinkle the slices with about half of the grated cheese. Smear a thin layer of bacon pâté, about ¼ inch thick, on 6 slices of bread. Sprinkle the remaining grated cheese over the pâté. Top with the remaining slices of bread.

4 Heat the corn oil in a large frying pan. Add the sandwiches two at a time and cook over medium heat, for 2 minutes on each side, until golden brown on both sides. Drain on paper towels.

To make the sandwiches easier to cut and serve, instead of cutting them right after frying them, transfer them to a platter and chill in the refrigerator for an hour. Then slice them into nice even squares, transfer to a baking sheet, and reheat in a 300°F oven for 6 minutes, or until warmed through.

The world is full of finger-pointing moralists who find foie gras to be ethically repugnant. California recently banned all foie gras products; Chicago tried to, but the city quickly came to its senses. Michael Ginor owns and oversees Hudson Valley Foie Gras in Ferndale, New York, where I buy my foie gras and duck products. I implore anyone with any misgivings about foie gras to go and visit his operation. It is a clean, resourceful, and humanely run farm that happens to sell duck livers. If you have any doubts, it will change your mind about foie gras.

EGGPLANT, RICOTTA, NEWSOM'S HAM,

AND FRIED BLACK-EYED PEAS WITH GRAPEFRUIT VINAIGRETTE

Salads fall into two categories: tossed and composed. I like serving this as a composed salad, which means that all the components are prepared separately and then put together on the plates at the last minute. There are many different types of eggplant out there, so be sure to experiment with some of the beautiful heirloom varieties. For an elegant salad like this, I will always go with the intensely salty Newsom's ham (see Resources, page 279). / **FEEDS 4 OR 5**

1 large or 2 medium eggplants, sliced into ¾-inch-thick disks

About 3 tablespoons olive oil

Kosher salt and freshly ground black pepper

1 cup ricotta

1 teaspoon grated grapefruit zest

3 ounces country ham, preferably Col. Bill Newsom's (see Resources, page 279)

½ cup cooked black-eyed peas (see note), patted dry with paper towels

Canola oil or corn oil for deep-frying

GRAPEFRUIT VINAIGRETTE

Juice of ½ grapefruit (about ½ cup)

2 tablespoons rice vinegar

¼ cup olive oil

1 teaspoon Dijon mustard

1 Preheat the oven to 400°F.

2 Arrange the eggplant disks in a single layer on a baking sheet. Brush on both sides with about 2 tablespoons of the olive oil. Sprinkle with salt and pepper on both sides. Roast for 16 to 18 minutes. Flip the slices of eggplant; they should look browned on the bottom and the skin should be slightly blistered. Cook for an additional 10 minutes. Set aside.

3 Meanwhile, mix the ricotta with the remaining 1 tablespoon olive oil, the grapefruit zest, ½ teaspoon salt, and ¼ teaspoon pepper in a small bowl. Reserve.

4 Slice the country ham; you want as many slices as you have eggplant disks. Set aside on wax paper or a cold plate until ready to use.

5 To make the black-eyed peas: In a skillet, heat about 1½ cups canola oil to 375°F (the oil should be ½ inch deep). Slowly add the black-eyed peas and fry them, stirring very slowly, for 6 to 7 minutes, or until the skins are very dark and crunchy. Immediately remove with a skimmer or slotted spoon and drain on paper towels. Sprinkle ½ teaspoon salt over the fried peas while they are still hot.

6 To make the vinaigrette: Whisk all the ingredients together in a small bowl. (The vinaigrette can be made ahead and refrigerated in a jar until ready to use. It will separate after a few minutes, but that's okay. Just shake it up a bit right before serving.)

7 To serve, divide the eggplant evenly among four or five salad plates. Place a spoonful of ricotta on each eggplant disk. Drape a slice of country ham over the ricotta. Sprinkle the fried black-eyed peas over and around the plates. Finish by drizzling the grapefruit vinaigrette over the salads.

Black-eyed peas came to America on the slave ships from Africa. They are one of the most common forms of beans in the world. To cook them, start with about ½ pound of dried beans. Rinse them under cold water and put them in a large saucepan along with 3 cups warm water. If you like pork, add a handful of ham trimmings to the pot. Bring to a boil, then cover the pan with a lid, reduce the heat to a simmer, and cook for about 45 minutes undisturbed. Check the beans. Are they tender enough to chew but still have a little resistance to them? That's how I like my peas, not at all mushy.

TAMARIND-STRAWBERRY-GLAZED HAM

To avoid ham confusion, it's important to note that this recipe calls for a city ham, which means a ham that has been injection-cured and usually very lightly smoked and sold partially cooked or ready to eat. Traditionally these hams are coated with a very sweet glaze—and I'm sure you've seen them decorated with rounds of canned pineapple slices and maraschino cherries. This tamarind glaze gets its sweetness and texture from ripe strawberries and brown sugar, but the intense tartness of the tamarind fruit cuts through the sweetness, as well as the ham's fat, bringing another layer of flavor to the dish.

Try this recipe for your next Easter ham, and serve it with your favorite roasted vegetables and a side of Cardamom Ambrosia Salad (page 194). / **FEEDS 8 TO 10 EASILY**

TAMARIND-STRAWBERRY GLAZE

¾ cup packed light brown sugar

½ cup fresh orange juice

¼ cup tamarind paste or concentrate (see Resources, page 279)

¼ cup honey

5 ounces fresh strawberries, washed and hulled

3 garlic cloves, chopped

2 teaspoons soy sauce

½ teaspoon freshly ground black pepper

½ teaspoon paprika

¼ teaspoon ground cloves

1 fully cooked spiral-cut ham (about 8 pounds)

1 To make the glaze: Combine all the ingredients in a medium saucepan and bring to a simmer over low heat, stirring to dissolve the sugar. Simmer for 8 to 10 minutes, until the strawberries are soft. Skim the foam off the top and discard.

2 Transfer the mixture to a blender and puree on medium speed. Pass through a strainer into a bowl or other container to remove all the strawberry seeds. Cover and set aside at room temperature.

3 Position a rack in the lower third of the oven and take out the other rack. Preheat the oven to 250°F.

4 Unwrap the ham and place it fat side up in a large roasting pan. Add about a cup of water to the bottom of the pan. Using a sharp chef's knife, make diagonal cuts into the fat of the ham about an inch apart and about ¼ inch deep to create a crosshatch pattern. Don't worry if you fumble a bit; this part isn't exact science. Wrap the entire ham in aluminum foil and place the pan on the bottom oven rack.

When using a brush to apply the glaze, use a real painter's brush. Seriously. Most pastry brushes are just cheap things that fall apart after a few uses. Buy yourself a good-quality painter's brush, wash it right after every use, and it'll last you for years.

5 Bake the ham for 10 minutes per pound (an 8-pound ham will take 1 hour and 20 minutes). Check the internal temperature of the ham with an instant-read thermometer: it should read 120°F.

6 Remove the foil and use a brush to apply a thick layer of the glaze onto the entire surface of the ham. The slits that you made earlier will have started to pull apart just a little. Get your brush into all the crevices and slits so the glaze will penetrate the meat. Increase the oven temperature to 450°F, return the ham to the oven, and bake for 10 minutes, or until the glaze has become candy-like and caramelized. Don't worry if you get a few burnt spots, those are the best bites.

7 Let the ham rest for 10 minutes, then transfer to a large platter, carve, and serve.

Tamarind is the fruit of a tropical tree that grows throughout West Africa, India, and Southeast Asia. The pod-like fruit is hard to come by in its fresh form, but there are many pastes and extracts that you can find at specialty markets. I use a brand called Tamicon. It is dark and rich and tastes like the actual tamarind fruit. Most brands, unfortunately, are watered down and/or blended with artificial flavorings.

COUNTRY HAM AND OYSTER STUFFING

Come the holidays, this is the stuffing you want on your dinner table. Try it for your next Thanksgiving dinner, or anytime you roast a large bird. Make sure you use cornbread that is not too sweet (or make your own; see page 208), because the chestnuts are going to add sweetness to the stuffing. If you are using a salty country ham, cut back on or omit the salt altogether. It doesn't really matter what oyster you use—pick your favorite ones. Just make sure they are fresh. / **FEEDS 8 AS A SIDE DISH**

2 pounds cornbread (see the headnote)

12 tablespoons (1½ sticks) unsalted butter, melted

5 tablespoons plus 2 teaspoons unsalted butter

2 cups chopped onions

1½ cups chopped celery

2 garlic cloves, finely minced

6 ounces country ham, finely diced

2 tablespoons chopped fresh sage

2 teaspoons chopped fresh thyme

1½ teaspoons sea salt

1 teaspoon freshly ground black pepper

½ teaspoon grated nutmeg

18 to 20 fresh oysters, shucked, their liquor reserved, and coarsely chopped

1 cup chicken stock

¾ cup whole milk

3 large eggs, lightly beaten

15 roasted chestnuts, peeled and coarsely chopped (see note)

1 Preheat the oven to 400°F. Lightly butter a 9-by-13-inch baking dish.

2 Cut the cornbread into ½-inch cubes. Toss the cornbread with the melted butter and spread out in a single layer on a baking sheet, crumbs and all. Bake, stirring occasionally, for 30 minutes, or until the cornbread is a nice toasty color. Set aside.

3 Meanwhile, melt 5 tablespoons of the butter in a large skillet. Add the onions, celery, and garlic and sauté until translucent, about 6 minutes.

4 Transfer the cooked vegetables into a large bowl and toss gently with the toasted cornbread. Add the country ham, sage, thyme, salt, pepper, and nutmeg, tossing well. Add the oysters, with their liquor, and mix gently with a rubber spatula.

5 Warm the chicken stock and milk in a small saucepan just until simmering. Add to the stuffing mixture. Fold in the eggs. Transfer the stuffing to the baking dish, dot with the remaining 2 teaspoons butter, and sprinkle the chopped chestnuts over the top. Cover the dish with foil.

6 Turn the oven down to 350°F and bake for 15 to 20 minutes. Remove the foil and bake for another 15 to 20 minutes, until the stuffing is browned on top but still looks moist. Serve hot.

In winter, you can find roasted and peeled chestnuts at many gourmet shops. If you have fresh chestnuts, make a slit down the middle of each one with a sharp knife, then dump into a pot of boiling water for 5 minutes. Transfer them to a baking sheet and roast in a 400°F oven for 15 minutes. Peel both the shell and inner skin. They peel easier when they are hot.

THE HAM LADY

Nancy Newsom is continuing a tradition of making country ham the old way, from hand-rubbing the salt onto the hams to curing them without nitrates. Hers was the first ham that I tasted and thought, "I would never miss prosciutto if I could have this every night." Nancy ages her hams for a minimum of 10 months, but most of the hams we get from her are 14 to 16 months old, with a 30- to 34-percent shrinkage rate, making for concentrated ham flavor. The shrinkage represents how much water has evaporated from the ham during the aging process. Her hams come from several different breeds, including Tamsworth, Red Wattle, Berkshire, and Duroc—all breeds that have a good meat-to-fat ratio.

"People may make history, but it is history that makes us who we are. With each generation that comes along, there is something lost. The ability to make country hams, and the love of nature, the morals, and the business ethics—these are things that our forefathers fell upon. They laid the foundation, and we need to take our forefathers with us and bring their ideas forward into our own lives."

—NANCY NEWSOM,
COL. BILL NEWSOM'S KENTUCKY COUNTRY HAMS,
PRINCETON, KENTUCKY

SEAFOOD & SCRUTINY

Always stir a pot clockwise
and tie your shoelaces
right foot first.
—MY SUPERSTITIONS DURING
TOP CHEF, SEASON 9

★ ★ ★

MY TOP CHEF RUN ENDED

with a can of oysters, a lot of hoopla, and temporary sadness. But like the many chefs who came before me and the many who will come after, I took the bitter pill of elimination and marched on. There's a lot of fuss over reality cooking shows, and rightfully so. They have changed the landscape for young cooks approaching their careers. Gone are the days when chefs lived and died by their oven doors. Chefs now have to worry about their public images as much as they do about their knife skills. This new cult of celebrity naturally brings out detractors as well as cheerleaders. It creates controversy, and the Internet lights up. We consume food blogs like jelly beans. We post every morsel of our daily comestibles like prayers. And the cooking shows keep coming, brash and merciless. It's not my intention to defend the reality of "reality" TV. People will always have an opinion about it either way, and I don't care to change their minds.

What I do want to talk about is the idea of public scrutiny, on *Top Chef, Iron Chef,* or any other show that pits talent against talent. According to the *Oxford English Dictionary,* scrutiny means "critical observation or examination." The word comes from the Latin verb *scruta,* meaning "to sort trash." How perfect! On *Top Chef,* our dishes were observed, examined, and criticized, and then the trash was sorted out. We were scrutinized and eliminated.

Art has become sport, and scrutiny has replaced idolatry. I know many who think this a turn for the worse. I don't. It's just the time that we live in.

I got my first job in a restaurant the summer I turned fifteen, busing tables at Terrace 5, a small, snooty restaurant on the fifth floor of the Trump Tower on Fifth Avenue in New York City. On my first day of work, I'd forgotten to buy a bow tie, so the manager sent me to a lady friend of his at Hermès who sold me a silk bow tie for cheap and taught me how to knot it. On my second day on the job, I made an espresso for Kim Basinger, and I thought I had the coolest job in the city. I saw a lot of celebrities that summer. Every day before lunch service, we were given a speech about how to serve them without intrusion, how to address them without making eye contact. I hung out with waiters who were cool as shit and sometimes let me smoke a cigarette with them. After the dinner rush, I would sneak back to the kitchen and see what was left over to eat.

I don't remember the name of the chef there. What I do remember was that it wasn't important. There was a time in the history of American dining when the chef was not the most important cog in the machine. There was a time when chefs did not get their photos taken or walk around the dining room shaking people's hands. There was a time when a chef was hired simply to cook, to remain anonymous. I didn't know much about food back then, but I loved watching the chef of Terrace 5 go about his day. He was quiet and humble, always working, sweating over a steam table. I remember him wiping the rim of every plate that left the kitchen and asking what people were saying in the dining room.

There was a time when a chef was hired simply to cook, to remain anonymous.

He always seemed a little beaten down. A little tragic. No one ever asked to shake his hand. No one ever wanted his autograph. At the end of each night, he would wring the sweat from the towel wrapped around his neck into a mop sink. His sumptuous plates of food were as anonymous as they were beautiful. In those days, André Soltner's name was in the paper a lot; so was Wolfgang Puck's. But the cult of food had not yet been born. There was no Food Network, only *The Frugal Gourmet.* And New York City's kitchens were filled with an army of anonymous chefs creating masterpieces.

This was around the time I started to really learn about food and restaurants. It was also,

coincidentally, about the same time the city cracked down on graffiti. Subway cars were fitted with graffiti-resistant stainless-steel finishes. Increased security in the train yards prevented the artists from doing their elaborate murals. Kids either went to jail or grew up, and I lost interest. So many masterpieces on the subway cars had vanished into memories, but I didn't mourn their loss. I was drawn to this new, even more transitory art form percolating beneath the surface of fine French cuisine. It was more intricate and dangerous than the graffiti I had been enamored of for so long.

Back then, I could never have imagined a world where chefs would become rock stars. All the chefs I worked for in my early days were chained to their kitchens, emblazoned with the scars of battle: fading slash marks from knife cuts, discolored blotches on their arms from old burns, and always a fresh bandage somewhere on their limbs. They were more artisans than artists. I could never have imagined a time when people would recognize me at airports or walking down the street. Truth be told, it is an uneasy experience, especially when you've been anonymous for most of your life.

All in all, I enjoyed the scrutiny I endured on *Top Chef.* How many of us, in our own endeavors, get to be analyzed so closely by the very best of our peers? To have your work picked apart layer by layer is mortifying and liberating at the same time. I could second-guess every criticism that was handed down to me, but after the dust settled, I realized that it was the most honest, objective scrutiny of my cooking that I've ever received. It was a privilege, really. And it is small potatoes compared to the scrutiny that is thrust upon you by the public at large. Here now, but gone tomorrow. It pushed us at a pace faster than most of us could follow: the adulation and the humiliation, the pursuit of eternity, and the fading memory of a single can of oysters. There is, at least, consolation in that.

Every year, the Southern Foodways Alliance holds a symposium in Oxford, Mississippi. It is an intimate gathering where anonymity is not allowed, but neither is scrutiny. Oxford is a place very different from the frenetic city I grew up in. Its pace is intentionally slower, and every step that much more meaningful. My first trip to the symposium was in 2005. I walked around with a name tag and a whiskey flush the whole weekend.

Oxford is a place to catch your breath. When you pull into the town square, it feels like home, even on your first visit. John T. Edge is the director of the Southern Foodways Alliance. Through him, I have met all of the great chefs of the South (and even some of the not-so-great ones), too many to name. I have stories with them all, with Linton and Sean and Ashley and Mike and Andrea and Tyler and Hugh and Currence and Angie . . . I collect these stories like tiles in a mosaic. But, unlike the fleeting murals of spray paint or even the fading memories of my childhood, and unlike the cult of celebrity, I want these stories to have permanence. I want to hoard them but at the same time ensure that they will live on forever. I want them to exist in a place insulated from the noise of artifice but at the same time to remain relevant. It is a contradiction, I know.

It feels like everything in the food world happens at a breakneck pace now. If there's something groundbreaking going on in a village in Spain, it will make the news in Louisville. The world is condensed to 140 characters and a DVR menu of cooking shows. Kitchens are full of good-looking young chefs with expensive Japanese knives. We can take a carrot, disassemble it, and reassemble it so it tastes like, well, a carrot. We can try things and eat things from every corner of the earth, and we react with a jaded ambivalence. Scrutiny has never been more public, more microscopic, more aggressive. Cooking as a sport is here to stay; poets and painters be damned. This is the generation belonging to chefs. And there is the next thing, always the next big thing just waiting to be discovered or manufactured for our consumption. I am frequently asked to predict what this will be. I have no answers, but I have faith that Oxford, Mississippi, will always be there. Indeed, its legend only grows.

RICE BOWL WITH TUNA,

AVOCADO, PORK RINDS, AND JALAPEÑO RÉMOULADE

I'll put pork rinds on just about everything. The great thing is that although they aren't a gourmet ingredient—you can find pork rinds at most gas station convenience stores—they add flavor and depth to almost any dish. It makes me think, "What other culinary secrets are truck drivers hiding?" Of course, you can make your own pork rinds too, in the form of cracklin' (see page 109), but I'm not a pork rind snob. I like 'em all. / **FEEDS 4 AS A MAIN COURSE OR 6 AS AN APPETIZER**

JALAPEÑO RÉMOULADE
¼ cup **Perfect Rémoulade**
    (page 6)
2 jalapeño peppers,
    seeded and finely diced

TOPPING
8 ounces sushi-grade tuna
1½ teaspoons Asian
    sesame oil
¼ cup coarsely chopped
    hearts of palm
1 avocado, halved, pitted,
    peeled, and diced
1 small romaine lettuce
    heart, coarsely chopped

4 cups cooked rice
    (see page 4)

GARNISH
1½ ounces pork rinds
1 tablespoon black sesame
    seeds

1 To make the jalapeño rémoulade: Mix the rémoulade with the jalapeño peppers in a small bowl. Reserve.

2 Dice the raw tuna into ½-inch cubes. Transfer to a medium bowl and toss with ½ teaspoon of the sesame oil. Add the hearts of palm, avocado, and romaine lettuce to another medium bowl and drizzle with the remaining sesame oil. Refrigerate both bowls.

3 To serve, scoop the rice into your rice bowls. Spoon a little romaine lettuce and avocado on top of the rice on one side of the bowl. Next add a little bit of the pork rinds, some sesame seeds, and the hearts of palm on the other side of the bowl. Dollop the tuna over everything. Dollop about a tablespoon of the rémoulade over the tuna in each bowl and serve immediately with spoons. It is best to mix everything together before enjoying.

RICE BOWL WITH SALMON,
ENDIVE, SHIITAKE, AND TASSO RÉMOULADE

Tasso is the famous spice-cured pork shoulder from Louisiana. It has a very distinctive cayenne-pepper-and-smoke flavor. If you can't find tasso, use any cured ham and add a pinch of cayenne and a few turns of freshly ground black pepper to the mix. / **FEEDS 4 AS A MAIN COURSE OR 6 AS AN APPETIZER**

TASSO RÉMOULADE

½ teaspoon olive oil

4 ounces tasso ham
(or any other aged ham, such as prosciutto), very finely diced

5 teaspoons Perfect Rémoulade
(page 6)

MARINADE

2 tablespoons soy sauce

2 teaspoons fresh lemon juice

1 teaspoon sugar

2 teaspoons grated fresh ginger
(use a Microplane)

TOPPING

8 ounces skinless salmon fillet,
cut into 1-inch pieces

2 teaspoons olive oil

1½ ounces shiitake mushroom
caps, sliced

1 teaspoon soy sauce

4 cups cooked rice
(see page 4)

GARNISH

1 large endive,
sliced lengthwise
into thin spears

1 ounce dried mango, sliced into
very thin strips

1 To make the tasso rémoulade: Heat the olive oil in a small sauté pan over medium heat. Add the tasso ham and sauté until crispy, about 3 minutes. Drain on paper towels and let cool.

2 Mix the rémoulade with the tasso ham in a small bowl. Reserve.

3 To make the marinade: Combine all the ingredients in a small bowl.

4 To make the topping: Toss the salmon into the marinade, turning to coat, and marinate in the refrigerator for 15 to 20 minutes. Drain the salmon and discard the marinade. Pat the salmon dry on paper towels. Heat a 10-inch skillet over medium-high heat. Add 1 teaspoon of the olive oil, then add the salmon and sauté for 3 to 4 minutes, until nicely caramelized but still pink on the inside. Press it gently—the flesh should bounce back but not flake apart. Transfer the salmon to a warm plate.

5 Add the remaining teaspoon olive oil to the pan and heat over medium heat. Add the shiitake mushrooms and soy sauce and cook for 4 to 5 minutes, until the mushrooms are wilted and caramelized.

6 To serve, scoop the rice into your rice bowls. Place the salmon and the shiitakes over the rice. Spoon about a tablespoon of the rémoulade over the salmon in each bowl. Garnish with a few spears of endive and a sprinkle of dried mango and serve immediately with spoons. It is best to mix everything together before enjoying.

POACHED GROUPER
IN EGG-DROP MISO BROTH

Whenever I'm in Florida, I eat as much grouper as I can. It's a fish that seems to go on and off of the trendy-menu radar, but for me it's always a favorite. If you find grouper that is fresh, poaching it, rather than frying or baking, gives it a tenderness that you can't achieve otherwise. / FEEDS 4

BROTH

6 cups water

2 pieces kombu, each about the
  size of a strip of bacon (see
  note)

1 cup packed bonito flakes

3 tablespoons white miso

7 teaspoons soy sauce

Juice of 1 lemon

6 ounces oyster mushrooms,
  cleaned

8 asparagus spears

1 zucchini

1 sweet potato

2 large eggs, preferably organic

4 dried apricots, thinly sliced

8 ounces skinless grouper fillet,
  thinly sliced

GARNISH

1 scallion, finely chopped

1 teaspoon toasted sesame seeds

> Kombu is dried kelp, mostly harvested off the Japanese island of Hokkaido. It is used, along with bonito flakes, to make dashi, an essential stock used as a base for Asian soups and stews. Kombu is often sold in cellophane bags and will keep indefinitely, as long as you store it wrapped in a cool, dry place.

1 To make the broth: Combine the water and kombu in a small pot and bring to a boil. Simmer for 5 minutes, then turn off the heat. Add the bonito flakes and let steep for 15 minutes.

2 Meanwhile, prepare the vegetables: Trim and slice the oyster mushrooms and place them in a medium bowl.

3 Hold each asparagus spear against a flat surface and run a vegetable peeler down the length of the stalk to peel off paper-thin ribbons: Hold the asparagus at the base and start the peeler about 2 inches above; discard the bottom of the stalk. Add to the bowl with the mushrooms.

4 Cut the zucchini lengthwise in half. Using the same method as for the asparagus, make thin ribbons of zucchini and place in the bowl. Discard the ends of the zucchini.

5 With a chef's knife, trim the sweet potato to a rectangle about 1 inch by 1 inch and about 3 inches long (it should look like half a stick of butter). Cut it in half and, using the same method as above, make thin ribbons of sweet potato. Add to the bowl and toss all the vegetables together.

6 Strain the broth into a bowl; discard the solids. Wipe out the pot and return the broth to the pot. Add the miso, soy sauce, and lemon juice and bring to a simmer over low heat. Add the vegetables to the broth and simmer for 3 minutes. Quickly add the eggs, whisking gently and slowly; the eggs will look like webs dancing underwater. Add the dried apricots.

7 Turn the heat off, add the grouper slices, and poach the fish for 3 minutes, no more. Ladle the broth, vegetables, and grouper into warmed bowls. Sprinkle with the scallions and sesame seeds and serve immediately.

WARM SHRIMP SALAD

WITH LEMONGRASS CRUMBS

I'm crazy about lemongrass. Use only the real thing: long, woody stalks with an aroma that is tantalizing and elusive. A lot of recipes call for cooking or steeping lemongrass to infuse its essence into a liquid. I find that that process mutes its brightness and intensity, which is what I love about it. I use only the hearts, about 2 inches of the inner part closest to the stem. Keep peeling it until you reach the part that has a smooth surface—that's the only part to use for cooking. The rest makes a nice tea for a relaxing evening. / **FEEDS 4 AS AN APPETIZER**

LEMONGRASS CRUMBS

3 ounces Lardo Cornbread (page 208), crumbled (¼ cup)
1 stalk lemongrass, trimmed to inner heart and grated on a Microplane (1 teaspoon)

1 tablespoon olive oil
12 ounces large shrimp (21 to 25 count), peeled and deveined
1 cup chopped seedless cucumbers
1 poblano pepper, diced
One 8-ounce can water chestnuts, drained, rinsed, and finely chopped
2 teaspoons fresh lemon juice
1 teaspoon soy sauce
Splash of fish sauce
¼ teaspoon cayenne pepper
9 stalks lemongrass, trimmed to inner heart and grated on a Microplane (3 tablespoons)
1 teaspoon chopped fresh mint
Salt and freshly ground black pepper to taste

1 Preheat the oven to 425°F.

2 To make the lemongrass crumbs: Spread the cornbread on a baking sheet and bake for 15 minutes, or until the crumbs are toasted and crunchy. Allow to cool, then add the grated lemongrass and mix well. The lemongrass will perfume your hands. Store in an airtight container until ready to use.

3 Heat the olive oil in a 10-inch skillet over medium heat. Add the shrimp and sauté for 2 minutes, or until they begin to turn opaque. Add the cucumbers, poblano peppers, and water chestnuts and cook for 3 minutes. Add the lemon juice, soy sauce, and fish sauce and simmer to reduce for a minute. Take the pan off the heat and add the cayenne pepper, lemongrass, mint, and salt and pepper to taste.

4 Spoon the shrimp onto four plates. Sprinkle the lemongrass crumbs over the shrimp and serve immediately.

If you don't want to make the cornbread for the crumb mixture yourself, you can use store-bought cornbread; just be sure to find one that has no added sugar. True cornbread does not have sugar in it. Sugar makes it taste like a corn muffin.

QUICK-SAUTÉED SQUID AND BACON SALAD

WITH GRATED GINGER AND APPLE

There's a lot going on in this salad, but it's all very well balanced. Squid has a wonderful texture when it is sautéed quickly, but it can get rubbery very fast, so watch the timing carefully. It is almost still raw, just a little warmed up—kiss it on the heat, as we chefs like to say. Squid can be bland, though, so it needs a strong supporting cast. Bacon is always good for that, and the combination of fresh ginger and raw apple adds a spicy tart note that brightens up the entire dish. Serve with a Riesling. / **FEEDS 4**

TAHINI VINAIGRETTE

2 tablespoons tahini

2 tablespoons Asian sesame oil

3 tablespoons water

1 tablespoon sherry vinegar

1 tablespoon fresh lemon juice

Salt and freshly ground black pepper

8 ounces bacon, cut into ½-inch-wide strips

8 cleaned squid, sliced into thin rings (see note)

1 teaspoon soy sauce

½ teaspoon fresh lemon juice

¼ teaspoon sea salt

Dash of freshly ground black pepper

GARNISH

1 Granny Smith apple

2 teaspoons grated fresh ginger (use a Microplane)

1 bunch arugula

1 To make the vinaigrette: Combine the tahini, sesame oil, water, vinegar, and lemon juice in a blender and blend on high until well combined. Season with salt and pepper to taste. Transfer to a jar or small bowl.

2 Heat a large 10-inch skillet over medium heat. Add the bacon and sauté for 5 minutes, or until it is slightly crispy and most of the fat has rendered out. Transfer to a paper towel to drain, then transfer to a bowl.

3 Remove all but 2 teaspoons of the bacon fat from the skillet. Heat the remaining fat over medium-high heat. Add the squid and sauté, stirring constantly, for 2 minutes. Add the soy sauce, lemon juice, salt, and pepper and sauté for another minute, then immediately remove the squid from the pan and add to the bacon.

4 Using a Microplane, grate about half of the Granny Smith apple into a bowl, avoiding the core. Mix 2 tablespoons of the grated apple with the grated ginger. (I make this toward the end so that the freshly grated apple doesn't oxidize and turn brown.)

5 To serve, place a small bunch of arugula in the bottom of each of four shallow bowls. Place the squid mix over the arugula. Spoon about a tablespoon of the tahini vinaigrette over the squid in each bowl, spoon a little of the apple-ginger mixture over the squid, and serve immediately.

Make sure your squid is super-fresh. Don't buy frozen. The trick here is to cook the squid hot and fast. Longer cooking will cause the squid to turn rubbery, so make sure all your ingredients and plates are ready to go before you heat up the pan.

FROG'S LEGS

WITH CELERY, CHILE PEPPER, FISH SAUCE, AND BROWN BUTTER

I used to live near Chinatown in New York City, and the frog's legs I'd get there were cheap and plump. People always joke that they taste like chicken, but they don't really. They have a poultry-like texture with a faint aquatic aroma that is a tasty union of land and sea. In the same spirit, here's a wonderful union of a classic French technique of cooking frog's legs in brown butter merged with my love for Southeast Asian fish sauce.

If you can get your hands on some of Robert Sinskey's Vin Gris of Pinot Noir rosé, it is a stellar pairing with this dish. / **FEEDS 4 AS AN APPETIZER**

1 Using kitchen shears, cut the legs at the joints and discard the feet if they came attached.

2 In a large skillet, melt the butter over high heat and, stirring constantly, allow the butter to brown slightly, 3 to 4 minutes. The butter will take on a nutty aroma. Turn the heat down to medium and add the frog's legs. Brown for 2 minutes on each side. Add the white wine, red pepper flakes, fish sauce, vinegar, salt, and pepper in quick succession. Sauté for 2 minutes, then turn off the heat.

3 Add the celery leaves, tat-soi leaves, and snow peas to the frog's legs and toss gently. Serve immediately.

Finding frog's legs takes a little patience. If you live in the South and you know a friend who is adept at frog gigging, then you are in luck, but that is probably unlikely. Otherwise, you can ask a fishmonger to order frog's legs for you. Most likely they will come frozen and skinless, but that's okay—they freeze well. Drain them thoroughly and dry with paper towels before cooking.

8 ounces frog's legs (see note)

2 tablespoons unsalted butter

1 tablespoon dry white wine

½ teaspoon red pepper flakes

¼ teaspoon fish sauce

¼ teaspoon rice vinegar

½ teaspoon sea salt

¼ teaspoon freshly ground black pepper

GARNISH

Leaves from 2 celery hearts

A small handful of baby tat-soi or watercress leaves

2 ounces snow peas, cut diagonally into thin julienne

FRIED TROUT SANDWICHES

WITH PEAR-GINGER-CILANTRO SLAW AND SPICY MAYO

This is my take on the famous Vietnamese banh-mi sandwich. Traditionally banh-mi is made with pork; this lighter version made with trout is fresh and crunchy. Brown and rainbow trout are the most prevalent varieties I find along the Kentucky-Tennessee waterways, where fly-fishing has a long history. You can make this dish with any trout that's found near you. When fresh, trout has a clean, nutty flavor and the meat is meltingly tender.

Serve the sandwiches with a bag of your favorite potato chips and bottles of Centennial IPA from Founder's Brewing Company. / **MAKES 4 SANDWICHES**

SPICY MAYO

1 cup mayonnaise, preferably Duke's

2 minced fresh Thai chile peppers

4 teaspoons fresh lime juice

1 teaspoon fish sauce

¼ teaspoon salt

PEAR-GINGER-CILANTRO SLAW

1 Asian pear, cored and cut into matchsticks (about 1½ cups)

1 cup fresh bean sprouts

1 cup coarsely chopped fresh cilantro sprigs (leaves and tender stems)

1 tablespoon grated fresh ginger (use a Microplane)

1 teaspoon rice vinegar

1 teaspoon fish sauce

Kosher salt and freshly ground black pepper

1 To make the mayo: Whisk together all the ingredients in a small bowl. Cover and refrigerate until ready to use.

2 To make the slaw: Combine the pear, bean sprouts, cilantro, ginger, vinegar, and fish sauce in a medium bowl. Season to taste with salt and pepper. Taste. Is it sweet and crunchy? Good. Let it rest for a bit in the refrigerator while you fry your fish.

3 To make the tempura batter: Combine the flour, cornstarch, and salt in a bowl. Whisk in the egg white and seltzer until a pancake-like batter forms. Do not overwhisk; small lumps are okay.

4 Heat ½ inch of oil to 375°F in a large cast-iron skillet over medium-high heat until hot. Season both sides of the trout fillets with salt and pepper. Dip 2 fillets into the tempura batter to coat evenly, letting the excess drip off, and fry in the oil, turning once or twice, until golden and cooked through, 3 to 4 minutes. Drain on a paper-towel-lined plate. The crust should be golden and flaky and the fish still moist inside. Keep the first batch warm, and repeat with the remaining trout.

5 To assemble the sandwiches: Using a serrated knife, split the baguette pieces lengthwise in half. Spread some spicy mayo on both sides of each piece of bread. Layer the lettuce on the bottoms of the bread, then top with the trout and slaw. Gently cover with the other halves of baguette and serve.

TEMPURA BATTER
1 cup all-purpose flour
1 tablespoon cornstarch
½ teaspoon kosher salt
1 large egg white
1 cup seltzer

Vegetable oil for frying
Four 4-ounce trout fillets
Salt and freshly ground
   black pepper

Four 6-inch pieces French
   baguette

1 head Bibb or Boston
   lettuce, leaves
   separated

PANFRIED CATFISH
IN BACON VINAIGRETTE

Farmed catfish has come a long way, and it's far from being muddy or mealy. Today's catfish is clean and downright delicate. So I don't like to blacken catfish—a quick panfry is more than enough. Grapes and bacon are great paired with catfish; they're just assertive enough to make a statement but subtle enough not to overpower it.

For a delicious light summer meal, serve this after a first course of Yellow Squash Soup with Cured Strawberries (page 190). / **FEEDS 4**

BACON VINAIGRETTE
3 strips thick-sliced bacon,
  finely diced
1 shallot, minced
10 ounces red seedless
  grapes (1½ cups)
2 teaspoons chopped fresh
  thyme
2 teaspoons sherry vinegar
1 teaspoon Creole mustard

4 skinless catfish fillets
  (about 4 ounces each)
Salt and freshly ground
  black pepper to taste
1 tablespoon unsalted
  butter
1 teaspoon olive oil

GARNISH
Chopped fresh thyme
Sliced red seedless grapes

1 To make the vinaigrette: Place the bacon in a medium skillet and cook over high heat until the fat is beginning to render, about 3 minutes. Add the shallots and continue to cook, stirring frequently, until the bacon and shallots are browned and crispy, another 5 minutes.

2 Meanwhile, place the grapes in a blender and pulse until they are crushed and juiced but still a coarse puree, 10 to 15 pulses.

3 Add the pureed grapes to the skillet and, using a wooden spoon, scrape up any browned bits on the bottom of the skillet. Add the thyme, vinegar, and mustard, turn the heat to low, stir gently, and simmer for 5 minutes. Take the pan off the heat and keep the vinaigrette warm until ready to serve.

4 Season the catfish fillets with a little salt and pepper. In a large skillet, heat the butter and oil over high heat. When the butter starts to smoke, add the catfish to the skillet. Cook on the first side for 3 minutes, then gently flip the catfish, lower the heat to medium, and cook the catfish for another 3 minutes, until crispy on the other side and cooked all the way through. Remove from the heat.

5 Ladle a few tablespoons of the bacon vinaigrette into the bottom of each of four warm shallow bowls. Place the catfish in the bowls, garnish with chopped thyme and a few slices of grapes, and serve immediately.

SEAFOOD BOIL

Charleston is one of the most beautiful waterfront cities on the East Coast. Whenever I'm there, I try to get invited to a Lowcountry seafood boil. There's nothing complicated about it. A seafood boil is all about abundance, lots of libations, and eating with your hands. I host seafood boils all summer long here in Louisville, and every one is a little different.

At first I was going to call this recipe Kentucky Seafood Boil, but really the only thing Kentucky about it is that I suggest you drink bourbon during the meal. Of course, you can drink whatever you want with it; just make sure you have fun. The most important ingredient of the meal is good company, so choose your invitees carefully. And make sure it's a sunny day—the mess is too much to eat indoors! Line a picnic table with newspaper and dump the boil out onto it. Have plenty of lobster crackers on hand for opening the crabs.

You can serve this with fresh lemon wedges, sea salt, hot sauce, drawn butter, Okra Tempura (page 196), Quick Caraway Pickles (page 173), and/or Lardo Cornbread (page 208) on the side. I like to open an abundance of drinks for my guests to choose from: Portuguese whites, ten-year-old bourbons, a clean pilsner, and loads of sweet tea. / FEEDS 8 TO 10

SPICE BAG

3 tablespoons cumin seeds

3 tablespoons coriander seeds

2 tablespoons black peppercorns

1 tablespoon ground sumac

1 tablespoon red pepper flakes

2 bay leaves

1 To make the spice bag: Wrap all the spices in a coffee filter or a piece of cheesecloth and tie tightly with kitchen twine.

2 Bring the water to a boil in the largest pot you have, at least a 10-gallon pot. Add the spice bag, lemon halves, garlic, bourbon, salt, and paprika, and bring to a boil, then reduce the heat and simmer for 15 minutes.

3 Add the potatoes and corn and simmer for 5 minutes. Add the sausages, shrimp, crabs, clams, and mussels, bring to a boil, and boil until the sausages are cooked, the clams and mussels have opened (discard any unopened ones), and the potatoes and corn are tender, another 10 to 12 minutes.

4 Lift out the vegetables, sausages, and seafood and dump onto a table covered with layers of newspaper.

6 quarts water

2 lemons, halved

6 garlic cloves

1 cup bourbon

½ cup sea salt

1 tablespoon smoked paprika

2 pounds small red potatoes, scrubbed

6 ears corn, shucked and cut into 1-inch-thick wheels

1 pound pork sausages

1 pound jumbo shrimp in the shell, head on if you can find them

4 whole blue crabs

8 ounces littleneck clams, scrubbed

8 ounces mussels, scrubbed and debearded if necessary

Sumac is a spice ground from the berries of a shrub. It has a mild tart-lemony flavor and is popular in Middle Eastern cuisine.

SOUTHERN-BRED OYSTERS

The last two regions on the planet to rely heavily on wild oyster harvests are the Gulf of Mexico and the Chesapeake Bay. Sadly, the Chesapeake oyster trade began tipping toward failure in the 1980s, and the Gulf's business is now on the ropes as well. Other areas decimated their populations of wild oysters hundreds of years ago. Oystermen in New York, for instance, have had to bring schooners full of Chesapeake Bay oysters to drop into the Long Island Sound to "finish" as bluepoints since the early 1900s. And the Gold Rush and ensuing demand and overharvesting resulted in Olympia oysters disappearing from the San Francisco Bay by the turn of the twentieth century as well. Fortunately, the Gulf and the Chesapeake Bay are just so massive that they were able to continue with harvest after harvest for quite a long time. Now they are both in a fragile state, and there is more at stake than just oyster beds: there are history and tradition, communities, and livelihoods.

Travis and Ryan Croxton run an oyster farming company along the Rappahannock River in eastern Virginia that is leading a movement to bring wildlife and clean waters back to the Chesapeake Bay with the *Crassostrea virginica,* the original Chesapeake Bay oyster. My two favorites of theirs are the Rappahannock River oysters and the Olde Salts. They are clean varietal oysters that are as good raw as they are baked, and they make a wonderful base for layering citrus and buttery notes on top.

Geographical identification of oysters is a recent trend and has made certain places in the Pacific Northwest and Cape Cod synonymous with sexy oysters. Along the Gulf Coast, most of the oysters are sold under the generic classification of "Gulf oysters," with the exception of the famous oysters from the Apalachicola Bay on the Florida Panhandle. Texas, with its great oyster beds off the Galveston coast, is also starting a movement to designate region-specific oysters from the Gulf. All of this excitement and awareness is ensuring that there will remain a vibrant oyster community in the South to rival the reputation of the cold-water oysters in the North.

RAPPAHANNOCK

GULF COAST

OLDE SALTS

RAW OYSTERS

WITH RHUBARB MIGNONETTE

As soon as rhubarb starts to sprout in the spring, I am all about this recipe. We are lucky to have an abundance of rhubarb around Louisville. The tartness of rhubarb is too much for some, but I'm a huge fan. It's sublime with the brininess of oysters. / **MAKES 2 DOZEN OYSTERS**

RHUBARB MIGNONETTE

¼ cup champagne vinegar

1 tablespoon water

¼ cup chopped rhubarb, plus 2 teaspoons minced (see note)

½ teaspoon sugar

2 teaspoons minced shallots

¼ teaspoon fish sauce

Sea salt

¼ teaspoon freshly cracked black pepper

2 dozen of your favorite oysters, scrubbed, shucked, and left on the half shell

1 To make the mignonette: In a small saucepan, warm the vinegar, water, chopped rhubarb, and sugar; do not let it come to a boil. When the vinegar is just hot to the touch, about 2 minutes, turn off the heat and let the rhubarb steep for 30 minutes. The vinegar will have a vibrant pink hue from the rhubarb.

2 Strain the vinegar into a small bowl and chill it completely in the refrigerator; discard the cooked rhubarb.

3 Add the minced rhubarb, the shallots, fish sauce, salt to taste, and pepper to the chilled vinegar.

4 Arrange the oysters on a bed of ice, and drizzle the mignonette over them, or serve it in small ramekins on the side.

Rhubarb should be bright pink to red; don't use green rhubarb, which has been picked too early. Rhubarb leaves are poisonous, and usually they are trimmed off before it goes to market, but in case you find some at a farmers' market, be sure to remove and discard the leaves before using.

WARMED OYSTERS
WITH BOURBON BROWN BUTTER

I like to cook oysters outdoors in my brick oven, but you can cook them in your kitchen oven as long as you can get it really hot—like 500°F. After I pull the oysters from the oven, I shuck them in front of the gathering crowd. I always keep a few extra oyster knives on hand, and people love to join in. It's fun, and oysters right out of the oven are heavenly. I think this is the best way to eat: getting your hands dirty with a bunch of people around you all wanting to get dirty too. / FEEDS 4 TO 6

1 Turn the oven to as high as it will go. Spread a layer of rock salt in a large cast-iron skillet and heat in the oven for at least 15 minutes.

2 Meanwhile, make the brown butter: Warm the butter in a small saucepan over medium heat until it begins to foam, about 2 minutes. Add the salt and cook until the butter begins to turn brown and a nutty aroma wafts through the air, about another 2 minutes. Turn off the heat and scrape the bottom of the pan with a wooden spoon to incorporate the milk solids (they're full of flavor), then very slowly add the bourbon to the butter. It will bubble up violently. Stir in the lemon juice, skim off the foam, and keep warm until ready to serve.

3 Arrange the oysters on the hot salt. Bake for 4 to 6 minutes. The oysters are ready when you see a slight bubbling coming out of the sides of the shells. When you bend down to grab the skillet, you should smell the mouthwatering aroma of gently simmering oyster juices.

4 The top shells of the cooked oysters should easily pop off with an oyster knife: Remove the top shells and place the oysters back onto the salt bed in their bottom shells. Serve with the warm brown butter drizzled on top or on the side. Garnish with the lime zest and chopped cilantro.

Enough rock salt to cover the bottom of a large cast-iron skillet

BOURBON BROWN BUTTER
6 tablespoons unsalted butter
½ teaspoon sea salt
¼ cup bourbon
A few drops of fresh lemon juice

12 oysters, scrubbed

GARNISH
Grated zest of 2 limes
1 tablespoon chopped fresh cilantro

The shells will be too hot to handle right out of the oven, so make sure you have a kitchen towel to hold the oysters. These are only good hot, so put them in the oven right before you are ready to serve.

CORNMEAL-FRIED OYSTER LETTUCE WRAPS

Oyster lettuce wraps are always a hit at cocktail parties, and I always run out. There's something about the combination of the umami-rich country ham and the warm oysters that takes this to another place. True Bibb lettuce has an earthiness to it that is unique. They say it comes from the limestone-rich soil of Kentucky. If you can't find Bibb lettuce, Boston or butter lettuce is a fine substitute. / **MAKES 4 WRAPS**

CAVIAR MAYO

¼ cup mayonnaise, preferably Duke's

1 ounce spoonbill caviar (see Resources, page 279)

A few drops of fresh lemon juice

Canola oil for frying

½ cup all-purpose flour

½ cup fine cornmeal

1 large egg

1 teaspoon water

1 teaspoon whole milk

8 oysters, shucked

Kosher salt

4 slices country ham

4 Bibb lettuce leaves

1 To make the mayo: Combine the ingredients in a small glass bowl and fold together gently with a rubber spatula or a plastic spoon. Refrigerate until ready to serve.

2 Heat ½ inch of oil in a large cast-iron skillet over medium-low heat until it reaches 320°F. Meanwhile, place the flour and cornmeal in two separate shallow dishes. Whisk the egg with the water and milk in another shallow bowl. Dredge the oysters in the flour, dip them into the egg wash, letting the excess drip off, and then dredge in cornmeal, turning to coat evenly.

3 Fry the oysters, turning once, until golden and crispy, 2 to 3 minutes. Drain on a paper-towel-lined plate and season with salt.

4 Place a slice of country ham on each lettuce leaf, top with 2 fried oysters, and roll up or fold into a packet. Spoon a little caviar mayo on top and serve right away.

Spoonbill caviar is sold all throughout the South. Also known as paddlefish roe, it is the roe of freshwater sturgeon. It has a nice texture and a briny, inky flavor. It's pricey, but nowhere near the exorbitant levels of Caspian Sea roe. And spoonbill caviar is sustainable, which is crucial for any ingredient that I choose to use in my restaurant.

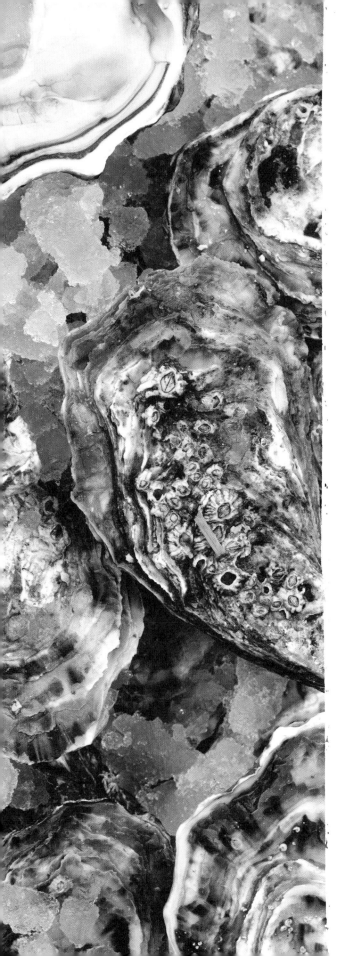

THE FISHERMAN

The first time I met Bryan Caswell, we were speaking on a panel about southern food in Charleston. Later that evening, I challenged two college kids to a beer-drinking contest—it was a two-liter "boot" of beer. I didn't have a partner, so I asked Bryan if he'd join me. He didn't even flinch. We crushed those college boys handily. It is this spirit of adventure that is apparent in everything he does. Bryan is the most avid fisherman I've ever met. When he talks about fishing in the Gulf, he is talking from the very depth of his soul.

"I was a fisherman long before I ever got behind a stove. Growing up in Houston, I've scoured the Gulf Coast from Apalachicola to Brownsville in search of all manner of fish and shellfish. With its hundreds of edible species, I am still constantly amazed at the diversity and bounty of the Third Coast. The Gulf Coast has the largest wild oyster population left in the world, grass flats and barrier islands as far as the eye can see, the Flower Garden's amazing coral reefs, and deep-blue ocean depths. From offshore to inshore, there is no place like it on earth, and I'm lucky enough to call it home."

—BRYAN CASWELL,
CHEF/OWNER, REEF, HOUSTON

PICKLES & MATRIMONY

If a young girl leaves rice in
her bowl after a meal, she
will end up with a pimply-
faced husband.
—KOREAN SUPERSTITION

PICKLES ARE A LOT LIKE LOVE

stories. They both take time, and you worry that it's not going to work out, but with patience, there is always a happy ending. Author Laurie Colwin once said, "The best way to feel at ease in the kitchen is to learn at someone's knee." I used to watch my grandmother make kimchi when I was a kid. It seemed like endless work, always salting cabbage or grating ginger or packing jars. As soon as the Napa cabbage was done, she'd start on the cucumbers and radishes and garlic

chives and perilla leaves. And then she'd work with stranger things still, like dried cuttlefish and wood ear mushrooms and fern bracken. When it was my turn to cook, I mimicked her movements. That's how I knew I was doing it right, even without recipes. I learned from my grandmother how to wipe the sweat off my brow using the back of my wrist, and that a finger is an instrument for dipping and tasting everything.

I loved my grandmother endlessly. And she loved me back, despite my faults. I once bought a duck from Chinatown and wanted to make a recipe I'd found in a Chinese cookbook. I used every pot and utensil we had in the kitchen, spilled grease and sauce in places no one would think to look (how do you get soy sauce on the ceiling?). The one thing I failed to realize was that ducks in Chinatown are sold undressed (i.e., with all the innards still in them). The cookbook assumed I would be

using a dressed carcass (i.e., with the gross stuff removed). I followed every instruction in the recipe to a T. The bird came out shiny and glazed—and distended. I brought it out to the dinner table. Usually dinner was just my grandmother and me, since my parents were working, but we would pretend there was a roomful of guests gathered for a feast. She would fold paper napkins into triangles to look fancy and pour tea. When I punctured the skin of the duck, green intestinal juices squirted out onto my lap. We picked some meat off the other end of the bird and then my grandmother patiently cleaned up my mess while I read through the recipe again and again, wondering where I'd gone wrong.

She had a patience and love that only a widowed grandmother could have for her grandson. Until she met my Jewish girlfriend. Deborah was in the eighth grade, a year ahead of me in school. She wore pastel colors, and under her auburn bangs, she had freckles like sesame seeds that drove me crazy. She'd come over and we'd watch hours of TV while I worked up the nerve to make a move. Meanwhile, my grandmother would tighten the lids on her kimchi jars and hide the reconstituted anchovies; and no way in hell was Deborah getting any of her dried persimmon tea. When Deborah was gone, she'd sit me down and tell me that her only prayer each night was for me to meet a nice Korean girl. That she would be ready to die with joy and serenity once she knew I had made the right choice in a wife. She was not above invoking God. She'd make me touch a Bible when I told her I would. I was thirteen. But my grandmother was a persistent woman. She outlasted Deborah and Sarah and Laurie and . . . , and none of them ever got to her kimchi. Her Bible was worn out at the seams.

Before she died, my grandmother made me promise I'd choose a good wife. I said I would. I knew she meant a Korean wife, but neither of us wanted to say it. I also told her I had just found a great job that would make me rich. I lied. But it made her relax, which meant her pain would go away for a few hours. My grandmother died on New Year's Day of 1997, the exact same day Townes Van Zandt died. I sometimes dream they are waiting in line next to each other at the heavenly gates. He plays her a song and she tells him how familiar it sounds. "My grandson listened to that song," she'd say, "always trying to impress some white girl." Then they'd laugh about it and walk peacefully into the next world.

When it was time for me to tell my mother that I was engaged to Dianne, I gathered my family at a Korean restaurant. She knew what was coming, because I'd never invited my parents to dinner. My mom is easier than most; she is progressive and funny and open-minded. But she is still a mother, and she is still Korean. She had a list somewhere of all the Korean girls I'd dated since high school, and she kept track of them. When she discovered Facebook, it was like it had been invented just for her. She noted my former girlfriends' stats on index cards like she was recruiting a baseball team. Each time one of them got married, she threw the card away—and with it, another chance at happiness. That night she clutched her handbag extra tight, as if she didn't want to lose the stray card or two that I knew were still swimming in there.

I told Dianne that whatever happened that night, just keep eating kimchi like there was no tomorrow. When I announced our engagement, all of a sudden everyone was talking in Korean, which we never did. Dianne was so brave and strong and beautiful and patient, and she ate about a pound of kimchi. My mom reacted bravely too. She even smiled. My dad hadn't smiled at me in ten years, but that night he reached in grinning and hugged Dianne. My mom got quiet, and I could tell she was fighting her emotions. She wanted to find something to like about Dianne, something she could say to welcome her into the family. After a long silence, she looked up at me and said, "She likes kimchi, huh?" She said it in English. And that was how she gave us her blessing.

Now it was my turn to meet Dianne's family. We drove up to Ferdinand, Indiana. Population: very small and very German-Catholic. I'd say it was a quaint town, but quaint implies cozy, and cozy implies imperfection, and Ferdinand is perfect. The lawns are configured in precise right angles, the modest houses are spotless, and the cars in the driveways seem like they've been detailed with a Q-tip. This was Dianne's world—humble yet resourceful. There is nothing more resourceful than cabbage. What is more brilliant than sauerkraut, the marriage of cabbage and salt and ingenuity? For a town whose mailboxes read like a Bavarian phonebook, sauerkraut is the ultimate expression of pride.

Dianne's sauerkraut is Kippenbrock sauerkraut, which means it comes from her mom's side of the family. They have a secret cupboard full of it—how many jars, only her mom knows. The shelves are lined with identical 8-ounce Ball jars with a small circle of muslin just underneath each lid to protect the fermented, crunchy goodness underneath. When we visit Dianne's family, it's usually with all her sisters and brother and nieces and nephews. We dine on under-salted turkey, mashed potatoes, overcooked green beans, ham sandwiches, sausage links, and a curious aspic they call "salad," which is lime Jell-O made with Sprite, with chunks of walnuts, pineapple, and cream cheese floating in it. But there's never sauerkraut at the dinner table. As if it's too precious to share. As if we haven't earned it yet.

There is nothing more resourceful than cabbage.

Dianne's mom presides over these family dinners with a watchful eye. She allows the banter to go on around her, but every so often she will toss in a remark a few minutes delayed, just to make sure everyone is on their toes. Not a thing gets by her, not the gossip about the neighbor's bad loans, not the inaccuracies in the *Ferdinand News,* not even the coded messages in the pamphlet of prayers printed by the local church.

The first time I tried her sauerkraut, I asked her if there was any juniper in it. I must have sounded like a rube. To me, it had anise notes and a garlicky must, followed by cider and yeast with a hint of clove. She looked at me with pity. Sauerkraut is cabbage and salt. But it's not just any cabbage, it's cabbage grown in the backyard by Dianne's dad, tended to lovingly and in exactly the same manner for generations. I asked Dianne's mom for the recipe once. I actually took out a pencil and paper. Let's start with the amounts. She said, "It's about as much as you can carry in your arms. Then you shred it thin." "How much?" I asked. "A tubful or two." "Salt?" I said. "As much as it needs and then you let it sit for a while until it's ready, you see. Then the important part is you have to pack it and punch it down. Then after a while you see how much juice it makes. And then you'll know when it's ready."

Smart lady.

Dinners with Dianne's family are never long-winded affairs. They are condensed and scripted. There is no unnecessary lingering. As each family member leaves, Dianne's mom carefully hands out jars of sauerkraut. It seems random—most get one jar, some get two, others get none. No one ever makes a fuss about it; they take what she gives them and that's that. I've never been able to figure out her system—I've stopped trying. Only she knows how many jars are left, and she controls the allocation. In different times, she would have been an empress.

When I made that important first visit to Ferdinand, I came with a letter I'd written to Dianne's parents. I read it to them in their living room. I told them how much I loved their daughter and how I wanted to spend my life with her. I asked for their permission. They gave me their blessings, but, like my parents, they kept their emotions restrained. We had a pleasant dinner and gossiped about everyone in Ferdinand. At the end of the night, as we were leaving, Dianne's mom gave us six jars of sauerkraut.

FOUR SEASONS OF KIMCHI

For me, cabbage is kimchi and vice versa. Napa cabbage is the variety
used for traditional kimchi—the spicy red version that accompanies every
Korean meal. But the word "kimchi" is not the name of this one dish only.
Rather, think of the word as a verb. You can kimchi anything: cabbage,
cucumbers, radishes, oysters, even fruit. It is the method that matters here:
It is the fermentation that makes it kimchi. I am constantly turning things
into kimchi. In this chapter, I've given four of my favorite ways to make
kimchi; they follow the seasons. Each recipe is separated into three sections: the cabbage, the paste, and the guts (which is all the other shredded
vegetables and spices that add flavor and texture to the kimchi). Once you
read through the recipes, you will understand that the process of kimchi
is simply the combination of these three elements—a fourth being time.
Once you have mastered that, you are free to go out and explore any kind
of kimchi you want. The options really are limitless.

SPRING

SUMMER

FALL

WINTER

RED CABBAGE-BACON KIMCHI

(WINTER)

The red cabbage gives this kimchi a brilliant color that is all the more attractive during the dark winter months when foods can get very monotone. Try it with bratwurst, Chicken-Fried Pork Steak (page 112), or T-bone Steak with Lemongrass-Habanero Marinade (page 67). Add some spinach or kale to this kimchi, and it'll work as a first-course salad. The bacon adds depth and saltiness, but it's just fine without it, if you want to keep this vegetarian. / **MAKES 1 TIGHTLY PACKED GALLON JAR**

CABBAGE

2 red cabbages (4 to 5 pounds total)

½ cup kosher salt

PASTE

3 cups water

½ cup sweet rice flour (see note)

¼ cup sugar

GUTS

2 small red onions, thinly sliced

12 ounces carrots, grated (use a box grater)

3 green apples, cored and thinly sliced

½ cup Korean chile flakes

½ cup fish sauce

3 garlic cloves, grated (use a Microplane)

A 2-ounce piece ginger, grated (use a Microplane)

3 strips bacon, fried until crisp, drained on paper towels, and crumbled

1 Shred the red cabbage by hand or in a food processor and transfer to a large bowl. Sprinkle the salt over the cabbage and toss thoroughly. Let rest for 40 minutes. Drain, rinse, and return to the bowl.

2 Meanwhile, make the paste: Combine the water, rice flour, and sugar in a medium saucepan and bring to a simmer, stirring constantly, until the mixture thickens, 1 to 2 minutes. Allow to cool.

3 To make the guts: combine the red onions, carrots, green apples, chile flakes, fish sauce, garlic, and ginger in a large bowl with the red cabbage.

4 Fold the guts into the cooled paste. Add the bacon and mix thoroughly. Wearing clean latex gloves, mix the guts mixture thoroughly into the red cabbage. Transfer the kimchi to a gallon glass jar or airtight plastic container with a tight-fitting lid. Let stand at room temperature for 24 hours, then refrigerate. The kimchi will be ready to eat in 4 or 5 days, and it will keep for another 2 weeks.

Rice flour, also called glutinous rice flour, is available in Asian markets.

GREEN TOMATO KIMCHI

(SPRING)

I'm always looking for new ways to use green tomatoes—we get so many of them in Kentucky. The green tomatoes give this kimchi a crunchy bite and a spring-like pale green color. The Brussels sprouts, which are a part of the cabbage family, add a delicate cabbage flavor and texture. This kimchi is insanely tasty on crab cakes, served as an accompaniment to pâtés or charcuterie, or paired with Adobo-Fried Chicken (page 82). / **MAKES 3½ QUARTS**

1 In a large colander, toss the Brussels sprouts and green tomato slices with the salt. Let stand at room temperature for 30 minutes. Drain, rinse, and transfer to a large bowl.

2 To make the paste: Combine the water, rice flour, and sugar in a medium saucepan and bring to a simmer, stirring constantly until the mixture thickens, 1 to 2 minutes. Allow to cool while you make the guts.

3 To make the guts: Combine the daikon, garlic, ginger, chile flakes, fish sauce, and vinegar in a food processor and process to a chunky puree.

4 Fold the guts into the cooled paste. Add the chopped cilantro.

5 Wearing clean latex gloves, mix the guts mixture thoroughly into the Brussels sprouts. Transfer to a large glass jar or an airtight plastic container with a tight-fitting lid. Let stand at room temperature for 24 hours, then refrigerate. The kimchi will be ready to eat in 4 or 5 days, and it will keep for another 2 weeks.

BRUSSELS SPROUTS
2 pounds Brussels sprouts, finely chopped
2 pounds green tomatoes, thinly sliced
¼ cup kosher salt

PASTE
1½ cups water
¼ cup sweet rice flour
2 tablespoons sugar

GUTS
6 ounces daikon radish, grated (use a box grater)
2 garlic cloves, grated (use a Microplane)
A 2-ounce piece ginger, grated (use a Microplane)
1 teaspoon Korean chile flakes
¼ cup fish sauce
¼ cup rice vinegar

½ cup chopped fresh cilantro

WHITE PEAR KIMCHI
(SUMMER)

This kimchi is vegan-friendly and very mild, as it has neither fish sauce nor chile pepper flakes. It is traditionally served only in summer, and I tend to eat it with cold dishes like shrimp salad or chop it up and add it to a corned beef sandwich. This is also one kimchi that you can serve right out of the container as a salad course. / **MAKES 1 TIGHTLY PACKED GALLON JAR**

CABBAGE

1 large Napa cabbage
   (4 to 5 pounds)
6 quarts water
1 cup kosher salt

PASTE

3 cups water
½ cup sweet rice flour
⅓ cup sugar

GUTS

1 cup chopped onions
1 Asian pear (about 10 ounces),
   peeled, cored, and diced
8 ounces daikon radish, grated (use
   a box grater)
A 4-ounce piece ginger, grated (use
   a Microplane)
6 garlic cloves, grated (use a
   Microplane)
¼ cup kosher salt
2 teaspoons ground coriander
1½ teaspoons ground fennel

1 small head broccoli, trimmed and
   cut into bite-sized florets
2 red bell peppers, cored, seeded,
   and cut into ribbons
2 yellow bell peppers, cored,
   seeded, and cut into ribbons
4 serrano or jalapeño peppers,
   thinly sliced
½ cup pine nuts

1 Slice the cabbage lengthwise into quarters. Cut out the core and discard it. Put the cabbage into a large container and add the water and salt. Let stand at room temperature for 2 hours; drain and rinse.

2 Coarsely chop the cabbage into approximately 2-inch strips. Transfer to a large bowl.

3 To make the paste: Combine the water, rice flour, and sugar in a medium saucepan and bring to a simmer, stirring constantly until the mixture thickens, 1 to 2 minutes. Allow to cool while you make the guts.

4 To make the guts: Combine the onions, pear, daikon, ginger, garlic, salt, coriander, and ground fennel in a food processor and process to a coarse puree.

5 Fold the guts into the cooled paste. Add the broccoli, red and yellow peppers, serrano peppers, and pine nuts.

6 Wearing clean latex gloves, mix the guts mixture thoroughly into the cabbage. Transfer to a gallon glass jar or airtight plastic container with a tight-fitting lid. Let stand at room temperature for 24 hours, then refrigerate. The kimchi will be ready to eat in 4 or 5 days, and it will keep for another 2 weeks.

SPICY NAPA KIMCHI
(FALL)

You'll probably recognize this kimchi—it's the most popular version. Traditional recipes call for adding salted/fermented shrimp, but it's too difficult to find a consistently good-quality brand; I find that high-quality fish sauce works just as well. The fermenting time is up to you. Some like to ferment kimchi longer to get that stinky, sour flavor—which I happen to love. Shorter fermentation times will give you fresher, crunchier results, though the flavors will seem a bit layered instead of harmonious.

This kimchi is great to eat with fatty meats—pork, beef short ribs, burgers, or hot dogs—and any meat that comes off a grill. / **MAKES 1 TIGHTLY PACKED GALLON JAR**

1 Slice the cabbage lengthwise into quarters. Cut out the core and discard it. Put the cabbage in a large container and add the water and salt. Let stand at room temperature for 2 hours; drain and rinse.

2 Coarsely chop the cabbage into approximately 2-inch strips. Transfer to a large bowl.

3 To make the paste: Combine the water, rice flour, and sugar in a medium saucepan and bring to a simmer, stirring constantly until the mixture thickens, 1 to 2 minutes. Allow to cool while you make the guts.

4 To make the guts: Combine the onions, chile flakes, daikon, ginger, garlic, and fish sauce in a food processor and process until well combined.

5 Fold the guts into the cooled paste. Add the chopped scallions.

6 Wearing clean latex gloves, mix the guts mixture thoroughly into the cabbage. Transfer to a gallon glass jar or airtight plastic container with a tight-fitting lid. Let stand at room temperature for at least 24 hours, and up to a day and a half, then refrigerate. The kimchi will be ready to eat in 4 or 5 days, and it will keep for another 2 weeks.

CABBAGE

1 large Napa cabbage
  (4 to 5 pounds)
6 quarts water
1 cup kosher salt

PASTE

3 cups water
¾ cup sweet rice flour
¼ cup sugar

GUTS

1 cup chopped onions
2½ cups Korean chile flakes
10 ounces daikon radish,
  grated (use a box grater)
A 4-ounce piece ginger, grated
  (use a Microplane)
6 garlic cloves, grated (use a
  Microplane)
⅓ cup fish sauce

2 cups chopped scallions

CABBAGE

Cabbages and the whole Brassica family have been important to many cultures and in many areas throughout history—the Chinese, Romans, and Egyptians, the Jews, the Middle East, India, Germany, Scandinavia, Poland, Russia, Ireland, and the list goes on. Cabbage has been said to cure everything from inflammation to hangovers to bird flu. Yet, though it has been so important in so many Asian and European cultures and cuisines, you'll never see it on anyone's favorite ingredient list. And it'll never make the cover of a food magazine. It's just too accessible. (It's like the girl who always picks up the phone on the first ring; that's not sexy.) But the very thing that makes cabbage overlooked—that it grows easily and quickly and results in bountiful harvests—is exactly what has made it arguably the most important vegetable in history. During times of war and plague and famine, entire civilizations have existed on little more than braised and pickled cabbage. And along the way, those cultures have each invented a delicious way to enjoy this unsung hero.

Brussels Sprouts

Green Cabbage

Red Cabbage

Napa

Savoy

PINEAPPLE-PICKLED JICAMA

Jicama is a sweet root vegetable that is widely used in Mexican and Southeast Asian cuisine. It has a white, crunchy interior that is perfect for pickling, because it readily absorbs the flavor of the pickling liquid without losing its own subtle sweetness. The pineapple juice here, spiked with chile flakes and fresh mint, gives the jicama a tropical flavor.

This is a quick pickle recipe. Adding the pickling liquid to the jicama while it is still hot allows it to soften and penetrate the jicama much more quickly than a traditional pickle brine. It'll be ready to eat in as little as a day.

I love this pickle with Asian BBQ. I also love it served just in a bowl, along with some nuts and marinated artichokes, at a cocktail party. / MAKES 1 QUART

1 small jicama (about
    1 pound)
1 small red bell pepper
1 small yellow bell pepper
1 pineapple
½ cup distilled white
    vinegar
¼ cup water
1½ tablespoons sugar
1 tablespoon salt
1 teaspoon red pepper
    flakes
2 star anise
3 cloves
A few fresh mint sprigs

1 Peel the jicama. Cut it into thin matchsticks about ¼ inch thick and about 1 inch long. Core, seed, and cut the bell peppers into thin ribbons about the same length.

2 Peel, quarter, and core the pineapple, then cut it into chunks. Place the pineapple chunks in a blender, along with the vinegar and water, and puree on low. Don't overblend—you don't want the pineapple juice to foam. Strain the juice through a sieve set over a bowl; discard the fibrous solids.

3 Transfer the pineapple juice to a small saucepan and bring it to a simmer. Add the sugar and salt and simmer for 5 minutes, stirring to dissolve them. Remove from the heat.

4 Pack the jicama and bell peppers into a quart glass jar, layering them with pepper flakes, star anise, cloves, and mint. Pour the hot pickling liquid into the jar. Cover tightly and refrigerate for at least 1 day before enjoying; this will keep in the refrigerator for up to 2 weeks.

QUICK CARAWAY PICKLES

If you only have one day to make pickles, make this recipe. While they'll have more flavor the next day, they can be eaten the same day. The caraway is a break from the usual dill flavor you are used to in pickles. I don't strain out the caraway seeds; they'll get soft enough to eat and are delicious. / MAKES 2½ QUARTS

1 Put the cucumbers in a large glass jar or plastic container.

2 In a large saucepan, combine the salt, both vinegars, water, sugar, caraway seeds, red pepper flakes, and cinnamon and bring to a boil, stirring until the sugar is completely dissolved. Turn off the heat and allow to cool for 10 minutes.

3 Pour the pickling liquid over the cucumbers. Cover with a tight-fitting lid or several layers of plastic wrap and refrigerate. The pickles will be ready in about 4 hours, although they are better the next day; they will keep for up to 3 days.

2½ pounds pickling cucumbers, such as Kirby, scrubbed and sliced about ½ inch thick

½ cup kosher salt

2 cups rice vinegar

2 cups apple cider vinegar

1 cup water

1 cup sugar

2 tablespoons caraway seeds

2 teaspoons red pepper flakes

1 cinnamon stick

BOURBON-PICKLED JALAPEÑOS

This recipe doesn't require much of an explanation—it's just good for so many reasons. I use the jalapeños as much for garnishing different dishes as I do for cocktails. / **MAKES 1½ QUARTS**

1   Wearing disposable gloves, slice the jalapeño peppers into ¼-inch-thick rounds. Transfer to a jar.

2   Combine the vinegar, bourbon, honey, coriander seeds, salt, mustard seeds, and bay leaves in a small saucepan and bring to a boil, then simmer for 5 minutes.

3   Pour the hot liquid over the peppers and seal the jar with a tight-fitting lid, let cool to room temperature, and refrigerate. The peppers will be ready in 3 days, and they will keep for up to 2 weeks.

1 pound jalapeño peppers
1¼ cups distilled white vinegar
1 cup bourbon
½ cup honey
2 teaspoons coriander seeds
1 teaspoon salt
1 teaspoon yellow mustard seeds
2 bay leaves

PICKLING

When I refer to "quick pickle" recipes, it means that I use vinegar to speed up the pickling process, rather than just fermenting the ingredients. True pickles, like the kimchi recipes in this chapter, take weeks to mature. Quick pickles are ready in a day or two. And true pickles require you to can the vegetables, which is an arduous task. With quick pickles, you can simply store them, tightly sealed in clean jars in the refrigerator. Yes, true pickles will keep longer, but these quick pickles are so good they wouldn't last long anyway. I developed the recipes in small enough amounts that you no doubt will consume them in less than 2 weeks, which is about the length of time you'd want to hold them.

PICKLED JASMINE PEACHES

WITH STAR ANISE

You need to flavor your pickles, but it's a hassle to strain out or remove loose spices that you don't want to eat. Using tea bags is the perfect solution—they are packed with flavor. You can steep the pickle liquid just like you would a cup of tea; then, when the pickles are ready, you can just toss out the tea bags. Of course, use only high-quality tea.

This pickle screams for a nice, fatty pork dish, but it's great with the gaminess of lamb and goat too. Or serve it with an aged sheep's-milk cheese and some crusty bread for a refreshing version of a cheese plate. / MAKES 2 QUARTS

2 pounds slightly underripe peaches

1 cup champagne vinegar

1 cup water

1½ cups sugar

1 teaspoon kosher salt

4 star anise

2 Serrano chili peppers, sliced in half

3 jasmine tea bags

1 Peel the peaches with a vegetable peeler. Slice into wedges, discarding the pits. Pack into a large glass jar or other heat-proof container.

2 Combine the vinegar, water, sugar, salt, and star anise in a medium saucepan and bring to a boil, stirring to dissolve the sugar and salt. Pour the hot liquid over the peaches and add the peppers and the tea bags. Cover with a tight-fitting lid and refrigerate.

3 Remove and discard the tea bags after 1 day. The peaches will be ready after 2 days, and they will keep for up to 3 weeks.

PICKLED CHAI GRAPES

I love pickling fruit. The combination of salty and sour tames the sweetness of the fruit, adding layers of flavor without taking away from the identity of the grapes. I eat pickled grapes (at right) with salty, aged cheese like Manchego or even aged cheddars. They're great with a charcuterie plate as well. Or try serving them with sliced pears and pomegranate seeds, for an aromatic fruit salad. / **MAKES 3 QUARTS**

3 pounds red seedless grapes, stemmed, washed, and dried

1 cinnamon stick

2 cups champagne vinegar

1 cup water

2 cups sugar

1 teaspoon salt

3 chai tea bags

1 Slice each grape in half and transfer to a large jar or other container. Add the cinnamon stick.

2 Combine the vinegar, water, sugar, and salt in a large saucepan and bring to boil, stirring to dissolve the sugar and salt. Pour the hot liquid over the grapes. Add the tea bags and cover with a tight-fitting lid. Refrigerate. Remove the tea bags after 2 days. The grapes will be ready to eat in 4 days, and they will keep for up to a month.

PICKLED COFFEE BEETS

I was having so much fun pickling using tea bags that one day I thought, "Would coffee work?" I tried pickling fennel and carrots and turnips with coffee beans and none of them worked. But then I tried beets. The beets work because they are so sweet, the coffee beans don't overpower them. In fact, the coffee is just barely detectable in the background, but it gives the beets a mysterious bitter note. / **MAKES 2 QUARTS**

2 pounds red beets

1 serrano chile pepper, cut in half

2 cups distilled white vinegar

1 cup water

½ cup sugar

4 teaspoons salt

2 teaspoons coriander seeds

½ teaspoon coffee beans

4 bay leaves

1 Trim and peel the beets. Using a mandoline, slice the beets into thin rounds. Transfer to a large glass jar, along with the chile pepper.

2 Combine the vinegar, water, sugar, salt, coriander seeds, coffee beans, and bay leaves in a medium saucepan and bring to a boil, stirring to dissolve the sugar and salt. Pour the hot liquid over the beets. Cover with a tight-fitting lid and refrigerate. The beets will be ready to eat in 4 days, and they will keep for up to a month.

PICKLED GARLIC
IN MOLASSES SOY SAUCE

I drew this recipe from memory; the pickled garlic in soy sauce was my grandmother's. She had a way of doing things that was a little different each time. So I made this recipe a little different too, with the addition of molasses. I think my grandmother would have liked it. I warn you: This pickle is as pungent as it gets. But if you are a garlic-head like me, you'll love it. It can accompany any grilled meat or stir-fry and is also great with fried quail. I sometimes puree the pickled garlic with the juices and use it as a condiment for lettuce wraps, spring rolls, or fried tofu. / MAKES ABOUT 1½ QUARTS

1 Place the garlic in a jar and add the distilled white vinegar; the garlic should be completely submerged. Cover with a tight-fitting lid and refrigerate for 5 days.

2 Drain the garlic, discarding the vinegar, and rinse under cold water. Return the garlic to the jar.

3 Combine the soy sauce, water, rice vinegar, sugar, molasses, and jalapeño in a medium saucepan and bring to a boil. Turn off the heat and let stand for 15 minutes.

4 Pour the liquid over the garlic and add the jalapeño pepper. Cover with a tight-fitting lid. Refrigerate. The garlic will be ready to use in 6 days, and it will keep for several months.

8 ounces garlic
   (about 4 heads),
   cloves separated,
   peeled, and rinsed
Distilled white vinegar
   to cover
2 cups soy sauce
2 cups water
¾ cup rice vinegar
½ cup sugar
½ cup molasses
1 jalapeño pepper

PICKLED CORN-BACON RELISH

These days you are as likely to find a producer of delicious, high-quality relishes—or, in the same category, compotes and preserves—at your local farmers' market as you are to make them yourself. I'm all for making things from scratch, but when you can find a jar that is as good as one you would make, I'm quick to give in. However, you won't find this relish just anywhere. If I can find a way to put a piece of bacon in something, I will.

This relish is a great addition to any picnic meal: in sandwiches, with the crusts cut off, or with pulled pork on soft buttery rolls. Don't forget the iced tea and salty potato chips. Now, that's my kind of afternoon. / MAKES 2 QUARTS

2 strips bacon

5 ears corn, shucked

1 red bell pepper, cored, seeded, and finely diced

1 orange bell pepper, cored, seeded, and finely diced

1 cup finely diced red onions

1½ cups apple cider vinegar

1½ cups water

⅓ cup sugar

2 teaspoons black mustard seeds

½ teaspoon fennel seeds

1 tablespoon salt

1 Cook the bacon in a medium skillet until crisp. Drain on paper towels.

2 Cut the kernels off the corncobs with a sharp knife. Combine the corn, peppers, and red onions in a bowl, cover with cold water, and soak for 10 minutes to rinse out some of the starch. Drain.

3 Combine the vinegar, water, sugar, mustard seeds, fennel seeds, and salt in a large saucepan and bring to a boil, stirring to dissolve the sugar and salt. Add the corn, peppers, and onions and bring back to a simmer.

4 Transfer the relish to a glass jar. Add the bacon, whole or crumbled, and cover with a tight-fitting lid. Refrigerate. The relish will be ready to eat in 2 days, and it will keep for up to a week.

PICKLED ROSEMARY CHERRIES

I paired these pickles with quail in one of the *Top Chef* challenges that I actually won (thanks, Ty-lor!). Cherries are sweet, but the rosemary tames the intense fruit and makes the pickle taste like a savory snack. Serve it with any chicken or game dish, like duck, quail, or pheasant. Try it next Thanksgiving instead of cranberry sauce. Or, for something really different, serve it over vanilla ice cream for a savory sweet dessert. / **MAKES 2 QUARTS**

2 pounds cherries,
   stemmed and pitted
2 fresh rosemary sprigs
1 cup rice vinegar
½ cup water
¼ cup sugar
1 teaspoon salt
½ teaspoon black
   peppercorns

1 Put the cherries into a large glass jar, along with the rosemary sprigs.

2 Combine the vinegar, water, sugar, salt, and peppercorns in a small saucepan and bring to a boil, stirring to dissolve the sugar and salt. Let cool for 10 minutes.

3 Pour the liquid over the cherries and cover with a tight-fitting lid. Refrigerate. The cherries will be ready to eat in 4 days, and they will keep for up to a month.

THE PICKLE MASTER

I first met Bill Kim at a restaurant show in Chicago; we'd both been hired by the Korean Ministry of Food and Culture. We were each asked to create a modern version of a classic Korean dish. I still remember Bill's braised kimchi with hominy and bacon, a traditional dish reimagined through his unique perspective. We became instant friends, and I love to call him up and compare notes. Bill's vision is filtered through his love of Latin cuisine and mine through a Southern lens. But we share a love for kimchi.

"Korean food has finally arrived. And kimchi is the condiment everyone has gravitated to. It's funky, smelly, spicy, and one of my favorite things to eat. My favorite vegetable for kimchi is the kirby, a seasonal cucumber, with garlic, garlic chives, ginger, Korean chile flakes, fish sauce, and shrimp paste. People argue about how they like their kimchi: fermented or 'fresh' made. I like the second method. It reminds me of a Latin salsa. The flavors come in layers: spicy, briny, garlicky, and earthy, all in a single bite. It's the bomb*!"*

—BILL KIM,
CHEF/OWNER OF URBANBELLY
AND BELLY SHACK, CHICAGO

VEGGIES & CHARITY

On New Year's Day, eat cabbage and black-eyed peas for good luck in the upcoming year.
—SOUTHERN TRADITION

IT STARTED WITH A JOHNNY

Cash song. On January 13, 1968, Cash performed a concert at Folsom Prison, and he released the live album later that year. It changed live recording forever. I bought the cassette when I was in high school; in college, I bought a CD version of it; and now I listen to it on my computer. I've listened to "Folsom Prison Blues" a thousand times, and it still moves me. I always wanted to create something that crazy, that important.

Like most chefs, I get asked to do charity work all the time. Often it's along the lines of donating a gift certificate or making a thousand canapés for people in tuxedos and gowns. A lot of money gets raised at these events, and I've always tried to be a good citizen about it, hoping to assuage the guilt I've built up over the years of leading a gluttonous life. I know how lucky I am to be surrounded by great food and rarefied libations. Good food is always a gift. The time, energy, and love needed to make delectable food exceeds any monetary value we can assign to it. Because, as my good friend author Francine Maroukian once said to me, time is our most valuable commodity. That extra night it takes to brine a pork loin, that extra hour it takes to let a dough rise, the time it requires to peel fresh garlic makes all the difference in the world.

About a year ago, I was driving home from a charity event where I'd cooked for four hundred people. There was wine and foie gras and profiteroles and a tequila sponsor and pretty people in shimmering attire, and we were all feeling so darn good about ourselves. Halfway into the drive, though, I realized that I had no fucking clue what charity I had just raised money for. This was no one's fault but mine. I'm sure it was printed on every twenty-foot banner that floated from the ceiling right next to the tequila and wine logos. I was confident that some unfortunate kid in some hospital got to have that surgery he really needed. And it made me feel both selfish and shallow for thinking that I was anything more than hired help in the organization's fund-raising efforts.

But that was not the concept of charity I grew up with. When my family moved into a new apartment building full of other immigrant families, there was an unspoken rule that the more established families would come by on random nights with dinner in

Tupperware containers, packed into a reused A&P shopping bag. My grandmother, always smiling at the door, would take these bags right to the kitchen sink and sniff them with disbelief. Why would anyone give us a free meal if not to poison us? When the North Koreans pushed south to invade the city she lived in, she'd had to flee her home with nothing more than her son (my dad) in one arm and a basket of clothes in the other. She'd had to camp out with thousands of strangers in overcrowded boats and trains, in unthinkable places, and she'd had to fight for every morsel of food, oftentimes against men twice her size. That defining experience turned her into a strong, cunning, and strategic woman, but it also made her cripplingly cynical. Who was this Jamaican family, really? And what was this stinky food they wanted us to eat? Once she determined that it was not poisonous, I was allowed to have a plate. She'd never touch it herself, simply watched as I downed bowls of okra and yellow rice. The Korean families would bring tofu soup and rice congee. The Indian family, curry with eggplant and chickpeas. It was mostly vegetables, cheap older vegetables bought at a discount. But the charitable gesture made their food taste good, comforting even.

Which brings me back to Johnny. What is so remarkable about that album is not just his singing but how the inmates reacted to his performance. Sure, it was a publicity stunt, and, yes, the final tapes were edited to make the cheers louder, but that doesn't take away from his contribution of time, playing a concert for a roomful of marginalized criminals. His time was a valuable commodity, but the inmates, well, all they had was time on their hands. The convergence of the two was a precious rare moment.

I decided soon after that charity dinner that I wanted to be more like Johnny. I would cook dinner in a prison for the hardened inmates. I

called a criminal-lawyer friend and set up a site visit at a Kentucky maximum-security prison. Now, I am no coward, and I've tussled my way through enough fights in my days, but I was not prepared for a prison tour. I never got within twenty yards of an inmate, but even from a distance, they looked like they would eat me alive if given the chance. The smell was the most frightening part of the tour. It wasn't the smell of dank violence; it was the noxious smell of ammonia everywhere. As if the constant mopping and cleaning hid something more unspeakable. We got to the bottom of a stairwell and I noticed blood splatters on an otherwise spotless floor. The guard's reaction was somber. "It happens sometimes," he said, with little emotion, and radioed in for a cleanup. My lawyer friend suggested that I might try a different route: there's a correctional facility for kids nearby, and he thought they'd appreciate my help.

Everyone deserves a good meal.

I ended up cooking dinner at the Louisville Metro Youth Detention Center, which is a place for teen offenders who are too young for penitentiaries. I made BBQ with an array of sides and peach cobbler, and the kids got fruit punch to drink. I scooped their dinner onto Styrofoam plates and talked to them as they walked through the buffet line. All of these kids had made bad choices, some more so than others, but what surprised me was that, in their eyes, they were still kids. Most were shy; they giggled at anything, like all teens do. They were inquisitive and curious and hungry. They were kids. The warden asked me to say something to them. I didn't give a lecture or tell my life story. All I said was that

I believed in my heart that everyone deserves a good meal and that included them. They gave me hugs and asked if I'd come back. They wrote me letters. As I said, I consider myself a pretty tough guy, and I thought I was ready for anything, but I never thought I'd have to swallow my tears as these kids smiled and waved good-bye to me in their brown jumpsuits and slippers.

Since then, I have quietly devoted time to dinners for small groups of families. I show them the farm and a few cooking tips, and I get to spend an afternoon squeezing limes and rolling dough with the kids. The kids learn fast; they absorb knowledge without prejudice or fear. I invite the families to have lunch at my restaurant, and we pour apple juice into wineglasses for the kids and use proper forks and crumb the table before dessert. I get thank-you letters from the families, and I keep each one. I don't call the media, I don't ask for sponsors; I just find a place and a time and a group of twenty or thirty people who are in need of something, and I cook them a good meal. I'm always inspired by the way the kids' faces light up when they taste a new sauce or learn how to chop an onion. Instead of writing a check, I try to give them a safe place for a few hours where they can let their imaginations wander and grow. And I try to teach them the importance of good food and all that that entails.

Sometimes when I want a quiet day where my cell phone is out of range, I'll head over to Jackson Farms, in Memphis, Indiana, where I get a lot of my produce. They have more than 150 acres and grow everything from corn to peaches to beets to hothouse tomatoes. They are always shorthanded, so they tolerate me on their farm, even though I'm not much help. I usually tinker with things. The farmers are always nice about it, always ready to listen to some new idea I have or to grow some new seed I've found in a catalogue. My favorite place to hang out, though, is the nurseries, where the young seedlings start to bud. It's amazing to see them at this early stage, when they are nothing more than sprouts, barely distinguishable from each other. Some will become melons and others tomatoes and others peppers, but here in this controlled environment, they are just pushing up through the soil, trembling to survive. Most of these seedlings and sprouts would not make it in the field. They'd be trampled on, flooded out by rain, or eaten by birds. They need the safety of the nursery to get strong before being transferred to the outside elements. Sort of reminds me of the kids I work with. And why should they have any less?

YELLOW SQUASH SOUP

WITH CURED STRAWBERRIES

A refreshing soup can taste like summer in a bowl. This is a delicious start to a light meal or a smart accompaniment to a toasted sandwich. Make this when yellow squash is in season—it's at its best in summer. It's the same with the strawberries. The curing process here both intensifies the flavor of the strawberries and cuts the tartness. It gives the berries an almost meaty texture. Pair this with a classic French Sancerre. / FEEDS 8

SOUP

2 tablespoons olive oil

½ cup chopped onion

2 pounds yellow squash, coarsely chopped

1½ teaspoons fresh thyme leaves

2 cups vegetable stock

½ cup sour cream

2 teaspoons salt

Freshly cracked black pepper

STRAWBERRIES

1 pound fresh strawberries, washed and hulled

½ teaspoon kosher salt

½ teaspoon sugar

1 To make the soup: Heat the olive oil in a large skillet over medium heat. Add the onion and cook until translucent, about 2 minutes. Add the yellow squash and thyme and sauté for 3 minutes. Add the vegetable stock and bring to a boil. Simmer for 10 minutes, or until the squash is soft all the way through. Take off the heat and let cool for a few minutes.

2 Transfer the soup to a blender, add the sour cream and salt, and puree on high until very smooth, about 2 minutes. Check the consistency: If the soup is a little gritty, strain it through a fine-mesh sieve. Chill in the refrigerator for at least 2 hours, or as long as overnight.

3 About 1 hour before serving, make the strawberries: Slice the strawberries into ¼-inch-thick slices and place them in a glass bowl. Sprinkle the salt and sugar over the strawberries and gently toss them with your fingers—making sure not to crush them. Let them cure for an hour at room temperature; no longer, or they will get too soft.

4 To serve, ladle the chilled soup into bowls. Top each one with a few cured strawberries. Crack some fresh black pepper over the top and serve immediately.

Try the cured strawberries on your next cheese plate, or as an accompaniment to a cured meat platter. Cure only what you need at the time, since they do not hold for very long.

SOUTHERN FRIED RICE

I had to put this recipe in the book. I originally thought, well, it's too cliche. It certainly isn't the kind of recipe that comes to me in a moment of deep introspection. It's the kind that slaps you in the face and says, "C'mon, get off your high horse and give 'em what they want." To make fried rice the right way, be sure to get your skillet or wok screaming hot and work furiously through the recipe. Practice it a few times before trying it in front of an audience. You'll look like a pro. / **FEEDS 6 AS A SIDE DISH**

2 tablespoons Asian sesame oil

½ cup finely chopped onion

1 jalapeño pepper, finely chopped

2 garlic cloves, minced

¾ cup black-eyed peas, cooked, cooled, and drained (see note, page 000)

¾ cup corn kernels

¼ cup finely diced green bell pepper

¼ cup finely diced seeded tomatoes, drained

2 tablespoons peanut oil

2 large eggs

¼ cup ham broth (see note)

Freshly ground white pepper

2 cups cold leftover long-grain white rice (see note)

2 tablespoons soy sauce, plus more to taste

2 teaspoons oyster sauce

2 teaspoons Worcestershire sauce

Salt

Chopped scallions for garnish

1 Heat the sesame oil in a large skillet until smoking hot, then reduce the heat to medium. Add the onions, jalapeño pepper, and garlic and stir-fry until the onions turn golden brown, 2 to 3 minutes. Add the black-eyed peas and corn and stir-fry for another 2 minutes. Add the green pepper and tomatoes and stir-fry for another 2 minutes.

2 Transfer the contents of the skillet to a bowl and clean out the skillet with paper towels. Heat 1 tablespoon of the peanut oil in the pan over high heat. Lightly beat the eggs with the ham broth and white pepper, then scramble the eggs in the pan. As soon as they come together in clumps, remove from the heat and add to the bowl with the cooked vegetables.

3 Clean out the pan again and heat the remaining 1 tablespoon peanut oil. When it is hot, add the cold rice and fry, stirring vigorously with a wooden spoon to separate the rice kernels, for 2 minutes. Add the soy sauce, oyster sauce, and Worcestershire sauce and cook for 1 minute, stirring the rice constantly but not smashing it. It is key to keep vigorously stirring the pan as you heat up the ingredients.

4 Stir the vegetables and egg into the rice and adjust the seasoning with a little salt, white pepper, and soy. Once the fried rice is hot throughout, transfer to warm bowls and serve, garnished with chopped scallions.

To make ham broth, combine about 6 ounces of ham trimmings and 2 cups water in a pot, bring to a boil, and boil for 1 hour. Strain the broth; discard the ham pieces. Store the broth in a jar in your fridge until ready to use; it will last for a week in the refrigerator, or for months in your freezer.

Use only cold leftover rice. This recipe won't work as well with freshly cooked rice—it will get too mushy.

BRAISED BACON RICE

I love braising bacon. It takes on a whole new identity and lends a smoky, rich texture to anything you add it to. This is good as a side dish with roast chicken or pork chops, but it's so flavorful and satisfying I eat it for dinner with a fried egg on top. / **FEEDS 6 TO 8 AS A SIDE DISH**

1 Cook the bacon in a large pot over low heat until it has rendered most of its fat, about 5 minutes. Add the onions, chopped celery, and the garlic and cook for about 6 minutes, stirring constantly to avoid burning the bottom of the pan.

2 Add the mustard, cayenne, and paprika and stir, then add the chicken stock and tomato juice and bring to a boil. Add the rice, stir, and lower the heat to a slow simmer. Let the rice cook, uncovered, for about 16 minutes, or until most of the liquid has been absorbed.

3 Add the chopped celery leaves, butter, and salt and pepper to taste to the rice. Turn off the heat and let the rice stand for a few minutes, stirring occasionally. Serve hot.

There are many great bacons in the world today, but Benton's in Tennessee is the mack daddy of them all. It's extra salty and extra smoky, and well worth making the effort to seek it out (see Resources, page 279).

8 ounces slab bacon, cut into ¼-inch dice (see note)
1½ cups chopped onions
1 cup chopped celery, plus 2 tablespoons chopped celery leaves
2 garlic cloves, minced
½ teaspoon dry mustard
¼ teaspoon cayenne pepper
¼ teaspoon smoked paprika
4 cups chicken stock
½ cup tomato juice
1 cup Carolina or other long-grain rice
2 tablespoons unsalted butter
Salt and freshly ground black pepper

CARDAMOM AMBROSIA SALAD

WITH BLUE CHEESE DRESSING

Most people think of ambrosia salad as a cloud of chunky white fruit in a glass bowl with neatly arranged canned mandarins on top. But we've evolved from those dark ages, and it's high time this salad got a makeover. Ambrosia can be *reeeaally* delicious, if made with the best, freshest ingredients. If you are even thinking about using dried coconut flakes from a bag, don't bother with this. Sweet fresh coconut meat is what makes it a standout.

I don't usually go for aperitifs, but a chilled glass of Lillet is perfect with this salad. / FEEDS 6 TO 8 AS A SIDE DISH

DRESSING

2½ ounces blue cheese

3 tablespoons buttermilk

3 tablespoons sour cream

2 teaspoons white wine vinegar

¼ teaspoon sugar

Salt and freshly ground black
    pepper to taste

SALAD

2 oranges, cut into suprêmes (see
    note)

1 grapefruit, cut into suprêmes
    (see note)

2 Champagne mangoes, peeled,
    pitted, and thinly sliced

2 Anjou pears, cored and thinly
    sliced

½ cup shredded fresh coconut (see
    note)

3 ounces pitted dates, coarsely
    chopped, plus more for garnish

¼ cup slivered almonds

¾ teaspoon ground cardamom

2 teaspoons coconut water (from
    the fresh coconut)

Chopped fresh flat-leaf parsley for
    garnish (optional)

1 To make the dressing: Mash the cheese in a small bowl with a fork. Add the remaining ingredients and whisk until combined but still a bit lumpy.

2 To make the salad: Combine the orange, grapefruit, mango, and pear slices in a medium bowl. Add the shredded coconut, dates, and almonds, then sprinkle with the cardamom, add the coconut water, and thoroughly toss the salad. Add the dressing and toss together.

3 Divide the salad among individual bowls or serve it in a large bowl for a family-style dinner. Garnish with more chopped dates and some parsley, if desired.

To make citrus suprêmes, using a sharp knife, cut off the top and bottom of the fruit. Cut away the rind and white pith in wide strips from top to bottom, following the shape of the fruit. Working over a bowl, use a paring knife to cut between the membranes to release the wedges of skinless fruit.

To prepare fresh coconut, start with a 2-pound coconut. Holding it firmly in one hand over a large bowl, use the back of a butcher knife to rap the coconut following the grain. When the shell cracks, catch the coconut water in the bowl. Drain the juice and reserve. Using a spoon, scrape out the coconut flesh. Grate on the large holes of a box grater. Freeze what you don't need in a resealable plastic bag; it will keep for weeks in the freezer.

OKRA TEMPURA
WITH RÉMOULADE

Surrounded by a feathery light, crispy batter, okra is just soft enough to give way but still retain its crunch. This is a great side dish, appetizer, or party snack, or just an indulgent bite on a lazy afternoon. Serve it on butcher or craft paper, or on a linen napkin for a more elegant look. The rémoulade makes this a culinary treat, but in all honesty it's just as good with a dollop of Duke's mayo and some Texas Pete hot sauce. Try serving this on its own with some Rogue Morimoto Soba Ale. / **FEEDS 4 TO 6 AS A SIDE DISH**

BATTER
1 cup all-purpose flour
⅔ cup cornstarch
1 teaspoon baking powder
¼ teaspoon salt
2 large egg yolks
2 cups club soda or seltzer

About 4 cups corn oil for deep-frying
1 pound okra, trimmed and halved lengthwise
Salt
Perfect Rémoulade (page 6) for dipping

1 To make the batter: Sift together the flour, cornstarch, baking powder, and salt into a medium bowl. Whisk in the egg yolks. Slowly add the club soda, whisking vigorously; the batter should have the consistency of pancake batter. Set aside.

2 Pour 2 inches of oil into a heavy pot and heat to 350°F. Working in batches, dip the okra in the batter, let the excess drip off (a long wooden skewer is perfect for dipping, so you don't get your fingers covered in batter), and gently lower it into the hot oil. Fry until golden, about 2 minutes. With a slotted spoon, transfer to paper towels to drain and sprinkle with a little salt. Let the oil return to 350°F between batches.

3 Serve hot, with the rémoulade for dipping.

When deep-frying, use a wide, deep pot, and work in batches. If you want to keep the fried okra warm while you're working on the next batches, put it on an unlined baking sheet in a 175°F oven; it will stay crisp until you're ready to serve.

ROASTED OKRA

AND CAULIFLOWER SALAD

Don't be put off by what you've heard about the sliminess of okra. That "slime," which is actually called mucilage, covers the seed pods and is released when the okra is cut into. Roasting okra in the dry high heat of your oven renders it tender while minimizing the mucilage. The cumin here gives the okra and cauliflower a spicy floral note, which is balanced by the sweetness of the dried apricots. / **FEEDS 6 TO 8 AS A SIDE DISH**

½ head (about 10 ounces) cauliflower, cut into small florets

8 ounces okra, trimmed (see note) and halved lengthwise

2 teaspoons olive oil

1½ teaspoons ground cumin

1 teaspoon salt

5 dried apricots, thinly sliced

¼ cup chopped roasted cashews

Grated zest of 1 orange (1 teaspoon)

Juice of ½ orange

1 Preheat the oven to 400°F.

2 Place the cauliflower on one baking sheet and the okra on another. Drizzle 1 teaspoon of the olive oil over the cauli-flower, sprinkle with ¾ teaspoon of the cumin and ½ teaspoon of the salt, and toss well. Repeat with the okra and the remaining 1 teaspoon oil, ¾ teaspoon cumin, and ½ teaspoon salt. Spread out the cauliflower and okra.

3 Place both pans in the oven and bake the okra for about 10 minutes, the cauliflower for about 25 minutes. They are done when they are soft, slightly shriveled, and just a little browned around the edges. Transfer the okra to a large bowl, then add the cauliflower when it is done.

4 Add the dried apricots, cashews, orange zest, and juice and toss well. (The salad can be kept warm in a 200°F oven until ready to eat.)

5 Serve in warm bowls.

Make this during the height of okra season, late spring to summer. Pick small, tender okra; when okra is young and fresh, there's no need to trim the tops—they are soft enough to eat.

EDAMAME HUMMUS

My chef de cuisine at 610 Magnolia, Nick Sullivan, came up with this dish when we were searching for an accompaniment to our braised beef short ribs. It's been a favorite at the restaurant ever since. It's also great paired with grilled kalbi, ham hocks, or any other slow-braised meat. We don't puree the hummus until it's smooth; we leave it lumpy and textured, so you can still taste the edamame. This is also great as a healthy snack, served with some raw vegetables. / **FEEDS 6 TO 8 AS A SIDE DISH**

1 In a large saucepan, heat the olive oil over medium heat. Add the shallot and garlic and sauté for 2 minutes, or until soft. Add the edamame and cook for 2 minutes. Add the water, tahini, lemon juice, soy sauce, salt, and cumin, stir, and bring to a simmer. Simmer gently for 6 minutes.

2 Transfer the contents of the pan to a food processor and process until you have a thick, crumbly puree. You can keep this warm in a pot on the stove until ready to serve, or serve at room temperature.

2 tablespoons olive oil

1 shallot, finely chopped

5 garlic cloves, finely chopped

2 cups shelled cooked edamame (see note)

1 cup water

½ cup tahini (see note, page 236)

½ cup fresh lemon juice

1 tablespoon soy sauce

2 teaspoons salt

2 teaspoons ground cumin

You can find shelled frozen edamame at Asian markets and gourmet stores. They are cooked and ready to eat. Unlike other beans, soybeans hold their texture and flavor even after being frozen.

COLLARDS AND KIMCHI

The most rewarding dishes to me are the ones that coax complex flavors from the humblest of ingredients. My first vinegary, salty bite of braised collards was a revelation. It took me back to the experience of eating cabbage kimchi, another precious dish that arose from poverty but has come to impress even the most sophisticated palates. I love these intense flavors from two cultures that are worlds apart, and somehow they work together harmoniously, as if they belong together.

Collards and Kimchi goes nicely with roast lamb or fried chicken. / **FEEDS 6 TO 8 AS A SIDE DISH**

1 tablespoon lard or
   bacon fat
1 tablespoon unsalted
   butter
1 cup chopped onions
1½ cups diced country ham
   (about 10 ounces)
1½ pounds collard greens,
   washed, stemmed, and
   coarsely chopped
2½ cups chicken stock
2 teaspoons soy sauce
1½ tablespoons apple cider
   vinegar
8 ounces (1¼ cups) Red
   Cabbage–Bacon Kimchi
   (page 166), or store-
   bought (see note),
   chopped

1 Heat the lard and butter in a medium pot over high heat. Once the butter starts to foam, add the onions and sauté for 5 minutes, or until they get a little color. Add the ham and cook for 3 minutes, until it is crispy but not too brown. Add the collards, chicken stock, and soy sauce, cover, and cook over medium heat for 30 minutes, stirring occasionally. Taste the collards: They should be tender but still have a little chew to them.

2 Add the vinegar to the greens and cook for 1 minute.

3 Toss the kimchi into the pot with the greens. Mix together, and serve immediately, juices and all.

If you're buying premade kimchi from an Asian market, pick one that is well ripened. Look for cabbage that is almost translucent and notice a smell. Ripe kimchi can smell pungent and sour even through a glass jar.

KABOCHA SQUASH MAC 'N' CHEESE

WITH PORK RIND CRUST

Who doesn't love mac 'n' cheese? My version is satisfyingly familiar but elegant enough that you won't have to share it with your kids. If you don't like pork rinds, you can substitute bread crumbs for the topping. But if you have any sense of what is good in this world, you'll never reach for bread crumbs to make a crunchy topping again. I know there's a lot of pork rinds in this book (as in my life), but I figure, hey, if you find something you like, you should stick with it.

Serve this with fried chicken, or at any meal where you want lots of sides. / **FEEDS 8 TO 10 AS A SIDE DISH**

---

1 small kabocha squash
   (about 1½ pounds)
2 tablespoons olive oil
Kosher salt and freshly
   ground black pepper
12 ounces elbow macaroni
1½ cups whole milk
1 cup chicken stock
3 ounces sharp cheddar
   cheese, grated
3 ounces Colby cheese,
   grated
3 ounces Pecorino Romano
   cheese, grated
2 tablespoons unsalted
   butter
½ teaspoon grated nutmeg
5 tablespoons crushed
   pork rinds (see note)
2 teaspoons black sesame
   seeds

1 Preheat the oven to 375°F. Butter a 4-inch-deep 9-by-12-inch baking dish or casserole.

2 Peel and halve the squash. Scrape out the seeds and membranes and cut into rough 1-inch cubes. Place them on a baking sheet, toss with the olive oil, and season with a little salt and pepper. Spread them out on the baking sheet and bake for about 25 minutes, or until the squash is fork-tender.

3 Meanwhile, bring a large pot of lightly salted water to a boil. Add the elbow macaroni and cook for 8 to 10 minutes, or until cooked but still with a slight resistance to it. Drain the macaroni in a colander and cool under cold running water. Set aside.

4 Transfer the cooked squash to a blender, add the milk, chicken stock, three cheeses, and the butter, and blend on high to a smooth puree. Add 2 teaspoons salt, ¾ teaspoon pepper, and the nutmeg and pulse to mix. Transfer the squash puree to a bowl, add the elbow macaroni, and mix thoroughly.

5 Transfer the mixture to the buttered baking dish. Sprinkle the pork rinds and sesame seeds over the top. Cover with foil and bake for 20 minutes.

6 Remove the foil, and continue baking until the mac 'n' cheese is lightly browned and crisp on top, another 25 to 30 minutes.

You can find pork rinds at any supermarket or gas station. Empty the package into a food processor and blend for a minute, or crush the pork rinds with your hands into a large bowl.

SPOON-BREAD WITH KALE AND BACON

As the name suggests, this dish is best eaten with a spoon, and you've got to eat it while it is piping hot. Spoonbread is somewhere between a bread and a custard, and it's one of those recipes that demands a well-seasoned cast-iron skillet. It just won't work without one. And you'll get better results making spoonbread in a few 6-inch cast-iron skillets than one large one. Maybe this recipe is a good reason to buy some of those little skillets—they are so darn cute. / **MAKES THREE 6-INCH SPOONBREADS OR ONE 14-INCH SPOONBREAD; FEEDS UP TO 10 PEOPLE**

8 ounces bacon, diced

⅓ cup chopped onion

4 ounces kale, cleaned, stemmed, and coarsely chopped

3 cups whole milk

1¼ cups white cornmeal

3 large eggs, beaten

2 tablespoons unsalted butter, melted, plus more for the skillet(s)

1¾ teaspoons baking powder

1 teaspoon kosher salt

Spoonbread will deflate and turn rubbery if it sits. Serve it right out of the oven. The spoonbread won't have another life as leftovers, so make just what you will need for a meal.

1 Heat a large cast-iron skillet over medium-high heat and add the bacon. Cook for 2 minutes, until the fat is beginning to render and the bacon is lightly crisped, then add the onions and sauté for 3 minutes, or until the onions are soft. Add the kale and sauté for 10 minutes, or until the kale is tender. Remove from the heat and set aside.

2 Preheat the oven to 400°F.

3 Bring the milk to a gentle boil in a small pot over medium heat. Stir the cornmeal into the boiling milk and cook, stirring constantly, until thick, 3 to 4 minutes. Remove from the heat, transfer to a bowl, and allow to cool.

4 Add the eggs, butter, baking powder, and salt to the cornmeal and beat with a hand mixer on medium speed for 6 minutes, until all the ingredients are thoroughly mixed together and the eggs have stiffened the batter slightly. Fold in the bacon and kale.

5 Heat a teaspoon of butter in each of three 6-inch cast-iron skillets, or heat 2 teaspoons butter in a 14-inch cast-iron skillet, over high for 2 minutes, or until the butter foams. Pour the batter into the hot skillet(s), transfer to the oven, and bake for 15 to 18 minutes for 3 small pans, 22 to 24 minutes for 1 large pan. Serve the spoonbread in the pan(s) hot from the oven.

CREAMED CORN AND MUSHROOM CONGEE

What I love about rice is that it can be cooked into so many different textures, and all of them are good. When slow-cooked (as in risotto), rice absorbs flavor but still retains a bite. It can be fried to a crunchy outer layer that gives way to a fluffy soft center. But perhaps the most comforting incarnation of all is when rice is cooked until it dissolves into a creamy porridge. Congee is traditionally a Chinese breakfast dish, but with the addition of fresh corn and mushrooms, it works brilliantly as a comforting first course or a very different side dish.

I love this on the first cold day of autumn, with a glass of Buffalo Bill's Pumpkin Ale. / **FEEDS 6 AS A STARTER OR SIDE DISH**

1 In a large pot, combine the rice, water, and fish sauce and bring to a boil over high heat. Lower the heat to a simmer, partially cover with a lid, and cook, stirring often, for 45 minutes.

2 Add the corn, mushrooms, salt, pepper, and soy sauce to the rice, stir well, and cook for another 20 minutes. If the rice gets dry and sticky, add a little more water to the pot. The congee should be loose and shiny, like a porridge.

3 When the congee is ready, turn off the heat, add the egg to the rice, and stir vigorously. Add the lemon zest and juice, ginger, and garlic and stir well.

4 Spoon the congee into small bowls. Drizzle a little sesame oil and sprinkle a few crushed peanuts over the top of each bowl and serve hot.

¾ cup jasmine rice

8 cups water

1½ teaspoons fish sauce

2 cups corn kernels

4 ounces shiitake mushroom caps, trimmed and thinly sliced

1½ teaspoons salt

¼ teaspoon freshly ground black pepper

½ teaspoon soy sauce

1 large egg

Grated zest and juice of 1 lemon

1 teaspoon grated fresh ginger (use a Microplane)

1 large garlic clove, grated (use a Microplane)

GARNISH
Asian sesame oil
Crushed peanuts

PARSNIP AND BLACK PEPPER BISCUITS

A good biscuit, buttery and light, can make the meal, but biscuits can sometimes be bland without the ladleful of gravy that usually accompanies them. Try this version for a biscuit that's floral and spicy and complex enough to be served without gravy. It ain't a breakfast biscuit, for sure. It wants to hang with the dinner crowd. Serve it with melted butter or a little honey brushed over the top. / **MAKES 10 TO 12 BISCUITS**

PARSNIP PUREE

2 tablespoons unsalted butter

12 ounces parsnips, peeled and finely chopped

½ cup water

½ cup buttermilk

2 tablespoons honey

½ teaspoon kosher salt

BISCUITS

2 cups all-purpose flour

2½ teaspoons baking powder

½ teaspoon kosher salt

6 tablespoons chilled unsalted butter, cut into small pieces

¼ teaspoon coarsely ground black pepper

Melted butter or honey for serving

1. To make the parsnip puree: Heat the butter in a large skillet over medium heat until melted and frothy. Add the parsnips and cook for about 8 minutes, until nicely browned and tender. Deglaze the pan with the water and use a wooden spoon to scrape up the browned bits on the bottom of the pan. Add the buttermilk, honey, and salt to the pan and simmer for 5 minutes.

2. Transfer the mixture to a blender and blend on high for 2 minutes, or until smooth. Add more water if needed to make a smooth puree. Pour into a bowl and chill in the refrigerator for 20 minutes.

3. Preheat the oven to 400°F. Line a baking sheet with parchment paper.

4. To make the biscuits: Combine the flour, baking powder, and salt In a large bowl. Cut in the chilled butter quickly with your fingers (or use your food processor and pulse about 10 times to make a crumbly mix). Chill for about 10 minutes.

5. Add 1 cup of the chilled parsnip puree and the pepper to the dough and gently knead just until combined. (Store leftover parsnip puree covered in the refrigerator for up to 1 week.) Turn the dough out onto a lightly floured surface. With a lightly floured rolling pin, roll the dough to about ½ inch thick. Dust the top of the dough with flour and fold it crosswise into thirds. Roll the dough again to about ½ inch thick. Cut out biscuits with a 2-inch biscuit cutter to get 10 to 12 rounds. Place the dough rounds 1 inch apart on a baking sheet.

6. Bake the biscuits for 12 minutes, or until golden. Remove and cool for 2 minutes on a wire rack.

7. Serve the biscuits warm, with melted butter or honey dripping over the tops.

You can find parsnips year-round at the grocery store or farmers' market. Choose parsnips that are firm and fragrant; they should smell floral, with a hint of licorice. If they're sold in a bag, pinch a little hole in it and take a sniff. Avoid parsnips that smell musty or moldy.

LARDO CORNBREAD

Cornbread is a matter of controversy in my house. I know enough not to add sugar to the batter; but my wife always drizzles sorghum or maple syrup on it. "That's different," she says. Because I find most cornbread a little dry, I add so much fat to the batter that you don't miss the sugar. "That's cheating," she says, as she pinches the last crumbs of this cornbread into her mouth. I can't win. / FEEDS UP TO 10

2 cups yellow cornmeal

2 cups all-purpose flour

1 tablespoon kosher salt

1 tablespoon baking powder

1 tablespoon baking soda

¼ cup plus 1 tablespoon corn oil

3 large eggs

1 large egg yolk

2½ cups buttermilk

4 tablespoons unsalted butter, melted and cooled

6 ounces lardo (see note), diced small

6 ounces aged sharp cheddar cheese, grated

Unsalted butter for serving

1. Preheat oven to 400°F.

2. In a large bowl, whisk together the cornmeal, flour, salt, baking powder, and baking soda.

3. In a medium bowl, mix together the ¼ cup oil, eggs, yolk, buttermilk, and melted butter. Pour into the bowl with the dry ingredients and mix thoroughly with a wooden spoon. Fold in the lardo and cheese.

4. Heat a 12-inch cast-iron skillet over high heat until very hot. Add the tablespoon of corn oil to the skillet and swirl it around to coat the bottom. Pour the cornbread batter into the skillet and cook on high heat for 2 minutes.

5. Transfer the skillet to the oven and bake for 40 minutes, or until a knife inserted into the center comes out clean. Serve warm, cut into wedges, with a pat of butter on top.

As the name suggests, you can use lardo for this recipe, but I actually use the fat trimmed off an aged country ham. It is smoky and renders beautifully. You have to use a cured fat, though. Don't use bacon fat, because it will melt away completely.

CURRIED CORN GRIDDLE CAKES

WITH SORGHUM-LIME DRIZZLE

Corn and curry are a natural pairing for me, and a perfect combination in these griddle cakes. It's important to make this recipe with fresh summer corn, which fills these little pancake-like treats with bursts of sweetness. I kept this recipe vegetarian, but you can just as easily add pork sausage or country ham to the batter. Serve as a snack before dinner or as a side dish to a hearty main course. / **MAKES ABOUT 30 SMALL GRIDDLE CAKES**

1 To make the drizzle: Melt the butter in a small saucepan. Add the sorghum, lime zest, and juice and stir until combined. Keep warm until ready to use.

2 To make the corn cakes: Heat the butter in a large cast-iron skillet over medium heat until it foams. Add the corn and cook over medium-high heat until soft, about 4 minutes. Transfer to a bowl and let cool.

3 In a small bowl, whisk together the cornmeal, flour, sugar, curry, salt, black pepper, cayenne pepper, baking powder, and baking soda. Whisk the buttermilk and eggs in a medium bowl. Add the dry ingredients to the buttermilk mixture and whisk until well combined. Fold in the corn and scallions.

4 Heat 1 teaspoon corn oil in a large skillet over medium heat. Add about a tablespoon of batter for each corn cake to the pan and cook, flipping once, until crisp and golden brown, about 2 minutes per side. Transfer the cakes to paper towels to drain, then keep warm on a baking sheet in a 200°F oven while you make the remaining corn cakes.

5 Transfer the corn cakes to a platter and serve with the warm sorghum-lime drizzle on top.

DRIZZLE

2 tablespoons unsalted butter

½ cup sorghum

Grated zest and juice of 1 lime

CORN CAKES

2 tablespoons unsalted butter

1½ cups fresh corn kernels (from 2 ears)

1 cup cornmeal

½ cup all-purpose flour

1 tablespoon sugar

1½ teaspoons madras curry powder

1 teaspoon salt

½ teaspoon freshly ground black pepper

¼ teaspoon cayenne pepper

½ teaspoon baking powder

¼ teaspoon baking soda

1¼ cups buttermilk

2 large eggs

6 scallions, chopped

Corn oil for panfrying

WTF POTATO SALAD

My neighbor and reliable taste tester Steven gave this dish its name. I'm not a fan of simple potato salads, which only hold my attention for a bite or two. So I came up with this version for those nights when I want to eat only vegetables but I don't want it to feel too healthy or boring. I invited Steven over and he arrived, wineglass in hand, to try my new potato dish. I hadn't decided what to call it, but after taking one bite, he shouted, "WTF, that's good!" And so the potato salad got its name.

Serve as a side with baked ham or steaks. / **FEEDS 6 AS A SIDE DISH**

DRESSING

¾ cup mayonnaise,
 preferably Duke's

2 tablespoons sour cream

2 garlic cloves, minced

2½ tablespoons fresh
 lemon juice

2 teaspoons Dijon mustard

5 dashes hot sauce
 (my favorite is
 Texas Pete)

½ teaspoon paprika

½ teaspoon ground cumin

½ teaspoon freshly ground
 black pepper

¼ teaspoon sea salt

POTATO SALAD

2 large eggs, preferably
 organic

2 teaspoons olive oil

4 ounces shiitake
 mushroom caps, thinly
 sliced

1 To make the dressing: Combine all the ingredients in a bowl and whisk well. Cover and refrigerate until ready to use.

2 To make the potato salad: Place the eggs in a medium saucepan, add 4 cups tepid water, and heat over medium-high heat. Bring to a gentle simmer and cook for 12 minutes. Drain the eggs and chill them under cold running water. Peel gently and reserve in a bowl of cold water in the refrigerator until ready to use.

3 Meanwhile, heat the olive oil in a small skillet over medium heat. Add the mushrooms, soy sauce, and pepper and panfry the mushrooms, stirring constantly, until wilted and nicely browned, 6 to 8 minutes. Transfer to a plate and set aside.

4 Combine 8 cups water and the salt in a large pot, add the potatoes, and bring to a boil over high heat. Cook for 16 minutes, or until the potatoes are tender but still have a little resistance when you insert a toothpick into one of them.

If you can, make the potato salad a day ahead and keep tightly covered in a glass container in the refrigerator overnight. Allow to come to room temperature before serving. The overnight rest allows the dressing to be absorbed into the vegetables and the flavors to become more harmonious.

5 Turn off the heat and add the sugar snap peas to the pot. Wait 2 minutes, then drain the potatoes and sugar snap peas in a colander and chill under cold running water.

6 Cut the potatoes into bite-sized pieces and toss into a large bowl. Add the sugar snap peas, shiitake mushrooms, diced ham, bell peppers, celery, and pickled okra. Add just enough dressing to coat the vegetables, tossing gently. Taste and adjust the seasoning with salt and pepper.

7 Transfer the salad to a large platter and top with the hard-boiled eggs, cut in half.

1 teaspoon soy sauce

¼ teaspoon freshly ground black pepper, plus more to taste

1 tablespoon sea salt, plus more to taste

2 pounds fingerling potatoes, scrubbed

4 ounces sugar snap peas

6 ounces country ham, finely diced

1 red bell pepper, cored, seeded, and sliced into ribbons

1 yellow bell pepper, cored, seeded, and sliced into ribbons

2 celery stalks, thinly sliced

4 pickled okra, thinly sliced (substitute 7 cornichons if you don't have pickled okra)

BUTTER BEANS

WITH GARLIC-CHILE AND CELERY LEAVES

This is my favorite way to eat beans. I can go all summer long eating this dish. Don't bother making it with frozen or canned beans; they lose their subtle flavor quickly after they are picked. If you can't find fresh butter beans, baby limas work fine. Just don't make the mistake of calling them one and the same.

A full-bodied Vermentino is a wonderful choice for this dish; I especially like the one from La Spinetta. / **FEEDS 4 AS A SIDE DISH OR FIRST COURSE**

¼ cup chopped bacon

1 cup chopped onions

1 cup finely chopped tomatoes

1 garlic clove, minced

1 pound shelled butter beans

1 cup chicken stock

1 cup water

2 teaspoons apple cider vinegar

¼ teaspoon red pepper flakes

1 tablespoon unsalted butter

Salt and freshly ground black pepper

A few drops of fresh lemon juice

A small handful of celery leaves (see note)

1 Cook the bacon in a large saucepan over medium heat until it begins to render out its fat, about 3 minutes. Add the onions, tomatoes, and garlic, stir, and cook for another 5 minutes.

2 Add the butter beans, chicken stock, water, vinegar, red pepper flakes, and butter and bring to a boil. Reduce the heat and simmer, stirring occasionally, until the beans are tender, about 30 minutes.

3 Season with salt and pepper, and add the lemon juice. Spoon into bowls and top each with a few celery leaves.

When using celery leaves, pick the palest, softest leaves from the heart of the bunch. They are packed with flavor, so use them sparingly. And leave them fresh on the stalks until just before serving.

SOFT GRITS

I get my grits from Anson Mills in Tennessee, and this recipe is adapted from their suggestions. All grits cook differently; depending on which brand you get, you will have to adjust your cooking time. The nice thing is, it's almost impossible to ruin grits. Just keep adding liquid and cooking it down until the texture feels right to you. Don't make them too pasty, though; that doesn't taste good. I don't add cheese to my grits, but you are welcome to grate a few teaspoons of your favorite cheddar right at the end before serving. Leftover grits hold well overnight; remember to add a little water when reheating and adjust the salt. / FEEDS 4 AS A SIDE DISH

1 In a medium pot over medium heat, bring the water to a simmer, about 3 minutes. Add the grits and cook, stirring constantly with a wooden spoon, for 6 minutes. Reduce the heat to low and cover the pot with a tight-fitting lid.

2 In a small pot, heat the chicken stock and keep warm. Every 8 to 10 minutes, uncover the grits and stir them thoroughly while adding ½ cup of chicken stock until all the chicken stock is used. If the grits are getting too pasty, add a little water too. After 35 minutes, check the texture of the grits. They should be creamy and tender but not mushy. Add the milk and continue cooking for another 10 minutes. I like my grits just a touch runny, but that's a personal preference. Cook until you get the texture that suits you.

3 Turn off the heat. Add the salt to taste and the pepper. Finish by stirring in the cold butter and the soy sauce with a wooden spoon and serve immediately.

1 cup water
½ cup (3 ounces) Anson Mills coarse grits (see Resources, page 279)
1½ cups chicken stock
½ cup milk
Fine sea salt
¼ teaspoon freshly ground black pepper
2 tablespoons unsalted butter, cold and cut in small cubes
2 teaspoons soy sauce

BOURBON-GINGER-GLAZED CARROTS

I'm one of those people who think that if a recipe has ginger in its name, it should really taste like ginger. There is no substitute for fresh ginger, and this recipe uses lots of it. Warmed by the bourbon and the brown sugar, the ginger zips these carrots into a yummy accompaniment to a hearty rib-eye steak or slow-cooked brisket. This dish is another great example of how Asian spices can really marry harmoniously with the flavors of the South. / **FEEDS 4 TO 6 AS A SIDE DISH**

Heat the butter in a large skillet over high heat. Add the carrots and sauté for about 6 minutes, until slightly softened. Add the brown sugar and ginger and cook, stirring, until the brown sugar dissolves, about 2 minutes. Deglaze the pan by stirring in the bourbon and orange juice. Cook until the carrots are fork-tender and the liquid is reduced and syrupy, 6 to 8 minutes. Season with the salt and pepper to taste and serve.

4 tablespoons unsalted butter

1 pound baby carrots, sliced lengthwise in half, or large carrots (about 5) sliced into ¼-inch-thick rounds (see note)

¼ cup packed brown sugar

3 tablespoons peeled, minced fresh ginger (see note)

3 tablespoons bourbon

Juice of 1 orange

2 teaspoons salt

Freshly ground black pepper

If you can, buy organic baby carrots that are crisp and heavy for their size. Thumbelina carrots are an amazing choice for this recipe. They are packed with flavor, and they are the prettiest carrots you will find at the farmers' market.

You can use a Microplane to grate the ginger if mincing is too much work.

FRIED GREEN TOMATO-CILANTRO RELISH

Relish is endlessly versatile. In fact, I don't even know what to specifically recommend eating with this relish, because the list goes on and on. Try it with brisket, cold cuts, or poached shrimp, or even on toast with a little butter. Frying the tomatoes first gives the relish that extra depth, making it almost a meal in itself. I've been known to eat it with salty potato chips and beer and not regret it at all. Make a double recipe, if you like—the relish keeps for a couple of weeks in the fridge. / **MAKES ABOUT 2 CUPS**

¼ cup olive oil

2½ pounds green tomatoes, sliced ¼ inch thick

½ cup chopped onion

2 garlic cloves, minced

3 tablespoons chopped fresh cilantro

1 tablespoon Dijon mustard

½ teaspoon sherry vinegar

1 teaspoon sugar

½ teaspoon ground fennel

½ teaspoon ground cumin

1¼ teaspoons salt

½ teaspoon freshly ground black pepper

1 Heat a teaspoon of olive oil in a large skillet over high heat. Working in batches, add the slices of green tomato in a single layer and fry for about 2 minutes on each side, adding more oil as necessary. Transfer to a plate.

2 When all the tomatoes are fried, add the remaining olive oil to the pan, then add the onions and garlic and cook over low heat until the onions are translucent and soft, about 4 minutes. Remove from the heat.

3 Finely chop the fried tomatoes and place in a medium bowl. Toss in the onions and garlic, add the cilantro, mustard, vinegar, sugar, fennel, cumin, salt, and pepper, and mix thoroughly. The relish can be stored in an airtight container in the refrigerator for up to 2 weeks.

When I chop cilantro, I use both the leaves and the stems. Store any extra cilantro standing in a glass of water in your refrigerator to keep it fresh for up to a week.

THE EDITOR

I first met Ethne Clark when she asked me to write a column for *Organic Gardening*. She devotes an entire magazine to vegetables, with an undying love and devotion to the seasons. It was not one of those give-me-a-recipe-along-with-a-tagline-about-why-you-love-this-or-that kind of columns. As a chef, I am constantly asked to reduce my love for vegetables into twenty-five-word sound bites. Here was someone who was going to give me eight hundred words. Ethne asked me to tell the story of winter spinach. A week after I submitted the first column, Ethne called me to ask if I would write the entire series the following year. It is an honor to write for her and to write about the infinite crops that spring up in our backyards and farmlands.

"Historically, in the Old World, vegetables and fruit were thought to be 'cold and wet,' capable of unbalancing the body's humors and causing ill health. That changed with the Age of Enlightenment and the seventeenth-century influx of New World produce that shook up tired European palates—and gardens. In homes where meat had been served in copious amounts, the vegetable course became a stand-alone entrée, and meat became the side dish. The diet of the rural poor was suddenly not only fashionable, but also good for you. Elizabethan philosopher Sir Francis Bacon wrote, 'God Almighty first planted a garden, and indeed it is the purest of human pleasures.' For centuries we've been finding our solace in the kitchen garden, tending neat rows of cabbages, gently thinning carrots, plucking herbs to revive our palates, and, at year's end, gathering in our harvest. A metaphor for a life well lived."

—ETHNE CLARK,
EDITOR, *ORGANIC GARDENING*

BOURBON & BAR SNACKS

To cure the grippe, hang your hat on the bedpost and drink whiskey until you see two hats.
—OLD KENTUCKY REMEDY

SIN ON A SUNDAY, REPENT

on Sunday. Words to live by. The biggest Saturday in Louisville is the Kentucky Derby. It is what first drew me here. It is where fortunes are made and heartbreaks are plentiful. It is a weeklong marathon of gluttony and drinking and gambling and prideful lust and any other kind of trouble you want to find, culminating in what is for me, and for most Louisvillians, the best weekend of the year. Everyone you talk to has a line on a favorite horse. Everyone's got a tip in exchange for a drink.

The Derby is a sporting event second and a party first, with outlandish hats and seersucker suits everywhere you look, and afterward, a confetti tide of losing tickets strewn all over the city. By the time that familiar bugle announces the start of the Derby, most of us have consumed more alcohol and bacon than the average person will consume in a month.

The Derby would not be the Derby if not for bourbon. Tradition says to drink mint juleps, but truth be told, most sensible drinkers will start with an obligatory mint julep in a pewter cup, then switch to the more civilized concoction of aged bourbon with ice and a splash of water. The history and lore of bourbon is so deeply ingrained in the identity of Kentucky it is hard to say which came first. Along with tobacco and horses (the first Derby was held in 1875), whiskey has been the backbone of the state's livelihood and identity. Tobacco

farming is on its way out, and the state's dominance in the horse industry has been losing ground to states like Louisiana and Pennsylvania. But bourbon is here to stay. Kentucky still makes more than 95 percent of the world's bourbon, and production has more than doubled since 1999. There is no distilled spirit more closely associated with a region than bourbon is with Kentucky. In my travels around the globe, I have been to some far-off places, and whenever I tell people I am from Kentucky, the first thing they mention is always fried chicken! The second is the Derby. And the third, invariably with a big fat grin, is bourbon.

There are many debates about which is the best bourbon. The older the bourbon, the more liquid has been lost to evaporation (what is respectfully called "the angel's share"), and the higher in price the bourbon gets. But that doesn't necessarily mean it is the best. Debates turn into arguments about what proof it should be, how much sunlight the barrels should see, what kind of water to cut it with. Arguments turn into feuds. Every bourbon maker will give you ten reasons why drinking any other bourbon is a waste of time. It took me a long time to drink my way through the fifty or so major brands of bourbon. I have spent hazy afternoons at the old D. Marie at the top of the Galt House, sipping my way through a shelf of bourbons. I have paid fifty dollars for a taste of some rarefied Stitzel-Weller bourbon salvaged from the ashes. I have sipped and I have slugged. I have rollicked in the simple joys of a Rebel Yell and pontificated on the complexities of a Col. E. H. Taylor. I have graduated to the holy grail of bourbons, Pappy Van Winkle's 23 Year, and, like an unworthy disciple, I have begged for more. Whiskey drinking is not a cheap endeavor. And it takes years to develop a strong opinion. Now, after eight solid years of drinking a whole lot of bourbon, I have come to this conclusion: I have never met a bourbon I didn't like. There are plenty of wines I won't drink and beers so awful I can't repeat their names. There are scotches that taste like a donkey's ass and gins so floral I feel like I'm drinking my wife's perfume. Vodkas are pretty much tasteless except for the flavored ones, which taste more like chemical agents. I do love the flavor of tequilas, but I hate the flavor of the floor, which is where I always end up after drinking it. Cognac is delicious but too expensive, and rum reminds me of dessert. So bourbon it is.

Bourbon starts as a neutral grain alcohol, mostly corn, and is then aged in oak barrels that have been charred on the inside. My bourbon axiom is this: any neutral alcohol that you put into a charred oak barrel and let sit for a few years is going to be, at the bare minimum, enjoyable. Yes, there are bourbons that are smokier, some that are more caramel, others more cedar, but these are distinctions of personal taste. Even the most egregiously commercial bourbons agree with me; I have never turned one away. So the answer to that often-asked question, "What is your favorite bourbon?" The one I have in my hand.

The reason goes beyond a personal preference for brown liquor. Bourbon distilleries have made a collective effort to preserve and protect the quality of what can be called a bourbon. Like "Scotch" in Scotland and "Champagne" in France, the word "bourbon" has a long and treasured history, with roots and traditions tied to the rolling hills of Kentucky and the Appalachians—and there are many bloodsuckers out there who circle around looking for a way to capitalize on the name. It is a constant and ongoing battle. For now, the use of the word "bourbon" on a label is strictly controlled by law and continues to represent the highest standards of what a whiskey can aspire to become in a bottle. All bourbon is whiskey, but not all whiskey is bourbon.

The best Sunday for me is always the first Sunday of the new year. I make it a point to go and listen to Pastor A. Russell Awkard of New Zion Baptist Church. It is a propitious way to start the year. The reverend is a friend and a dedicated gourmand. He is a tall man who leans forward at a slight angle, as most tall men do, so they can hear you better. And he talks in a voice so soft and deliberate he makes you lean in to listen, which makes everything he says that much more important. To hear one of his sermons is to feel electricity pulse through your blood. Every word is carefully chosen. But as with every great public speaker, it is the delivery and the weight of those words that resonate. Reverend Awkard's gentle demeanor builds steadily into a rhythmic sway that soars to a communal rapture of love and harmony and charity. All the while, the organ chimes and the choir claps with generosity of spirit. To try to describe the experience in words is to demean it. It is a rich tradition of the South so powerful and so loaded with history that I am drawn to it as if it were a window into history.

I am not a religious man, but I believe in faith. I believe in community. Reverend Awkard restores his community's faith every Sunday. The first time I walked into his church, I was nervous about standing out in a community whose struggles and history I had not shared in. I was nervous about being different, about being viewed as an outsider looking in. Which I was. It helped to have my wife, who has never been uncomfortable talking to anyone in her life, with me. I was deeply moved not only by just how generous everyone was, but by how they were able to read my anxiety and actually went out of their way to make me feel at ease. The members of the community made me feel so welcome that by the end of that first sermon, I too was clapping and saying "Amen."

I have never met a bourbon I didn't like.

As tradition goes, we follow up the Sunday service with a meal at Franco's, one of Louisville's best soul food restaurants. We feast on smothered pork, smoky beans, pig's feet, liver and onions, braised collards, and the saltiest and tastiest fried chicken in town. The restaurant is filled with not simply customers, but a gathering of friends and family. They are bound together by many traditions, but one of the strongest is the love of good food. Whenever I eat at Franco's, there are always a few laughing children misbehaving at a family dinner, and I am always surprised at how much it reminds me of my own family eating in a Korean restaurant when I was a child. No one ever looks at a menu, because you always order the same things; children are allowed to wander off, because you know everyone in the restaurant. And no matter how good the food is, someone always has a complaint about something. It makes me laugh, these similarities.

And then there's the food. It's so different, but the feeling of being comforted and those salty, spicy, and sweet tastes are all so familiar. Not having grown up on soul food, I can still understand how a warm bowl of collards and a plate of boiled ribs can make everything seem right. And I would trade my sous vide circulators for a Styrofoam container of salty, crunchy fried chicken any day. The first time I ate at Franco's was also the beginning of finding my way back to the memories of my own culture's cuisine that I had long buried in the back of my mind. I started to overlap the images of all my childhood foods with the cultural complexities of soul food, and what I saw was an unlikely parallel, like I was drawing the same curves on a sheet of tracing paper laid over those images. If my grandmother were alive today, I'd tell her how much I miss her food. But I'd also tell her that I have found her spirit in a soul food restaurant—and in some of the bawdiest kitchens throughout the American South. And that there's not much difference, after all, between a bowl of congee and a bowl of grits.

Whenever I eat at Franco's, I stuff myself with fried chicken and beans and collard greens and pig's feet and whatever the special might be that Sunday. I sip overly sweetened iced tea, and I lean back in the pink upholstered booth and think, "Oh, this would be nice with some bourbon iced tea, wouldn't it?" But it's Sunday—no bourbon on Sundays, for heaven's sake.

JALAPEÑO-SPIKED BOURBON JULEP

Mint juleps are a part of the Derby celebrations, and everyone partakes in the ritual. But, to be honest, most juleps I've had are overly sweet, cloying, and hard to finish. This is my twist on the julep: It's minty and verdant, with a kick of spice at the end that makes you want another sip. Serve this in pewter or silver julep cups, and drink it outside on a porch sheltered by a magnolia tree. / **MAKES 1**

4 to 6 fresh mint leaves, plus a
    sprig for garnish
1 ounce Jalapeño Simple Syrup
    (recipe follows)
Crushed ice
2½ ounces bourbon
Splash of club soda
A jalapeño slice for garnish

Place the mint leaves in the bottom of a julep cup, add the simple syrup, and gently bruise the leaves with a wooden muddler or a wooden spoon. Add enough crushed ice to fill the cup almost two-thirds of the way. Add the bourbon and stir gently, then fill the cup almost full with more crushed ice. Top with a splash of club soda. Garnish with the mint sprig and slice of jalapeño and serve immediately.

JALAPEÑO SIMPLE SYRUP

MAKES 1½ CUPS

1 cup water
1 cup sugar
2 jalapeño peppers, chopped
(seeds and all)

1 In a small saucepan, combine the water, sugar, and peppers and bring to a boil, stirring to dissolve the sugar. Turn off the heat and let steep for 20 minutes.

2 Strain the syrup and allow to cool. Keep in an airtight container in the refrigerator.

This syrup keeps forever in the fridge. It is delicious in other cocktails too, or drizzle it over a fruit salad to give it a little zing.

KENTUCKY MULE

If I know it's going to be a long night, I'll start off with one of these. The fresh ginger will help to settle your stomach, and it also opens up your sinuses—and the bourbon wakes up your senses. Be careful, though; this drink is so good, it's easy to have one too many before dinner and end up not being able to taste anything. The fresh ginger simple syrup is key here, so don't skip this step. / **MAKES 1**

1½ ounces bourbon

¼ teaspoon fresh lime juice

1 ounce Ginger Simple Syrup (recipe follows)

3 ounces club soda or ginger beer

A lime wheel for garnish

A thin slice of fresh ginger for garnish

Fill a rocks glass with ice. Pour the bourbon, lime juice, and simple syrup into the glass. Add the club soda and stir gently. Garnish with the lime wheel and slice of ginger and serve immediately.

GINGER SIMPLE SYRUP

MAKES 1½ CUPS

1 cup water

1 cup sugar

A 3-ounce piece of ginger, chopped

1 In a small saucepan, combine the water, sugar, and ginger and bring to a boil, stirring to dissolve the sugar. Turn off the heat and let steep for 20 minutes.

2 Strain the syrup and allow to cool. Keep in an airtight container in the refrigerator for months.

Try this in other cocktails, or drizzle it over vanilla ice cream.

COCKTAILS

I could go on for days about the intricacies of how to make a proper mint julep or a decent old-fashioned. And I respect the passions of the best mixologists as much as I do those of chefs, though I try not to fret too much when mixing a cocktail—a cocktail should not take longer to make than to drink. I do, of course, have a few favorite mixed drinks that are elegant and uncomplicated. Cocktails are like a dinner course for me: I'll start my meal with one and usually end with one, but I avoid them during dinner itself.

I always keep a few good bourbons of varying ages on hand; the older they are, the less they get mixed with other ingredients. For most bourbons worth drinking, it's blasphemy to taint them with colas or sweet mixes. The oldest ones just get a cube of ice, nothing more, but my favorite way to drink bourbon is 2 parts bourbon to 1 part water and an ice cube. It just feels right. When it comes to deciding which bourbon to use for mixing in cocktails, I generally choose one that is a little better than average, but I never use anything aged longer than ten years in a mixed drink. I'd also avoid using the stuff that comes in plastic gallon jugs.

THE LOWDOWN ON BOURBON

To be called bourbon, whiskey must be made from 51 percent corn, it must be made in America, and it must be aged in charred American oak barrels. It must be bottled at no less than 80 proof. Most bourbon is made by a handful of distilleries in Kentucky, and most bourbons are made the same way they have been for generations and stored in massive warehouses where the windows let in the sun and the warmth. There are many flavors that describe a bourbon's character. For me it is the history and the stories that fill each bottle: secret blending recipes, surreptitious barrel trading, moonshine running, floods, and tornados. Many people will tell you that bourbon was invented in Kentucky because of the limestone water, because Louisville was a major trading post, because of Prohibition, and/or because of the weather. All that may be true, but it seems to me that it was because the stubborn, crazy folks of Kentucky resolved to produce this brown water despite nature's tribulations, rebellions, wars, government bans, and all-out treachery. Bourbon may be the new favorite of the bold young mixologists of today, but it is still made by the same kind of resilient people who have kept it alive for all these generations.

BOURBON SWEET TEA

I make this spiked sweet tea in pitchers or big Ball jars. It's impossible to drink just one glass, and it keeps fine all day long. The type of tea you use is up to you; choose your favorite. Then add a mild bourbon. I use a lot of sugar, because this is sweet tea, after all. If peaches are in season, garnish it with peach slices too. Make sure to keep lots of ice on hand for serving.

Don't serve this in iced tea glasses—someone will inevitably think it's just iced tea and take a huge gulp, ruining his or her evening (or not, depending on who it is). Instead, serve it in small wine or cordial glasses.   /   **MAKES 1 LARGE PITCHER; SERVES 6 TO 8**

3 cups water
½ cup sugar
2 or 3 black tea bags
1 lemon, sliced into wedges
1 lime, sliced into wedges
1 orange, sliced into wedges
1 cup bourbon
Lemon wheels for garnish

1 To make the tea: Combine the water and sugar in a small saucepan and bring to a boil, stirring to dissolve the sugar. Pour the sugar water into a jar, add the tea bags, and let steep for 5 to 10 minutes, depending on how strong you want your tea. (If you like your tea very strong, leave the bags in the tea for longer.)

2 Remove the tea bags and add the lemon, lime, and orange wedges. Pour in the bourbon. Cover the jar and chill.

3 Serve in small glasses and garnish with thin lemon wheels.

THE REBEL YELL

I always make this infamous drink with nothing less than Rebel Yell bourbon. I know it's not the best bourbon out there, but, hey, it was good enough for Keith Richards, so it's good enough for me. Rebel Yell is actually a lot better than most people give it credit for. I always keep a bottle of it at home. / **MAKES 1**

2 ounces bourbon

½ ounce fresh orange juice

A dash of fresh lemon juice

A dash of sugar

2 dashes Regan's orange bitters (see Resources, page 279)

1 large egg white

Ice cubes

An orange slice for garnish

Combine the bourbon, orange juice, lemon juice, sugar, orange bitters, and egg white in a shaker filled with ice. Shake vigorously and pour into a rocks glass. Garnish with the orange slice and serve immediately.

Anytime you use raw egg whites in a cocktail, make sure the eggs are fresh and preferably organic. You can tell the egg is fresh because the egg white will be thick and cling to the yolk.

THE NEW-FASHIONED

Everyone's got their own modern twist on the old-fashioned. It's a great classic cocktail, but all too often it's overly sweet—and the idea of adding a maraschino cherry doesn't scream refreshing and natural to me. Blackberries and thyme are a great pairing, and they play nicely together with the bourbon. This is elegant, contemporary, and a great way to celebrate an old classic. / **MAKES 1**

3 blackberries

2 fresh thyme sprigs

1 brown sugar cube

2 dashes Fee Brothers' orange bitters (see Resources, page 279)

A small orange wedge

2 ounces bourbon

Ice cubes

Splash of club soda

1 To make the garnish: Skewer one blackberry on a sprig of thyme to mimic the idea of a cherry with a stem.

2 Drop the brown sugar cube into a large old-fashioned glass and add the bitters, orange wedge, and the remaining 2 blackberries and thyme sprig. Muddle into a paste using a wooden muddler or a wooden spoon. Pour in the bourbon, fill with ice cubes, and stir. Top off with the club soda, garnish with your thyme-blackberry "cherry," and serve immediately.

RHUBARB-MINT TEA
WITH MOONSHINE

You probably won't find moonshine at your corner wine shop, but if you can get your hands on some, this is one of the most delicious and pretty drinks I've ever had. Before whiskey is aged in barrels, it is distilled as a clear corn liquor, also known as white dog or white lightning or, basically, moonshine. White dog is available more widely today; a number of bourbon distilleries are bottling white dog for eager imbibers. It has a clean, sweet, and refreshing flavor. If you don't have access to moonshine, the mint tea is great all by itself. This recipe makes more tea than you need for the cocktail, so enjoy the tea straight up on low-key days. / **MAKES ABOUT 2 QUARTS**

6 cups water

1 cup cranberry juice

2 cups sugar

8 stalks rhubarb, trimmed
   and cut into 2-inch
   lengths

1 bunch fresh mint

FOR EACH DRINK

Ice cubes

2 ounces moonshine or
   white dog (optional)

½ lime wheel for garnish

1 sprig cilantro for garnish

1 Combine the water, cranberry juice, and sugar in a medium pot, bring to a boil, and add the rhubarb. Turn the heat to low and simmer for 20 minutes. Turn off the heat and let cool for 15 minutes.

2 Reserve 1 mint sprig for garnish; add the rest of the mint to the rhubarb mixture and let steep for 1½ hours.

3 Strain the tea and chill in the refrigerator.

4 For each drink: Fill a small Mason jar with ice. Add the moonshine and fill the jar with tea. Garnish with the half lime wheel, sprig of mint, and sprig of cilantro and serve immediately.

SOY SAUCE FROM KENTUCKY

The gift of bourbon does not end with the libation. The old barrels still have an abundance of flavor left in them, and they are used to add a bourbon touch to everything from scotch to beer to hot sauce. The first time I heard about microbrewed soy sauce aged in bourbon barrels, I was skeptical. And then I saw a picture of Matt Jamie in the local paper. Soy sauce made by a white guy? I was convinced it was going to suck, but the world is full of surprises. Matt's Bluegrass Soy Sauce (see Resources, page 279) is some of the best I've ever had. You can use it in any recipe where you would normally use soy sauce, but it is milder and rounder than commercially produced soy sauce. Matt's brewing facility is less than ten minutes from my restaurant. I drop by all the time just to sit in the middle of that smelly warehouse. It is unreal for me to be in the middle of Louisville, looking out over train tracks and old Butchertown, and to be surrounded by the aroma of what I can only describe as the primordial, hereditary comfort of fermented soy juice.

BOILED PEANUTS

An enduring Southern tradition, boiled peanuts are one of those things that Yankees just don't quite understand. It took me a while to like them too. But they're good; trust me. I add a little soy sauce to my recipe, and it gives the peanuts a rich umami note. Make this with raw or green peanuts in the shell, not roasted. / **MAKES 2½ CUPS**

1 Combine the peanuts, 8 cups water, salt, and soy sauce in a large saucepan and bring to a boil. Reduce the heat, and simmer for 4 to 6 hours, depending on how much time you have on your hands. (Longer is better, but isn't that always the case?) Every hour or so, check the water level. Add about a quart of water each hour to make sure the water level stays high.

2 Drain the peanuts and chill.

3 Serve the boiled peanuts in bowls, and let your guests shell the peanuts themselves. Have an empty bowl handy for the shells—or, if you are eating outside, throw the shells into your herb garden; they make excellent compost. Leftover peanuts will keep in the refrigerator for 1 week.

1 pound raw or green peanuts in the shell
¼ cup salt
2 tablespoons soy sauce

EDAMAME AND BOILED PEANUTS

When I originally thought of this dish, it was as if a 120-watt lightbulb had gone off in my head. I've eaten edamame, the ubiquitous Japanese soybean snack, my whole life. When I first tried boiled peanuts, the soft, meaty texture reminded me of edamame, but the deep umami flavor was the total opposite of the green vegetal bite of fresh soybeans. Then I thought, why not put them together—the great snack of Japan meets the ultimate snack of the South. The creamy tahini dressing brings the two together.

I first made this for a Southern Foodways Alliance Symposium lunch in 2011, and I've been making it ever since. It's a great way to start a meal, along with a glass of Noilly Prat dry vermouth with ice and a twist of lemon. / **FEEDS 4 TO 6 AS A SNACK**

TAHINI DRESSING

½ cup tahini (see note)

3 tablespoons Asian sesame oil

¼ cup water

2 tablespoons fresh lemon juice

1½ tablespoons soy sauce

½ teaspoon salt

2 teaspoons sesame seeds

1 cup shelled cooked edamame (see note)

1 cup Boiled Peanuts (page 235), shelled

1 To make the tahini dressing: Combine all the ingredients except the sesame seeds in a blender and pulse until smooth. If it is too thick, add more water to reach the thickness of a creamy vinaigrette. Transfer to a bowl and fold in the sesame seeds. Refrigerate until ready to use.

2 Combine the edamame and the peanuts in a bowl, add the tahini dressing, and toss to combine. Serve in small bowls.

Tahini is a thick sesame paste used in Middle Eastern and Indian cuisines. It's sold in jars or cans, and when you open it, oil will usually have separated from the paste and floated to the top. You want the oil—don't discard it. Dump the entire contents into a large bowl and blend the oil back into the paste using a strong whisk. Pour it back into the jar, and it's ready to use.

Edamame is the Japanese word for young soybeans in the pod. You can find frozen edamame in most gourmet stores. They defrost quickly, and then the soybeans pop right out of the tough shells.

BACON CANDY AND CURRIED CASHEWS

Salty nuts and sweet bacon: the best of both worlds. Whenever I entertain, I put this snack out in small bowls, because if I serve more of it, my guests tend to finish it all and get too full to eat dinner. It's a great accompaniment to a bourbon cocktail before dinner. This simple recipe just goes to show you how a little effort can go a long way. The recipe works equally well with peanuts, pecans, and almonds. I wouldn't recommend making it with macadamia or pine nuts, though. / **FEEDS 4 AS A SNACK**

6 slices applewood-
  smoked bacon, diced
2 tablespoons sugar
1 cup cashews
2 teaspoons Madras curry
  powder
¼ teaspoon cayenne
  pepper
Pinch each of salt and
  freshly ground black
  pepper

1 Preheat the oven to 350°F.

2 Heat a large skillet over medium heat. Add the diced bacon and cook for 5 to 6 minutes, until most of the fat has rendered and the bacon has started to get crispy. Drain off all but about a tablespoon of the bacon fat into a small bowl; reserve.

3 Add the sugar to the skillet and cook, stirring, for 2 to 3 minutes, until it has coated the bacon and the bacon starts to look shiny. Add the cashews, curry powder, cayenne, salt, and black pepper and toss together to coat the nuts. If they seem a little dry, add another teaspoon of bacon fat and toss to coat.

4 Spread the nuts out on a baking sheet lined with parchment paper. Bake for 12 minutes, or until lightly toasted. Let cool to room temperature. Store in an airtight container at room temperature for up to a week.

PORTOBELLO MUSHROOM JERKY

WITH TOGARASHI

To make "real" jerky, you need a dehydrator and a lot of time on your hands, neither of which I have at home—you probably don't either. This recipe mimics the taste and texture of jerky but is made in a fraction of the time. It's a great healthy snack—perfect for your vegan friends. I like it as a topping for winter salads too. Serve with mugs of Old Rasputin Imperial Stout from North Coast Brewing Co. / FEEDS 3 TO 4 AS A SNACK

1 Position a rack in the middle of the oven and preheat the oven to 325°F. Set a wire rack on a baking sheet.

2 Clean the portobello mushrooms and slice thin, about ⅛ inch wide. Put the mushrooms in a small saucepan, add the remaining ingredients, bring to a light simmer over low heat, and simmer until the sorghum has dissolved, 4 to 6 minutes.

3 Drain the mushroom slices. Reserve the marinade. Lay the mushroom slices on the wire rack on the baking sheet. Using a pastry brush, brush them with the marinade. Flip the mushroom slices and brush the other side.

4 Roast for 25 minutes, or until the mushrooms are shriveled and dark but still chewy. Turn the oven heat up to 375°F and roast for another 10 minutes. Remove from the oven and let the mushrooms cool on the wire rack.

5 Serve the mushrooms piled high on small plates. Any leftovers will keep in an airtight container in the refrigerator for up to a few days.

2 large portobello
  mushroom caps (10 to
  12 ounces total)
⅓ cup olive oil
3 tablespoons soy sauce
1 tablespoon sorghum or
  honey
2 teaspoons fresh lemon
  juice
1 teaspoon togarashi
  (see note)

Togarashi is a Japanese spice blend that you can find in Asian markets. It comes in cute bottles shaped like shotgun shells. There are a number of different varieties, but the basic ones contain a mix of chili powder, dried orange peel, dried seaweed, sesame seeds, and other seeds.

Try this preparation with shiitake, oyster, cremini, or chanterelle mushrooms as well. Some wild mushrooms, like black trumpets or morels, won't work, because they're too delicate.

ASPARAGUS AND CRAB FRITTERS

Not all bar snacks have to be tributes to indulgence. I make these in the spring, when asparagus is everywhere. The mint adds an herbal punch at the end, but sometimes I use tarragon instead when I'm feeling a little more French. I make small quarter-sized fritters to serve as a snack, but you can make the fritters larger and serve as a first course, with a salad of dandelion greens and a lemon vinaigrette.

For a wine, I'm crazy about the simplicity and brightness of Torrontés from Argentina, but pick a good one; there are a lot of inferior ones on the market. / **FEEDS 4 TO 6 AS A SNACK**

1 cup all-purpose flour

1 tablespoon cornstarch

1 large egg

1 cup whole milk

8 asparagus spears
    (see note), thinly sliced

8 ounces jumbo lump
    crabmeat

4 dashes hot sauce
    (my favorite is
    Texas Pete)

1 teaspoon Dijon mustard

¼ cup chopped fresh mint

1 teaspoon salt

½ teaspoon freshly ground
    black pepper

Olive oil for panfrying

Lemon wedges for garnish

1 In a medium bowl, whisk together the flour and cornstarch. Crack the egg over the flour and whisk it in. Slowly add the milk, whisking, to make a pancake-like batter. Add the asparagus, crabmeat, hot sauce, mustard, mint, salt, and pepper and mix well.

2 Drizzle 1 tablespoon of olive oil over the bottom of a medium skillet and heat over medium heat. Add small mounds of the fritter batter, about a tablespoon each, to the skillet, without crowding, and cook for 2 minutes, or until they are browned and crispy on the bottom. Flip and cook for 1 to 2 minutes, until the second side is a dark brown and the middle is cooked through. Drain on paper towels. Repeat with the remaining batter.

3 Transfer the fritters to a platter and serve immediately, with lemon wedges.

Use only very fresh asparagus for this recipe. The tips should be tightly closed, the stems firm, and the color bright green.

CRISPY FRENCH FRIES

My favorite way to make fries is with the blanch-and-fry method typically used by restaurants. It yields crispy brown fries like the ones you get in French bistros. This recipe makes more than you need for Kimchi Poutine (page 242), but it is impossible not to snack on the fries as you make them. / **FEEDS 2 OR 1 VERY HUNGRY PERSON AS A SNACK OR 4 AS A SIDE**

3 large Idaho potatoes, scrubbed

8 cups peanut oil for deep-frying

Sea salt and freshly ground black pepper

1 Cut the potatoes lengthwise into ¼-inch-thick fries. Transfer the cut potatoes to a large bowl of ice water; make sure the fries are completely submerged in the water. Refrigerate for 30 minutes.

2 Pour the oil into a heavy deep pot and heat to 325°F. (The oil should be ½ inch deep; make sure there is at least 3 inches of room above the oil in the pot.)

3 Drain the potatoes on paper towels and pat dry with more paper towels. You want them to be as dry as possible. When the oil reaches the desired temperature, add the cut potatoes, in small batches, and fry for 4 to 6 minutes, or until limp and lightly browned. Using a skimmer, gently remove the fries from the oil and drain on paper towels for 15 minutes. (Set the pot of oil aside.)

4 Heat the oil to 375ºF. Return the fries to the hot oil, again in batches, and fry for 2 to 3 minutes, or until golden brown and crispy. Drain the fries on fresh paper towels, immediately sprinkle with salt and pepper, and serve.

KIMCHI POUTINE

This recipe falls under the category of "everything tastes better with kimchi." I first had poutine at Martin Picard's restaurant Au Pied de Cochon in Montreal, and it has haunted me ever since. Poutine is a perverse homage to all things fatty and oozy: it is a plate of french fries topped with melted cheese curds and gravy. Recently poutine has made its mark stateside in various incarnations. Chef Picard tops his with foie gras; I timidly drape mine with kimchi.

Serve the poutine with one of those big bottles of Delirium Tremens by Brouwerij Huyghe. / **FEEDS 2 OR 1 VERY HUNGRY PERSON AS A SNACK**

1 tablespoon unsalted butter

1 tablespoon all-purpose flour

¾ cup heavy cream

¼ cup chicken stock

1 teaspoon soy sauce

Pinch of cayenne pepper

Salt and freshly ground black pepper to taste

As many freshly made Crispy French Fries (page 241) as will fit in a 6-inch cast-iron skillet in a single layer

½ cup cheese curds (see note)

¼ cup chopped Red Cabbage–Bacon Kimchi (page 166)

1 teaspoon chopped fresh flat-leaf parsley

1 Preheat the oven to 350°F.

2 Melt the butter in a 6-inch skillet. Stir in the flour and cook, stirring, over low heat for 3 minutes to make a roux. Gradually add the cream, chicken stock, and soy sauce, stirring until smooth. Season the gravy with the cayenne and salt and pepper to taste. Keep warm until ready to serve.

3 Place the french fries in the bottom of a 6-inch cast-iron skillet. Sprinkle the cheese curds and kimchi over them. Heat the skillet in the oven until the cheese is warm and melty, about 5 minutes.

4 Remove the skillet from the oven and pour the gravy over the fries. Top with the chopped parsley and serve right away, in the skillet.

Cheese curds are the milk solids from soured milk traditionally used in poutine. They're hard to find fresh, so a good melty Havarti or Jack cheese, grated, works just fine.

PIMENTO CHEESE

There are as many versions of pimento cheese as there are families in the South. I've collected these recipes on my travels, and now make a sort of hybrid of my own. The recipe is simple, it tastes the way it should, and it's easy. There are so many uses for pimento cheese—in a grilled cheese sandwich, on a burger, in mac 'n' cheese, stuffed into olives (see opposite)—that you should really have a batch in your fridge at all times. / MAKES ABOUT 3½ CUPS

14 ounces sharp cheddar
    cheese, grated
1 garlic clove, chopped
A dash of Worcestershire
    sauce
A dash of hot sauce
    (my favorite is
    Texas Pete)
½ cup mayonnaise,
    preferably Duke's
One 4-ounce jar pimentos,
    drained, juice reserved,
    and chopped
Salt and freshly ground
    black pepper

Combine the cheese, garlic, Worcestershire sauce, hot sauce, and mayo in a food processor and pulse until combined but still crumbly. Transfer to a bowl and stir in the drained pimentos. If it needs it, add a little pimento juice to make it creamy. Season with salt and pepper to taste. Stored in airtight jars in the refrigerator, this will keep for up to a week.

FRIED OLIVES

STUFFED WITH PIMENTO CHEESE

There's nothing more inviting than a jar of pimento cheese sitting out on the bar next to some crusty bread. But I've always found that a mouthful of creamy cheese is not the best thing to pair with my favorite bourbon drinks. So I came up with this bourbon-friendly snack. I know fried olives are nothing new, but stuffing them with pimento cheese adds just the right note of tangy creaminess. / **MAKES 12 FRIED OLIVES**

1 Drain the olives and pat dry. If there are red peppers stuffed inside the olives, remove them using a toothpick. Fill a small resealable plastic bag with the pimento cheese. Push the cheese toward a bottom corner and twist the top tightly so that you've made what resembles a small pastry bag. Snip a small triangle off the bottom corner. Pipe the pimento cheese into the olives.

2 Set up three small bowls for breading the olives: Put the flour in one. Lightly beat the egg with the olive oil in the second one. Put the bread crumbs in the third bowl. Dredge each olive in the flour, then coat with the egg wash, and finally roll in the bread crumbs to coat, and put on a plate. Fry immediately or refrigerate for up to an hour until ready to fry.

3 Pour the peanut oil into a large heavy pot and heat over medium heat to 350°F. Carefully drop the olives one at a time into the oil and fry, turning occasionally, until golden brown, 2 to 3 minutes. Gently lift the olives out of the hot oil using a spider or slotted spoon and drain on paper towels.

4 Serve the olives warm on small plates. And, yeah, go ahead and have that gin martini you've been craving.

12 large pitted olives
¼ cup Pimento Cheese (opposite)
¼ cup all-purpose flour
1 large egg
1 teaspoon olive oil
¼ cup fine dried bread crumbs
2 cups peanut oil for deep-frying

I don't generally salt these after they come out of the oil because the olives are salty enough, but depending on the brand you use, you may want to add a little salt. Taste one to see before salting the whole batch.

FRIED PICKLES

One of the great food debates is what shape makes a better fried pickle: spears or chips. I am sympathetic to the arguments of both parties. The spear gives you a higher hot-pickle-juice-to-batter ratio, making each bite a juicy, briny mess, but the batter tends to fall off the pickle before you get to the end.

The chips have more surface area to grip the batter, but too much batter can lead to dipping into too much ketchup, which can overpower the pickle inside. Either way, fried pickles are delicious. I've made all sorts of fancy condiments to accompany fried pickles, but, as it turns out, there's nothing better than straight-up Heinz ketchup. You can use the Quick Caraway Pickles (page 173) or good-quality artisan pickles.

Serve the pickles hot on newspapers with ketchup and lots of napkins, and pair with large bottles of Sofie from Goose Island Beer Company. / **FEEDS 4 AS A SIDE DISH**

BATTER

2 cups all-purpose flour

1 tablespoon garlic powder

1 tablespoon onion powder

1 tablespoon kosher salt

2 teaspoons cayenne pepper

1 teaspoon smoked paprika

1 teaspoon ground cumin

1 teaspoon freshly ground
    black pepper

One 12-ounce bottle lager beer

3 cups corn oil

1 cup sliced pickles, drained
    and patted dry

Kosher salt

Ketchup for serving

1 To make the batter: Combine the flour, garlic powder, onion powder, salt, cayenne pepper, smoked paprika, ground cumin, and black pepper in a large bowl and mix well. Slowly pour in the beer, whisking steadily. Let the batter rest for 15 minutes.

2 Heat the oil in a large heavy pot to 350°F. *If using pickle spears,* dip each pickle into the batter, shake off the excess batter, and gently drop into the hot oil. Working in batches, fry for 2 to 3 minutes, until the batter is golden and crispy. *If using pickle chips,* add all of the chips to the batter. Using a spider or a strainer, lift the chips from the batter and let the excess batter drip from the chips (this will take a little time), then gently drop the chips into the fryer and fry as for the spears. Drain on paper towels and season with a little salt. Serve immediately, with ketchup.

PRETZEL BITES
WITH COUNTRY HAM

Soft pretzel are best eaten right out of the oven, while they are still warm. The pillowy dough, wrapped around the salty ham and the melty cheddar, is a perfect snack with bourbon or a Belgian-style beer. I like to make these in small bite-sized rounds, but feel free to make them into knots or a braid. / **MAKES 50 TO 60 BITES**

1½ teaspoons active dry yeast

3 tablespoons plus 1 teaspoon brown sugar

¼ cup warm water (105 to 115°F)

1 cup whole milk, warmed (105 to 115°F)

2½ cups all-purpose flour

½ cup finely diced country ham

¼ cup finely diced sharp cheddar cheese

4 cups hot water

4 teaspoons baking soda

Pretzel salt (see Resources, page 279)

2 tablespoons seeded and finely diced jalapeño peppers

½ cup Dijon mustard

1 tablespoon honey (optional)

4 tablespoons unsalted butter, melted

1 Mix the yeast, 1 teaspoon of the brown sugar, and the warm water in a cup and let the yeast activate until foamy, 5 to 8 minutes. In a separate cup, mix the remaining 3 tablespoons brown sugar and the warm milk and stir to dissolve.

2 In the bowl of a stand mixer fitted with the dough hook, combine the flour with the yeast and milk and mix on low for about 4 minutes, until combined. Raise the speed to medium and mix until a ball of dough forms; do not overwork the dough.

3 Transfer the dough to a bowl, cover with plastic wrap, and let rise in a warm spot for about 2 hours until double in size.

4 Once the dough has risen, transfer it to a floured work surface and cut into 4 pieces. Shape each piece into a ball. As gently as you can, knead 2 tablespoons of the country ham and 1 tablespoon of the cheddar into each ball. Roll each piece of dough into a long rope about ¾ inch in diameter. Using a pastry cutter or a sharp knife, cut into 1-inch pieces and arrange on baking sheets. Let the dough rest for about 30 minutes.

5 Preheat the oven to 400°F.

6 Combine the water and baking soda in a medium saucepan and bring barely to a simmer. Using a slotted spoon, dunk the pretzel bites about 5 at a time into the bath for exactly 20 seconds and immediately transfer to another baking sheet, ½ inch apart.

7 Sprinkle the pretzel salt over the bites. Bake for 8 to 12 minutes, or until golden brown and nicely puffed.

8 In a small bowl, stir the jalapeños into the Dijon mustard. If you like some sweetness, add the honey. Set aside.

9 Brush the baked pretzels with the melted butter and serve hot, with the jalapeño mustard.

THE DISTILLER

If you think all bourbons are the same, you need only pick up a bottle of Pappy Van Winkle to see that generations of whiskey knowledge and a purist approach to bourbon will result in a bourbon in a class by itself. Julian Van Winkle is the man behind this highly sought-after bourbon. I have known Julian for close to a decade, and though I have read much and even written about this mythical libation (and drunk more than my fair share), every time I talk to him, I learn something new.

"All the color and most of the flavor of bourbon come from the whiskey expanding past the charred layer into the wood of the barrel staves. This happens in the hot weather here in Kentucky. When the weather cools, the whiskey passes through the char layer again as it leaves the wood staves and goes back into the barrel cavity. Most bourbon barrels are made of American charred white oak, so they are basically the same. The only difference is that the staves may come from different parts of the tree, producing a slightly different flavor in the whiskey. We prefer staves made from the heartwood part of the tree rather than the sapwood or outer part of a log. The sapwood can give the whiskey a young, or green, flavor, which is unacceptable. We can alter the flavor of the whiskey in the barrels by placing them in different warehouses and different areas of the warehouses. We prefer a metal-clad warehouse with more airflow, which will produce the best flavor profile."

—JULIAN VAN WINKLE,
PAPPY VAN WINKLE BOURBON,
FRANKFORT, KENTUCKY

BUTTERMILK & KARAOKE

Don't throw the eggshells away until after your cake is finished baking.
—SOUTHERN SUPERSTITION

THERE'S ALWAYS MUSIC

playing in my kitchen. Different tempos for different times of the day. Just before service, it's something fast and loud to get us motivated. Earlier in the day, it's a mix of classic metal and hillbilly rock. Sometimes in the mornings, when it's only the pastry chef and me, I'll play some folk songs, sometimes Hazel and Alice, sometimes John Prine. There's a rhythm in what we do in our kitchens. I hear it in the steady chop of a knife against a cutting board, a whisk picking up speed in a bowl, or the

constant movement of a stir-fry. I can tell how good a chef is just by listening to the sound of her knife work. It is quiet but steady and strong—like a Gillian Welch song. Music surrounds me at all hours. At night, Louisville becomes a stage. I roam the city in search of music, whether it's a bluegrass festival, to hear the lightning fiddle of Michael Cleveland; or a concert hall, to dance to Johnny Berry and the Outliers; or a neighborhood bar, to hear Tyrone Cotton bend the blues and gospel into folk.

Critics have always used musical descriptors to talk about food. Dishes sing, ingredients have notes, flavors harmonize, BBQ rocks; the metaphors abound. I like metaphors because they can express thoughts in a way that the literal cannot. When I say I want to cook like Elvis, you know what I mean. I don't literally want to cook the way Elvis cooked, I want to cook the way

Elvis lived his life—bold and untethered and agitated. I have admired and learned from so many great cooks, both in homes and in restaurants, and the best ones have always inspired a melody. A good bowl of soup is like a love song. I have eaten meals that were symphonies, and I have had the occasional dish so perfect it made me sad the way a mind-blowing live concert does. Dessert is like a feel-good song, and the best ones can make you dance in your chair. I rarely made desserts before moving to Louisville. They always seemed to come out a bit morose—like a Townes Van Zandt song. I was too serious, too worried to just make fun desserts. But Southern meals always end on a happy note. (And usually with the promise of more libations.) It's hard not to smile. Merriment is contagious. That may sound obvious, but it took me a while to learn it. It's one more part of a journey that carried me from a Korean apartment in

Brooklyn to a cozy kitchen in the South. There's a country song in there somewhere.

Anyone who knows me knows my fondness for karaoke. Put a mike in my hand, and something primal takes over. Picture me in a cowboy shirt singing karaoke off-key, and you get the idea. I used to be shy about it—I don't have much of a voice. But it's an exhilarating feeling to sing, whether you are skilled at it or not. Scott Mertz is a friend and musician who is always good for a drink and a song. At the slightest suggestion, he'll sit in my dining room, pull out his vintage guitar, and belt out a gut-wrenching version of "Dead Flowers." He knows I'm tone-deaf, but he will ask me to join in anyway. He has always encouraged me to sing my heart out, no matter the outcome. He says it's about the passion, not the pitch. One song always turns into another, and then we sing a few more. As the bourbon flows, I begin to sound better—at least to myself.

The first time I had buttermilk, I didn't like it.

I could fill a book with pages and pages on complicated pastry skills, but that doesn't get at why we want desserts and what we want out of them. We want them to make us sing and put a smile on our faces. I find that most people who like to cook feel intimidated by desserts, as if making them requires a different skill. It doesn't. It does require a different vocabulary, and it requires you to be a bit more quiet, more patient. You may find that making dessert is a lot like singing karaoke: It's awkward at first, but once you start, you won't want to stop. You may not be any good at it, but so what? You practice and you persevere and you learn. You do

it because you know a good dessert will fill a room with jubilance. Even a halfway decent dessert makes people happy. And that's reason enough to keep trying.

Sometimes when I'm singing karaoke, I feel like I'm alone in a crowded room. It's just me and the synthesized melody and the moving highlights of the lyrics. The feeling is transcendent. It may be funny to everyone else, but if you have ever seen an Asian businessman swaying and crooning into a microphone lyrics he knows by heart, with his eyes closed so tight a tear actually flows down his cheek, well, that's what it's all about. I can get that way too. I have traveled so far from my roots in Brooklyn, even farther from my ancestry in Korea, and the farther I go, the more I am reminded of the home I had as a kid. I grow older and yet I find myself becoming the little Korean kid singing in my underwear in front of the TV. Maybe the person I was born to be is inescapable. Maybe it just takes a lifetime to appreciate it.

The first time I had buttermilk, I didn't like it. I expected it would taste buttery, not sour. Turns out you have to mix it with something else to bring out what is remarkable about it. I feel that way about Louisville too. It has brought out the best in me. It has given me an incredible new identity while at the same time allowing me to rediscover the one I started with. Buttermilk is a symbolic ingredient for me. It is a happy ingredient. So I turn to it often when making desserts. People always say "ooh" when they hear that their dessert has buttermilk in it. They must have their own story about buttermilk, their own happy endings. All of the desserts in this chapter have buttermilk in them in some form or another. You can make them using regular milk instead, but you'll miss the tart component. Also I like it when people ooh and aah over my food, don't you?

In 2011, I had the chance to visit Korea for the first time in almost twenty years. It was an unsettling experience. I wasn't sure how I would react to my countrymen or how they would react to me. Seoul is a beautiful city full of colors and perfumes and energy. I was warmly embraced, and it was fascinating to look into these strange people's faces and see my own. It was a dream to walk the streets that my great-great-grandparents might have walked. I circled the same streets many times, eating my way through street carts and outdoor grills. I pointed to familiar plates and inhaled fermented aromas that brought me back to a cosmic infancy of ancestral consciousness. I ate lots of garlic and sang karaoke. On the plane back to Louisville, I sat next to a stranger who recognized me from the restaurant. We got to talking a bit, and we realized we had a couple of friends in common. He promised he'd come to see me at my restaurant. As we landed and parted ways, he said to me, "Welcome home." It was a beautiful reminder of why I live here.

I have a lunch of a fried bologna sandwich and fries at Wagner's Pharmacy. It is an old landmark diner next to Churchill Downs, where horse trainers and jockeys like to hang out. It's a comfortable place and the food is decent enough. The customers end up talking to each other and the waitresses are as friendly as they are opinionated. It's always a lively place. It has a music all its own, very different from my restaurant but no less perfect. And that is what I have learned feels the most like home to me. It is not a *place* that I call home, but a familiar song or a salutation, or a taste of something that makes me stop and appreciate my surroundings. Home is a place of gratitude. And good food is the best reason to say, "Thank you." We all encompass so many identities, wear so many

hats, how do we call one place home? In my kitchen, I can travel to so many places just by switching out the ingredients in my pantry. And they all feel like home to me. That's the transformative beauty of all of our kitchens. I hope I have given you a window into mine, and that the invitation was worth it.

Ooh, and they're playing Old Crow Medicine Show on the radio. I'm ordering cherry pie with extra whipped cream on top.

TOGARASHI CHEESECAKE

WITH SORGHUM

When I was a kid, if I was well behaved (which wasn't often), I might get a rare treat of cheesecake from Junior's in Brooklyn. A single slice was probably bigger than my head. Those were magical times, and I guess I've been searching for that emotional cheesecake connection ever since. This is my adult version of cheesecake, full of togarashi. I use it a lot in savory recipes to add spice, but here it gives the cake a sharp, spicy note that helps balance the denseness. Serve with strong green tea or chai. / FEEDS 8 TO 10

CRUST

2 cups gingersnap cookie
    crumbs
2½ tablespoons sugar
5 tablespoons unsalted
    butter, melted

FILLING

4 ounces fresh goat cheese,
    at room temperature
6 ounces cream cheese,
    at room temperature
½ cup buttermilk
½ cup plus 2 tablespoons
    sugar
4 large eggs
Grated zest and juice of
    1 lemon
1 teaspoon togarashi (see
    note)

About 1 tablespoon sorghum
    for garnish

> If you can't find togarashi, substitute a little cayenne pepper and a sprinkle of sesame seeds.

1 Preheat the oven to 350°F.

2 To make the crust: Stir the cookie crumbs, sugar, and melted butter together in a medium bowl with a fork until the crumbs are evenly moistened. Press the mixture evenly onto the bottom of a 9-inch springform pan. Bake until golden brown and crispy, about 10 minutes. Cool completely. Reduce the oven temperature to 325°F.

3 To make the filling: In the bowl of a stand mixer fitted with the paddle attachment (or using a handheld mixer), beat together the goat cheese, cream cheese, and buttermilk until smooth and fluffy, 4 to 5 minutes. Gradually beat in the sugar until smooth. Beat in the eggs one at a time. Beat in the lemon zest and juice. Beat in ½ teaspoon of the togarashi.

4 Pour the filling into the springform pan. Sprinkle the top with the remaining ½ teaspoon togarashi. Wrap the pan in aluminum foil to prevent leaks and place the pan in a large roasting pan. Pour enough hot water into the roasting pan to come one-third of the way up the sides of the cake pan.

5 Bake the cheesecake for 1 hour and 20 minutes, or until slightly puffed. Remove the cake pan from the water bath and allow it to cool to room temperature, then chill in the refrigerator for at least 2 hours. (The cheesecake can be refrigerated, tightly wrapped in plastic wrap, for up to 5 days.)

6 To serve, run a thin knife around the sides of the cake pan and release the sides of the pan. Slide the cheesecake onto a serving platter. Drizzle the top with a little sorghum, slice, and serve.

GOAT CHEESE

Goat cheese gets its distinctive tart, herbaceous flavor from the fatty acids in the goat's milk and from the goat's diet, which is more diverse than a cow's. And goat cheese is more easily digested than cow's- or sheep's-milk cheeses. Even some lactose-intolerant people can happily eat goat cheese.

I love using goat cheese instead of cow's-milk cheese in recipes that call for a lot of cheese, like a cheesecake, because it is lighter, more pungent, and higher in protein. I'm lucky because Greenville, Indiana, just about forty minutes north of Louisville, is home to some of the country's best goat cheese. Judy Schad has been making her famous Capriole surface-ripened goat cheeses for more than twenty-five years. Her Sophia is marbled with ash and has a wrinkled geotrichum rind so delicate it belongs in a whole other category of deliciousness. Her Crocodile Tear is hand-molded, dusted with just a suggestion of paprika, and ripened to a dense, creamy texture that is best enjoyed by the teaspoon. When I want an over-the-top dessert, I replace the fresh goat cheese in the Togarashi Cheesecake with Sorghum (opposite) with the same amount of one of her surface-ripened cheeses. I use the rind and all, just blending it together. The result is a cheesecake so divine it's an insult to call it a cheesecake. I call it simply Capriole for Dessert.

CHILLED BUTTERMILK-MAPLE SOUP

WITH BOURBON-SOAKED CHERRIES

Make this soup with the best buttermilk you can find. I get mine from Willow Hills Farm in Kentucky. Try a local dairy farmer, if you can. You need to use the best buttermilk because this recipe is essentially straight buttermilk with a little sweetener. The simple flavor of the buttermilk goes so well with the complex depths of the bourbon. This soup is a yin-yang play on cream and fruit that is timeless. / FEEDS 6

1½ cups good-quality
    bourbon
½ cup plus 2 tablespoons
    fresh tangerine juice
¾ cup sugar
1 teaspoon vanilla extract
8 ounces fresh cherries,
    pitted
1½ cups buttermilk
    (see note)
5 tablespoons pure maple
    syrup

1 Combine the bourbon, ¼ cup of the tangerine juice, the sugar, and vanilla extract in a medium heavy saucepan, bring to a boil over high heat, and boil for 6 minutes. Turn off the heat and add the cherries. Stir gently and allow to cool to room temperature; the gentle heat will poach the cherries but not turn them to mush.

2 Transfer the cherries, with their liquid, to a bowl and chill in the refrigerator for at least 1 hour.

3 Meanwhile, combine the buttermilk, maple syrup, and the remaining 6 tablespoons tangerine juice in a separate bowl. Chill in the refrigerator for at least 1 hour.

4 Divide the buttermilk soup among individual bowls. Spoon a few cherries into the middle of each bowl and drizzle a little of the bourbon syrup over the soup. Serve cold.

If your buttermilk is a bit thin, add a little crème fraîche or sour cream to it to give it more body.

BUTTERMILK AFFOGATO

Sometimes it's the little things that bring the greatest joy. After a long, heavy meal, there's nothing more appropriate than a small cup of affogato, a traditional Italian dessert of vanilla gelato and a shot of strong espresso. In Louisiana, it is traditional to spike your coffee with a bit of roasted chicory. My buttermilk ice cream is light and tangy. The two together are a lovely match. You'll have more ice cream than you need for the recipe, but you will be glad to have it handy in your freezer. / **FEEDS 4**

4 small scoops
  Buttermilk Ice Cream
  (recipe follows)
Pinch of ground chicory
  (optional)
4 shots espresso

Scoop the ice cream into small bowls. If you want, add a small pinch of ground chicory to the warm espresso. Add a shot of espresso to each bowl and serve immediately.

BUTTERMILK ICE CREAM

MAKES ABOUT A QUART

2 cups heavy cream
1 cup sugar
1 cup buttermilk

1 Combine the heavy cream and sugar in a medium saucepan and stir over medium heat until the sugar is dissolved. Transfer to a bowl and let cool to room temperature.

2 Gently whisk the buttermilk into the cream mixture and chill in the refrigerator for 1 hour.

3 Churn the buttermilk-cream mixture in an ice cream maker according to the manufacturer's instructions. Pack into a freezer container and freeze until ready to use.

TOBACCO COOKIES

Tobacco farms are a rich part of Kentucky's history, and even today you can drive through Winchester and see huge tracts of tobacco leaves. I know it is very un-PC to indulge in tobacco, but I still find something romantic about it, and I make these gooey cookies as a tribute to the historically important crop. The coconut flakes are cooked down to resemble cut chewing tobacco. Then, I add a little tobacco flavor to the dough too, but you can omit it if you don't want that tantalizing sting at the end of your last cookie bite.

Serve the cookies warm with a cold glass of half and half—that's half milk and half buttermilk. For an adult version of milk and cookies, try these with a glass of slightly warm milk spiked with a shot of whiskey. / **MAKES ABOUT 24 COOKIES**

TOBACCO COCONUT FLAKES

1 cup firmly packed sweetened coconut flakes

1½ cups brewed coffee

¾ cup cola

2 teaspoons molasses

2 tablespoons sugar

2 tablespoons Tobacco Water (recipe follows; optional) or 2 tablespoons water

1 Preheat the oven to 355°F. Line a baking sheet with parchment paper.

2 To make the coconut flakes: In a medium saucepan, combine the coconut, coffee, cola, molasses, sugar, and tobacco water. Bring to a boil over high heat and boil for about 20 minutes, until all the liquid has been cooked off. Transfer the coconut flakes to a baking sheet and allow to cool to room temperature.

3 To make the cookies: In a small bowl, combine the flour, baking powder, and salt and stir together with a fork. Melt the chocolate and butter over a double boiler. Allow to cool slightly.

4 In a separate bowl, whisk together the eggs, sugar, buttermilk, vanilla, and tobacco. Stir into the chocolate mixture, then stir the flour mixture into this batter.

The tobacco leaves should be taken from a good-quality cigar. When you unroll the cigar to make Tobacco Water (see opposite), reserve a small amount to be chopped for the cookie batter.

5 Spoon the dough 1 tablespoon at a time onto the prepared baking sheet. Leave room in between for the cookies to spread while baking.

6 Top each cookie with a little of the tobacco coconut flakes. Bake for 10 to 12 minutes, until the cookie tops crack but the cookies are still soft in the center. Let cool for 3 minutes before handling. Lift with a spatula and transfer the cookies to a wire rack. Or let cool completely and store in an airtight container for up to a week.

COOKIES

1¼ cups all-purpose flour

¼ teaspoon baking powder

Pinch of salt

14 ounces semisweet chocolate, chopped

2 tablespoons unsalted butter

2 large eggs

⅓ cup sugar

1 tablespoon buttermilk

1 teaspoon vanilla extract

2 teaspoons chopped tobacco leaves (see note)

TOBACCO WATER

MAKES 3 CUPS

1 good cigar

3 cups warm water

1 Peel half of the layers off the cigar and discard. Separate the inner tobacco leaves and rinse under warm water for 3 minutes.

2 Fill a small bowl with the 3 cups warm water and steep the tobacco leaves in the water for 10 minutes. Strain the water and discard the tobacco leaves. The tobacco water will be quite strong, with a nicotine sting.

MUTSU APPLE TEMPURA
WITH BUTTERMILK CARAMEL

When apples begin to appear in abundance in the farmers' markets, it is my reminder that autumn has arrived. Mutsu is a succulent variety and the very best of the lot. Fried fruit may seem blasphemous, but this is really tasty: crispy and flaky on the outside and warm, sweet, and moist on the inside. You have to slice the apples just right—too thin, and the apple loses its crispness when fried; too thick, and the center won't get warm. I slice them into wedges about the thickness of my thumb, on the skin side. You can peel the apples if you want to, but I like leaving the skin on. A little caramel and a wisp of cinnamon is all you need to finish this addictive dessert snack.

The apples should be served hot out of the fryer, but make the whole recipe even if you are serving a smaller group, because people will eat the hell out of them. My buddy Greg Hall makes a virtuoso hard cider called Red Streak and, needless to say, it pairs really, really well with these fried apples. / **FEEDS 4 TO 6**

CARAMEL SAUCE

1 cup sugar

¼ cup water

½ cup heavy cream

2 tablespoons unsalted
 butter, softened

1½ tablespoons buttermilk

3 cups corn oil for deep-
 frying

1 To make the caramel sauce: Heat the sugar and water in a small saucepot over medium-high heat until the sugar caramelizes into a deep amber color, about 10 minutes; tilt the pan back and forth for even cooking, but do not, under any circumstances, stir the caramel. When the caramel is dark amber, turn off the heat and let cool for 3 minutes.

2 Whisk in the cream and stir. Let the sauce cool to near room temperature, then add the butter and buttermilk and mix well. Transfer to a container and refrigerate until ready to use.

3 Heat ½ inch of corn oil in a heavy pot to 350°F.

4 Meanwhile, make the batter: Combine the flour, cornstarch, sugar, and salt in a medium bowl. Pour in the Red Bull and whisk until combined.

5 Working in batches, using a fork or a toothpick, dip the apple slices into the batter, and gently drop into the hot oil. Fry for 45 seconds to 1 minute, until the batter is crisp and the apple is just warmed through. Lift the apples out of the oil with a skimmer or strainer and drain on paper towels.

6 Serve immediately on small plates, dusted with a little powdered sugar and a very light sprinkling of cinnamon and drizzle with the caramel sauce.

When making tempura, it is important to skim out any bits of batter remaining in the oil before frying your next batch. This will help keep the oil from burning. Watch the oil carefully and try your best to maintain it at a constant 350°F the entire time.

TEMPURA BATTER
1 cup all-purpose flour
⅓ cup cornstarch
1 tablespoon sugar
Pinch of kosher salt
1¼ cups Red Bull

2 Mutsu apples, cored and cut into ½-inch-thick wedges
Powdered sugar for dusting
Cinnamon for dusting

PEACH AND RHUBARB KUCHEN

The German influence is strong in the part of Kentucky where I live. Most of the old-country cuisine has disappeared from the regional foodways, but you can still find a few shops selling German-style cakes, or kuchens. *Kuchen* simply means "cake" in German, so there are a lot of versions. This one is unfathomably light and dense at the same time. I make it in the early part of summer, when both peaches and rhubarb are plentiful.

Serve this with a light Moscato d'asti, and watch your guests squeal with delight. / FEEDS 6 TO 8

KUCHEN

6 tablespoons unsalted
    butter, softened, plus more
    for the baking dish
1½ cups all-purpose flour
1 teaspoon baking powder
¼ teaspoon salt
3 ounces cream cheese,
    at room temperature
¾ cup sugar
1 teaspoon vanilla extract
2 large eggs
½ cup buttermilk
2 large peaches, peeled,
    pitted, and cut into
    wedges
4 ounces rhubarb, trimmed
    and cut into ½-inch pieces
    (about ¾ cup)

TOPPING

½ cup crushed pistachios
¼ cup sugar
2 tablespoons unsalted
    butter, cut into pieces

Buttermilk Whipped Cream
    (recipe follows)

1 Preheat the oven to 375°F. Smear a little soft butter on the bottom and sides of a 9-by-13-inch baking dish.

2 To make the kuchen: In a small bowl, combine the flour, baking powder, and salt and stir together with a fork.

3 In the bowl of a stand mixer fitted with the paddle attachment (or using a handheld mixer), combine the butter, cream cheese, sugar, and vanilla and cream together on medium-high for 2 minutes, or until smooth and creamy. Add the eggs and buttermilk and mix until thoroughly combined, 2 to 3 minutes. Slowly add the flour mixture, mixing until a smooth batter is formed; stop to scrape the sides of the bowl with a rubber spatula as necessary.

4 Pour the batter into the baking dish. Place the fruit over the batter and press it in just slightly. To top, sprinkle the crushed pistachios and sugar over the fruit and dot the cake with the butter.

5 Bake for 50 to 60 minutes, or until a toothpick inserted in the center of the kuchen comes out clean and the top is golden brown. Remove from the oven and allow to cool for a few minutes, then slice and serve warm with buttermilk whipped cream. Leftovers, if there are any, will keep, covered with plastic wrap, in your refrigerator for several days.

BUTTERMILK WHIPPED CREAM

MAKES ABOUT 2½ CUPS

1 cup heavy cream
6 tablespoons buttermilk
3 tablespoons powdered sugar

Combine the heavy cream, buttermilk, and powdered sugar in a large bowl and beat with an electric mixer on low until firm peaks form. Cover and refrigerate until ready to use.

CHESS PIE

WITH BLACKENED PINEAPPLE SALSA

There are as many versions of chess pie as there are stories about the origin of its name. Folklore has it that the name comes from the tradition of making the pie in the afternoon and storing it in a chest until ready to serve later that evening; over time, the word "chest" came to be "chess." Chess pie is rich and sugary as hell. I brighten it up with pineapple that is panfried in a little peanut oil. Some might think a pineapple salsa has no right to intrude into a classic Southern dessert, but it works—as odd as the combination might sound at first.

This is a sweet dessert, so there's no need for a dessert wine: crack open the bourbon, or maybe serve snifters of aged rye whiskey. / MAKES 2 PIES, EACH SERVING 6

PINEAPPLE SALSA

About ⅓ cup peanut oil

1 pineapple, peeled, cored, and sliced into ½-inch-thick rings

Grated zest and juice of 2 limes

1 tablespoon dark rum

3 tablespoons light brown sugar

DOUGH

2¾ cups all-purpose flour

3 tablespoons sugar

1½ teaspoons salt

8 tablespoons (1 stick) unsalted butter, cut into ½-inch cubes and chilled

¼ cup vegetable shortening, cut into ½-inch cubes and chilled

4 to 6 tablespoons ice water

1 To make the pineapple salsa: Heat 2 teaspoons of the oil in a large heavy skillet over high heat. Add 2 or 3 pineapple rings and fry until blackened on both sides, about 3 minutes on each side. Transfer to paper towels to drain briefly, then move to a cutting board. Repeat until all the pineapple rings are blackened, adding more oil to the pan as needed.

2 Chop the blackened pineapple rings into fine chunks. Transfer to a bowl and mix in the lime zest and juice, rum, and brown sugar. Cover and refrigerate until ready to use.

3 To make the dough: Combine the flour, sugar, and salt in a food processor and pulse a few times to mix together. Add the butter and shortening and pulse 10 to 12 times, until the mixture is crumbly, with butter bits the size of small peas. Add the water a tablespoon at a time, pulsing until a rough dough is formed; stop as soon as the dough gathers into a ball.

4 Turn the dough out, divide it in half, and shape into 2 disks. Wrap each disk in plastic wrap and chill in the refrigerator for at least an hour.

5 Chill two 9-inch pie pans in the refrigerator for 30 minutes.

6 Transfer one disk of dough to a work surface dusted with flour. Using a rolling pin, roll out the dough to a 12-inch circle, occasionally lifting the dough and turning it a quarter-turn; dust with more flour underneath if needed. Lift the dough up and drape into one chilled pie pan, pressing it gently against the

bottom and sides of the pan. Trim any excess overhang of dough with kitchen scissors or a knife. Roll out the other disk of dough; refrigerate both piecrusts for 30 minutes.

7 Position a rack in the center of the oven and preheat the oven to 350°F.

8 To make the filling: Whisk all the ingredients together in a medium bowl. Fill each piecrust about three-quarters full. Bake the pies for 30 to 35 minutes, until a toothpick inserted into the center comes out almost clean and a light crust has formed on top. Let cool on a rack. The pie can be served at room temperature or, better yet, slightly warm. Once cooled, the pies can be wrapped and left in a cool, dry place (like a chest or cupboard) for up to a day.

9 To serve, slice each pie into 6 slices, transfer to plates, and top with the pineapple salsa.

FILLING
6 large eggs
3 large egg yolks
3 cups sugar
6 tablespoons unsalted butter, melted
5 tablespoons fine cornmeal
1 cup buttermilk
1 tablespoon distilled white vinegar
1 teaspoon salt
1 tablespoon vanilla extract
1 teaspoon grated nutmeg

WHISKEY-GINGER CAKE
WITH PEAR SALAD

My neighbor, pastry chef Leah Stewart, created this for a Jack Daniel's dinner in Louisville. I liked it so much, I "borrowed" the recipe. Hey, come on, we all do it: take a recipe and adapt it into our own. Most whiskey-flavored desserts are too heavy and syrupy for me. I wanted the whiskey flavor, but in something refined and regal. We fussed around with the recipe to get it just right. Adding fresh pears to a traditional ginger cake gives it a contemporary feel.

Serve this as an elegant end to an important meal, with some good whiskey or a cocktail like The New-Fashioned (page 231). / FEEDS UP TO 10

CAKE

½ cup neutral oil, such as grapeseed or canola

10 tablespoons (1¼ sticks) unsalted butter, softened

2⅔ cups packed light brown sugar

4 large eggs

1 tablespoon grated fresh ginger (use a Microplane)

1½ cups buttermilk

½ cup unsweetened coconut milk

4⅓ cups cake flour, sifted

2½ teaspoons baking soda

1½ teaspoons ground ginger

1 Position a rack in the middle of the oven and preheat the oven to 325°F. Lightly grease two 8-inch round cake pans.

2 To make the cake: In the bowl of a stand mixer fitted with the paddle attachment, cream together the oil, butter, and brown sugar for 3 minutes. Beat in the eggs one at a time, beating well after each addition, then beat in the grated ginger and mix until smooth, about 2 minutes. Scrape down the sides of the bowl with a rubber spatula as necessary.

3 Combine the buttermilk and coconut milk in a small bowl. Whisk together the cake flour, baking soda, and ground ginger in a large bowl.

4 Alternating between them, slowly add the buttermilk mixture and the flour mixture, a little at a time, to the egg mixture, mixing on medium-low speed until well blended.

5 Pour the batter into the prepared cake pans. Bake for 45 minutes, or until a toothpick inserted into the center of a cake comes out clean. Let cool for 10 minutes, then remove the cakes from the pans and cool completely on a wire rack.

→ CONTINUED

FROSTING

¾ pound (3 sticks)
   unsalted butter,
   softened
4 ounces cream cheese,
   at room temperature
¼ cup good-quality
   whiskey
1 teaspoon vanilla extract
Two 1-pound boxes
   powdered sugar

GARNISH

1 Anjou pear
Grated zest and juice of
   1 lime
Unsprayed borage
   blossoms (optional)

6 To make the frosting: In the bowl of a stand mixer fitted with the paddle attachment, cream the butter and cream cheese together on medium speed until smooth, about 2 minutes. Add the whiskey and vanilla and continue mixing until smooth. Turn the speed to low and slowly add the powdered sugar, a little at a time, mixing until smooth. Set aside at room temperature until ready to use.

7 To assemble the cake, place one cake layer on a cake stand or a serving plate. Using a small offset spatula, spread a thin layer of frosting over the sides and top of the layer. Place the second layer on top, and spread the remaining frosting over the top and sides. Smooth out the sides, but don't worry about making it too perfect. (Homemade cakes should always tilt a little. It makes them more fun to eat.)

8 Just before serving, core the pear, slice into thin rounds and matchsticks, and toss with the lime zest and juice. Decorate the top of the cake with the pear and finish with a few borage blossoms, if desired. Slice and serve. The leftover cake will stay moist, well wrapped, in your refrigerator for at least 3 days.

BUTTERMILK

There are two kinds of buttermilk. Originally, buttermilk was the liquid, whey, that was the by-product of churning cream into butter. Milky and acidic, it was taken as a drink and used in a variety of recipes. Cultured buttermilk, what is sold today in our modern markets, is fermented by adding a lactic acid culture, *Streptococcus lactis,* to low-fat milk. It is more tart and thicker than old-fashioned buttermilk.

If you can get your hands on unpasteurized milk, you can make dreamy buttermilk out of it by allowing it to sour slightly in a warm, dark place for a few days. But most commercially sold milk, as well as buttermilk, has been pasteurized, which means it has been heated to kill off pathogens, and that kills the good enzymes too. If possible, get your buttermilk from a local dairy. Even pasteurized milk from their healthier cows will have a thicker, tangier texture and is better for you. Buttermilk is high in acid and protein and, despite its name, low in fat. Baking with it is useful not just because it adds a tangy flavor. When mixed with leavening to make everything from biscuits to pancakes, cakes, pie fillings, or cookies, it results in a moister, softer product.

NOTE: All of the buttermilk recipes in this chapter were tested with pasteurized cultured buttermilk for the sake of consistency.

SWEET SPOONBREAD SOUFFLÉ

Soufflés are tricky little devils. They seem to rise or fall with no rhyme or reason. This version combines the custardy nature of spoonbread with the meringue of a traditional French soufflé, so it's a bit more forgiving. It's also a bit more dense. It will still fall once out of the oven, so serve it quickly. I love to make this in summer when corn is ripe and sweet. Serve with powdered sugar or a little caramel. / FEEDS 6 TO 8

FOR THE MOLDS

4 tablespoons unsalted butter, softened

½ cup sugar

SOUFFLÉ

1 cup yellow cornmeal

1 cup buttermilk

4 tablespoons unsalted butter

2 cups corn kernels (from 3 large ears corn)

2 cups whole milk

½ cup plus 2 tablespoons sugar

1 teaspoon vanilla extract

½ teaspoon ground cinnamon

Pinch of kosher salt

5 large eggs, separated

Powdered sugar for dusting

1 Preheat the oven to 400°F. Generously butter six to eight 4- to 5-ounce soufflé molds (oven-safe coffee cups work great for this in a pinch). Add a small handful of sugar to one buttered mold and turn to coat the bottom and sides with an even layer of sugar. Tap out the excess sugar into the next mold and coat the mold. Coat the remaining molds, adding more sugar as necessary. Refrigerate the molds until ready to bake.

2 To make the soufflé: Whisk the cornmeal and buttermilk together in a medium bowl; set aside.

3 Melt the butter in a large sauté pan over medium-high heat. Add the corn kernels and sauté for 4 to 5 minutes, until tender. Add the milk, 2 tablespoons of the sugar, the vanilla, cinnamon, and salt, bring to a simmer, and simmer for 5 minutes.

4 Transfer the corn mixture to a blender and puree on high. Transfer to a bowl and stir in the cornmeal mixture, then let cool to room temperature.

5 Whisk the egg yolks into the cooled corn mixture.

6 In the bowl of a stand mixer fitted with the whisk attachment (or using a handheld mixer), beat the egg whites until they form soft peaks. Gradually add the remaining ½ cup sugar and continue to beat until stiff peaks form; this is your meringue. Gently fold the meringue into the corn mixture. Don't worry if it isn't all smoothly combined; a few streaks are okay.

7 Scoop the batter into the prepared molds, filling them almost all the way to the rim. Place the molds on a baking sheet and bake for 35 minutes, or until the tops are golden brown and puffed. Serve immediately, sprinkled with powdered sugar.

CORNBREAD-SORGHUM MILKSHAKE

(OR, "BREAKFAST")

This is not even a dessert, really. It's a recipe without any real measurements or rules, fast and loose. It's a Southern thang, a friend told me. I had to try it to believe it. And, boy, is it good. Your cornbread has to be stale and crumbly. I suggest buttermilk ice cream here, but I've made it with strawberry and even coffee ice cream too. Drink the morning after a long night. / FEEDS 2 TO 4, DEPENDING ON HOW HUNGRY YOU ARE

2 large scoops Buttermilk
    Ice Cream (page 258) or
    other ice cream
A fistful of crumbled
    leftover Lardo
    Cornbread (page 208)
2 tablespoons sorghum

Combine the ice cream and cornbread in a blender and pulse until roughly blended. Add the sorghum and pulse a few more times. Serve in large mugs or Ball jars.

Try this drink a few times to see how much sweetness you like in it. If you like it a little sweeter, just add more sorghum.

SORGHUM

Sweet sorghum comes from the sorghum plant, which looks like tall sugarcane stalks. It's different from grain sorghum, which is used in everything from animal feed to ethanol production. Sweet sorghum is juiced like sugarcane—by pressing the stalks between two heavy rollers. The juice is then slowly boiled until it turns into a sticky amber syrup, which is cooled and bottled. In color, it is somewhere between honey and maple syrup, but there are many different grades and varieties.

Kentucky farmers have been growing sorghum for generations. And Danny Ray Townsend is a rock star among sorghum producers—a two-time winner of the National Sweet Sorghum Producers and Processors Association's National Champion Award. His farm is near Winchester, Kentucky,

which, conveniently, is where they make my favorite chewing tobacco. I took a road trip to see Danny Ray recently with Matt Jamie, who sells Danny Ray's sorghum under his Bourbon Barrel Foods label (see Resources, page 279). Danny Ray sliced off a sorghum stalk and showed us exactly which section has the sweetest juice. And he showed us his old-time furnace and his mule that he keeps around just to remind people of how things were done in the ole days. To listen to him speak so eloquently about an obscure crop that he and his family have devoted their lives to for generations is a lesson in fortitude and devotion. I use Danny Ray's sorghum in everything from pancakes to tea to milkshakes. As long as people like Danny Ray are producing sorghum, I will be drinking it up.

COCONUT RICE PUDDING BRÛLÉE

Rice pudding was a popular dessert at the diners I worked at in New York City. But those puddings were pretty awful—the texture was heavy and starchy, and the only relief came in the form of dusty cinnamon powder that made me cough every time I inhaled a bit. I never gave up on rice pudding, though. My version is more exotic, and the caramelized top makes it elegant. Coconut milk has a higher fat content than cow's milk, so I generally serve this in small portions, in decorative ramekins. The rich dessert is perfect with a Framboise Lambic from Lindemans. / FEEDS 6

RICE PUDDING

½ cup long-grain white rice
(see note)

2½ cups whole milk

½ cup heavy cream

2¼ cups unsweetened
coconut milk

1 vanilla bean, split

1 star anise

1 cup sugar

½ cup buttermilk

2 tablespoons brown sugar

GARNISH

18 raspberries

Fresh basil leaves,
preferably Thai basil

1 To make the pudding: Combine the rice, milk, cream, coconut milk, vanilla bean, star anise, and sugar in a heavy pot, bring to a simmer over low heat, and simmer for 55 minutes to 1 hour 10 minutes, stirring occasionally, until the rice is soft. Transfer to a bowl and let the pudding cool to room temperature, about 1 hour; it will thicken as it cools.

2 Discard the vanilla bean and star anise. Add the buttermilk to the pudding, stirring it in gently with a wooden spoon. Divide the rice pudding among six 4-inch ramekins and chill in the refrigerator for at least 2 hours, and up to overnight.

3 Just before serving, spoon 1 teaspoon of the brown sugar evenly over the surface of each rice pudding. Using a blowtorch, gently heat the sugar until it turns a dark amber color. Cool briefly, until the sugar hardens.

4 Garnish each pudding with 3 raspberries and a few basil leaves and serve. (The sugar will start to pick up moisture and become tacky if you don't serve these right away.)

I use sushi rice for this recipe. Feel free to use arborio, but it will take a little longer to cook.

You can use the broiler to brûlée the puddings. Make sure you are using oven-safe ramekins. Place them on a baking sheet, add the sugar, and place them directly under the flame of your broiler. Watch carefully, as the sugar can burn quickly. With most broilers, I find that you have to rotate the pan every 40 seconds; it takes longer this way, but you'll get an even brûlée and you won't burn it.

THE MUSICIAN

Johnny Berry is a real-life honky-tonk country musician, and with his band, The Outliers, he tears up stages around the country with his gospel of songs that harken back to a time when country music was less glitzy, more gritty. His live shows are a marathon of up-tempo hooks and lyrics that make people want to get up and dance. He and I were up late one night talking about where to get good shirts (Leatherhead) or drink good beer (Holy Grale) in Louisville, when I discovered how much he loves cooking. He loves to cook as much as I love music. And when we cross paths, it's always a good time.

"For me, cooking and writing music are exactly the same when it comes down to it—you want to catch the moment. Man, when I look out and see ripe tomatoes in my garden, I just put them on the grill and let them sit there for a good long time 'til the flavor gets concentrated, to get rid of all that excess water and just get to the essence of it. Well, writing a song is no different. I can be inspired by anything that's happening in my life; I can see something just driving down the road and it hits me. All these thoughts and words. Then I just cook it down to get it to where it's flavorful; I get everything else out of its way."

—JOHNNY BERRY
OF JOHNNY BERRY AND THE OUTLIERS

RESOURCES

I have a lot of ingredients in my pantry, some of which you might not be able to easily access. I know there's nothing worse than finding a recipe you want to make and then realizing there's an ingredient that you can't find in your city. I use a lot of Korean ingredients, but the one ingredient I did not include in any recipe is the popular Korean chile paste *gochu jang*. Some might find this exclusion odd, but it is not easily found unless there is a real Korean market in your neighborhood. (Also, it is more often used as a condiment, and I chose to feature recipes that use chile as a layered note, not a sauce-on-the-side.) The remaining ingredients can be found in this list of resources—and don't underestimate the power of a good Internet search.

BACON

BENTON'S SMOKY MOUNTAIN COUNTRY HAMS
2603 Highway 411 North
Madisonville, TN 37354-6356
Tel: 423-442-5003
www.bentonscountryhams2.com

BITTERS

FEE BROTHERS' ORANGE BITTERS

FEE BROTHERS
453 Portland Avenue
Rochester, NY 14605
Tel: 800-961-FEES or 585-544-9530
www.feebrothers.com

REGAN'S ORANGE BITTERS

BUFFALO TRACE DISTILLERY
113 Great Buffalo Trace
Frankfort, KY 40601
Tel: 800-654-8471 or 502-696-5926

CAST-IRON PANS

LODGE MANUFACTURING COMPANY
Tel: 423-837-7181
www.lodgemfg.com

CHEESE

GOAT CHEESE

CAPRIOLE GOAT CHEESE
10329 New Cut Road
Greenville, IN 47124
Tel: 812-923-9408
www.capriolegoatcheese.com

SHEEP'S-MILK CHEESE

EVERONA DAIRY
23246 Clarks Mountain Road
Rapidan, VA 22733
Tel: 540-854-4159
www.everonadairy.com

FISH SAUCE

RED BOAT FISH SAUCE
Tel: 925-858-0508
www.redboatfishsauce.com

GRITS

ANSON MILLS
1922-C Gervais Street
Columbia, SC 29201
Tel: 803-467-4122
www.ansonmills.com

HAM

BROWNING'S COUNTRY HAM
475 Sherman Newton Road
Dry Ridge, KY 41035
Tel: 859-948-4HAM
www.browningscountryham.com

COL. BILL NEWSOM'S AGED KENTUCKY COUNTRY HAM
Newsom's Old Mill Store
208 East Main Street
Princeton, KY 42445
Tel: 270-365-2482
www.newsomscountryham.com

D'ARTAGNAN
Tel: 800-327-8246
www.dartagnan.com
For tasso ham

FATHER'S COUNTRY HAM
6313 KY 81
Bremen, KY 42325
Tel: 270-525-3554
www.fatherscountryhams.com

FINCHVILLE FARMS
5157 Taylorsville Road
Finchville, KY 40022
Tel: 800-678-1521 or 502-834-7952
www.finchvillefarms.com

THE HONEYBAKED HAM COMPANY
Tel: 866-492-HAMS
www.honeybakedham.com
More than 400 retail stores nationwide

PENN'S HAMS
P.O. Box 88
Mannsville, KY 42758
Tel: 800-883-6984 or 270-465-5065
Available at fine stores in Kentucky and by
mail-order

SCOTT HAMS
1301 Scott Road
Greenville, KY 42345
Tel: 800-318-1353 or 270-338-3402
www.scotthams.com

MAPLE SYRUP
**BLIS BOURBON BARREL MATURED
PURE MAPLE SYRUP**
www.blisgourmet.com
Sur La Table: www.surlatable.com
Williams-Sonoma: www.williams-sonoma.com

MAYONNAISE
DUKE'S
Tel: 800-688-5676
www.dukesmayo.com

OYSTERS
RAPPAHANNOCK RIVER OYSTERS, LLC
Tel: 804-204-1709
www.rroysters.com

PRETZEL SALT
www.nuts.com

RICE
CAROLINA RICE
Tel: 800-226-9522
www.carolinarice.com
Available at most supermarkets, in bulk from
their Web site, and from other online retailers

KOKUHO ROSE RICE
KODA FARMS
22540 Russell Avenue
South Dos Palos, CA 93665
Tel: 209-392-2191
www.kodafarms.com

SORGHUM
**BOURBON BARREL PURE CANE SWEET
SORGHUM**
BOURBON BARREL FOODS
Tel: 502-333-6103
www.bourbonbarrelfoods.com

SOY SAUCE
BLUEGRASS SOY SAUCE
BOURBON BARREL FOODS
Tel: 502-333-6103
www.bourbonbarrelfoods.com

SPOONBILL CAVIAR

SHUCKMAN'S FISH CO. & SMOKERY
3001 West Main Street
Louisville, KY 40212
Tel: 502-775-6487
www.kysmokedfish.com

TAMICON TAMARIND CONCENTRATE

Available at most Indian markets

OTHER GOOD STUFF

DVD OF FRED PROVENZA
Western Folklife Center: www.westernfolklife
.org/vmchk/Foraging-Behavior-by-Dr.-Frederick-
D.-Provenza-DVD/flypage_wfc.tpl.html

LE CREUSET DUTCH OVENS
cookware.lecreuset.com
Also available at www.chefsresource.com and
major department stores

SOUTHERN FOODWAYS ALLIANCE
www.southernfoodways.org

keep Louisville weird.®
support L   DEPENDENT businesses

ACKNOWLEDGMENTS

There are so many folks who made this book possible. A heartfelt thank you to all of them!

To Francine, who is a champion of the underdog

To Ann Bramson, who welcomed me into her esteemed family at Artisan

To Judy Pray, for her precision and her limitless hard work; let us eat more pig's feet

To Kim Witherspoon, for her wisdom and honesty, and to Maria, for introducing us

To Grant, for his talent and patience, cheers, and Rebel Yell

To Dimity, for her tireless devotion and good humor; Clay lives on

To Mike Anderson, for capturing "my" Kentucky with his camera

To Darra, for publishing my first essay

To Dean, for his thoughtful opinions and for reminding me of why Yeats is so relevant

To Mary W., for treating me like the rock star I'm not

To Eddie and Sharon, for believing in me when no one else did

To Brook, for his endless support and countless bottles of wine

To my late grandmother, she is in heaven

To my parents, for the childhood they gave me

To my sister, Julie, because she made every day of growing up an adventure

To Justin and Laura, for being awesome!

To my crew: Nick, Kevin, and Caleb, for all the infinite details in making service a triumph

To Mindy, Robert, and everyone else at 610; I don't thank them enough, I am always in their debt

To Kay Chun and Susan Nguyen, for their diligent recipe testing and good humor

To all the insanely talented chefs who welcomed me to their Southern homes

To John T., for bringing us all together

To Louisville, for adopting me

To every single person who has ever dined at my restaurant,

To anyone I've ever shared a drink with

And to my wife, Dianne, who taught me that love is boundless

INDEX

Note: Page numbers in italics refer to photographs

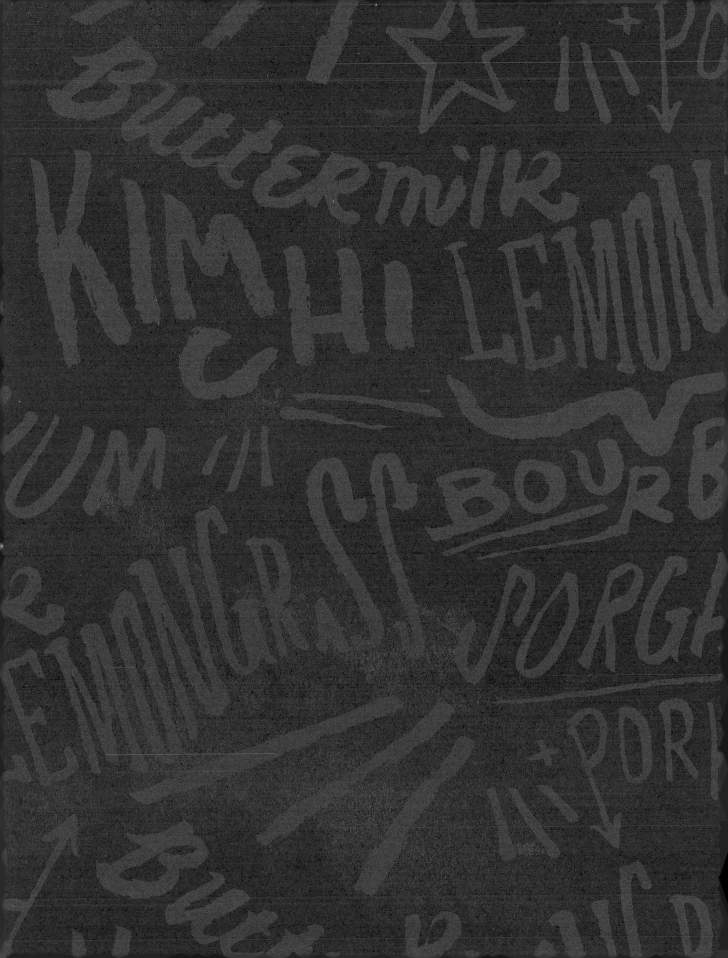